The Ecumenical Councils
of the Catholic Church

The Ecumenical Councils of the Catholic Church

A History

Joseph F. Kelly

A Michael Glazier Book

LITURGICAL PRESS
Collegeville, Minnesota

www.litpress.org

A Michael Glazier Book published by Liturgical Press

Cover design by David Manahan, OSB. Painting in Kiev, Sofia. Photo by Sasha Martynchuk. © Sasha Martynchuk and iStockphoto.

1   2   3   4   5   6   7   8   9

Library of Congress Cataloging-in-Publication Data

Kelly, Joseph F. (Joseph Francis), 1945–
    The ecumenical councils of the Catholic Church : a history / Joseph F. Kelly.
      p. cm.
    "A Michael Glazier book"—T.p. verso.
    Includes bibliographical references (p.   ) and index.
    ISBN 978-0-8146-5376-0 (pbk.)
  1. Councils and synods, Ecumenical—History. I. Title.
    BX823.K45 2009
    262'.5209—dc22   2009009757

To Gerard Anthony Kelly,
a good man, a good teacher,
and a good father

Contents

Preface

Like most church historians, I often wish that my fellow believers knew more about the forces and people who shaped the church over the centuries. Part of this problem is that many church historians, unlike theologians and biblical exegetes, have little interest in writing for general audiences. Years ago, my friend Joseph Tylenda, SJ, of the University of Scranton, told me that, after years of focusing on scholarly writings, he also wished to write for an educated but general audience, which he did with some fine books on the Jesuits. I never forgot what Joe said, and it has been my hope to do the same. The ecumenical councils have always interested me, and a study of them seemed a good topic.

But a book needs a publisher. I approached Liturgical Press, publisher of several other titles of mine, and the director, Peter Dwyer, and the editorial director, Hans Christoffersen, were both interested and supportive, as they have traditionally been for my efforts, and they encouraged me to go ahead with the book. My thanks to them for their confidence.

As an undergraduate teacher, I routinely taught church history surveys and so had a broad knowledge of the field, but the councils demanded more specialized knowledge, and so I turned to some friends for help. My thanks to Joseph Lienhard, SJ, of Fordham University, who read over the chapters on the first eight councils and offered valuable advice. For the late medieval councils and Trent, my friend and colleague at John Carroll University, Dr. Paul Murphy, director of JCU's Institute of Catholic Studies, provided valuable help on a number of historical points. Joseph Tylenda, who inspired this work some time ago, also read the chapters that Dr. Murphy did along with the one on Vatican I. He provided much valuable help on the history but especially the theology of those councils along with very useful advice. For Vatican II, my thanks to my department colleagues Dr. Joan Nuth and Rev. Jared Wicks, SJ, who drew from his virtually unrivaled knowledge of Vatican II to aid me with the book's most difficult chapter. All these scholars helped to make this a better book; the book's deficiencies are solely the responsibility of the author.

John Carroll University has a history of supporting scholarship, a history continued by my department chairperson, Dr. John Spencer, who recommended me for reduced loads to pursue my writing, as well as by Dr. Linda Eisenmann, dean of the College of Arts and Sciences, who approved Dr. Spencer's recommendation, and by Dr. David LaGuardia, academic vice president at the time I started this work, who officially granted me the reduced loads. Thanks also to Dr. Lauren Bowen, associate academic vice president and chair of the University Committee on Research and Service, who approved research funds for me to purchase books necessary for the research. My final academic thanks go to Mrs. Elizabeth England, my graduate assistant, who read this book more times than anyone should have to.

As always, my sincerest thanks go to my wife Ellen, a loving, thoughtful, and generous spouse, who took time from her own busy schedule and made myriad sacrifices, both large and small, so that I would have time to write.

This book is dedicated to my younger brother, Gerard Anthony Kelly, my childhood companion with whom I share so many warm memories.

Joseph F. Kelly
John Carroll University

Introduction

This book deals with the twenty-one councils considered ecumenical by the Roman Catholic Church, which would make it of interest to Catholic readers, but hopefully it will attract readers from other churches and traditions as well. The first eight councils were held before the eleventh-century schism between the Western, Latin Christians—ancestors of modern Catholics and Protestants—and the Eastern, Greek Christians—ancestors of the Orthodox churches of today. In fact, all eight councils met in Greek-speaking areas and were conducted in Greek. The next ten councils, all Western, Latin-speaking councils, occurred before the Protestant Reformation. To be sure, Protestants do not consider these councils to be in any way authoritative, but they do form part of the common history of Western Christians in the pre-Reformation period. Even the archetypal Catholic council, Trent, which met intermittently from 1545 to 1563, opened while some Protestant and Catholic leaders were still negotiating to prevent the split in the church from becoming permanent, and Protestant observers attended some sessions at Trent. This book is meant to be ecumenical, but not like a council.

Councils

What exactly is an ecumenical council? The word "council" refers to a meeting of any group of people with responsibility to deal with issues facing the group, for example, a student council or a parish council. In the Catholic Church the term usually means a meeting of bishops, either on their own or with the pope. Most common are provincial councils or synods, where the bishops of a particular ecclesiastical province get together, usually under the presidency of the metropolitan or senior bishop of the province. These bishops can legislate for the province, providing that their decisions do not contradict those of higher authorities.

When bishops from several ecclesiastical provinces or from an entire country meet, they constitute a plenary council, such as the three plenary

1

councils of Baltimore (1852, 1866, 1884), which determined the institutional development of Catholicism in the United States for the nineteenth and early twentieth centuries. Sometimes, especially in missionary areas, councils call together bishops from various countries and territories under the presidency of the bishop senior in status, for example, a cardinal, or of a papal representative. Thanks to modern transportation and communication, bishops can meet as often as annually.

Distinct from all these is the ecumenical council, a gathering of the bishops of the entire world under the presidency of the pope or, more likely on a day-to-day basis, one or more papal representatives. The pope alone can now summon a council, and he alone can give the decrees final approval. The word "ecumenical" comes from the Greek *oíkoumene*, meaning "the inhabited world." Often the pope invites to the council important ecclesiastical figures such as superiors of religious orders and abbots. Since a council's business routinely involves theological and canonical issues, "experts" (*periti* in Latin) in theology and canon law take part as advisors, some of whom exercise great influence.

In past centuries, Catholic monarchs sent representatives to the councils to make sure that their interests were served or at least preserved. In fact, several ecumenical councils were called by monarchs, not popes. Strange as this sounds today, in past centuries Christian countries did not separate church and state. Most people, including popes and bishops, considered monarchs to be sacred figures whose voices had to be heard or who often had power within the church itself, for example, in the appointment of bishops. Until the twentieth century, some Catholic monarchs could actually veto the election of a pope. Royal intervention prevailed throughout many Christian churches. For instance, the czar headed the Russian Orthodox Church, while even today the British monarch is head of the Church of England.

Given the enormous authority of the papacy within Roman Catholicism, one might ask, why does the church even have councils, at least since the advent of the papal monarchy? *The Church in Crisis*, the title of a dated (1961) but still helpful book on the councils by Monsignor Philip Hughes, sums up why councils have been called. At different points in history, the church has faced crises of such magnitude that the popes or the church at large felt it necessary that all the bishops should meet to decide what to do. As we shall see, some of these crises dealt with doctrinal issues of the greatest importance, such as the nature of the Trinity and of Christ, while other "crises" involved papal disputes with European monarchs, but the point remains that the pope felt the need to meet with the bishops.

Change and Development

As currently constituted, that is, in union with the pope, the ecumenical council is the supreme teaching authority in the Catholic Church. Its doctrinal decisions have, for Catholics, the same authority as Scripture and the traditional teachings of the episcopal *magisterium*, that is, the bishops' role as teachers in the church. This leads to another issue—do councils change Catholic teaching?

Up to the twentieth century, the answer was simple: no. "The bishops in council do not define new doctrines; they define or give witness to the teachings received from Christ and handed down in the Church from the beginning" (*Maryknoll Catholic Dictionary*, 198). This attitude reflected the traditional Catholic dependence upon the scholastic theologians of the Middle Ages, who, for all their theological brilliance, lived with a static worldview, which supported the notion that the church had never really changed its teachings.

But John Henry Cardinal Newman (1801–90) wrote about the development of doctrine, stressing that doctrines do change, not in the sense that the church teaches one thing on Monday and the exact opposite on Tuesday, but, rather, that in the course of centuries of lived Catholicism and theological reflection, the church advanced from a particular formulation of a doctrine to a more nuanced one, informed by new developments. Following Newman, most modern theologians accept that doctrine develops, although they often differ about whether a particular doctrinal formulation represents true development.

Let us consider a classic example of development, on an issue that still stirs up controversy.

In the fifth century the great North African theologian Augustine of Hippo (354–430) formulated the traditional doctrine of original sin (a phrase he created), that is, that all humans shared in the sin of Adam and Eve because we were born with the guilt of that sin on our souls and would be damned to hell forever if we did not receive baptism and have that guilt removed. But even after the guilt was removed, concupiscence, the inclination to sin, remained, and we live in constant need of God's freely-given divine grace, which we can do nothing to earn. Augustine's theology was, of course, far more nuanced than this, but these are the basics. Note that it depends upon the actual existence of Adam and Eve.

Many believers over the centuries resented and objected to this theory because it seems so unfair, but Augustine's brilliance maintained the theory, which received new life in the Protestant Reformation. In the eighteenth century, however, Enlightenment rationalists mocked original sin: two prehistoric people took a bite out of a piece of fruit and now all humanity is condemned to hell! But the theory held on in the churches.

Two nineteenth-century developments undermined the theory in its traditional form. One development is well known and still controversial. Two Englishmen, the geologist Charles Lyell (1797–1885) and the biologist Charles Darwin (1809–82), proved that a literal interpretation of the Garden of Eden story conflicted with scientific evidence about the origins of the earth and its creatures, evidence that has steadily increased since their day. A less well-known but equally important development was the rise of modern biblical exegesis, led mostly by German Protestant scholars, who demonstrated that the Garden of Eden story is an etiology, that is, a myth of origins, common in the ancient Semitic world, and thus should not be taken as a historical account.

These new developments traumatized many Catholics and conservative Jews but were especially difficult for evangelical Protestants. Yet as Catholic scholars accepted these new developments, the church moved away from the traditional interpretation, recognized the value of understanding the Bible in terms of the culture that produced it, and discarded the nonscriptural idea that we are all born damned, although retaining the belief that we are all sinners in need of divine grace. Recent evidence of this development is Pope Benedict XVI's 2007 abandonment of the notion of limbo, which had been formulated in the Middle Ages partly to alleviate the fears of parents that their deceased but unbaptized children were burning forever in hell.

The church's changing attitude toward the historicity of the Garden of Eden provides an excellent example of doctrinal development. While recognizing that the cultural particulars of ancient Israel cannot be *historical*, the church continues to teach the *religious* basics of Genesis: that sin separates us from God, that we sin on our own and must face the consequences, that God never deserts us and continues to aid us, and that God wishes all people to be saved (a very different view from that of Augustine, who thought that 90 percent of humans ended up in hell). The church has availed itself of modern knowledge and still maintained the importance of the Genesis account.

To this example many more could be added. John Carroll, SJ, founder of the American Catholic hierarchy (and namesake of my university), owned slaves, as did the Maryland Jesuit province, and in the antebellum South many Catholic bishops—along with rabbis and Protestant ministers—vigorously defended slavery, something that modern believers completely reject.

In some cases the change is more subtle. Many early Christian theologians accepted much of the philosophy of Plato (424–347 BCE), for whom true reality was spiritual. For these Christians, the "real presence" in the Eucharist did not have to involve a physical change in the elements of the bread and wine. Later theologians had a more material understanding of the real presence and, accepting much of the philosophy of Aristotle (384–322 BCE), created the formula of transubstantiation to explain the real presence.

The development of doctrine rarely proceeds smoothly, and every theologian with new ideas encounters Catholics who insist on an unchanging church in an unchanging world. Popes and bishops, entrusted with preserving the deposit of faith, look cautiously at some new theories, but the Catholic Church does accept and practice the development of doctrine. We must bear that in mind when examining conciliar teaching.

History and Theology

The definition of an ecumenical council given on page 2 is a theological one, but we must be very careful not to read theology back into history. Many Christians transport the church of their own day into previous eras. Inevitably, they experience disappointment when they discover discrepancies in this scenario. For example, modern Christians cannot conceive of the church without the New Testament, but the New Testament could not exist until all the books had been written, which did not happen until circa 125. But just because the books were written did not mean that they were recognized as forming a collection entitled the New Testament. Not until 367 did Athanasius, bishop of Alexandria, become the first person to list the canon of the New Testament and include the familiar twenty-seven books, no more and no less.

Today a pope must call an ecumenical council. But no pope called any of the first eight councils. Roman or Byzantine emperors called seven of them, while a woman, the Byzantine empress Irene, called the Second Council of Nicea in 787. The second ecumenical council, Constantinople I, was called in 381, met, decided the issues, and adjourned without informing the pope, Damasus I (366–84), that a council was being held. The Council of Constance (1414–18) met when three popes contested for the loyalty of Western Europe's Catholics. The "pope" who actually convoked the council was known as John XXIII, now regarded as an antipope (false pope). So how can these councils be considered authentic?

By ecclesiastical tradition, which the popes accepted. Let me quote the last century's greatest authority on the councils, Monsignor Hubert Jedin:

For the first millennium, and even beyond it, the ecumenical character of these assemblies is not decided by the intention of those who convened them, even if they wished them to have that character; in fact, during the whole of this period even papal approval of the decisions does not, from the first, bear the character of a formal confirmation, as was the case with regard to the ecumenical councils of a later period. The recognition of the ecumenical character of the twenty assemblies [Jedin wrote in 1959] cannot be traced back to one comprehensive legislative act of the popes. Their ecumenical character was only established by the theological schools and by actual practice. (Jedin, *Councils*, 3–4)

The first authoritative list of councils was drawn up for Roman Catholics in 1612 by the Jesuit theologian, cardinal, and saint Robert Bellarmine, who worked on the councils at the request of Pope Paul V (1605–21).

Another historical issue that may present a problem to the modern reader is the consistent and often influential role played in councils by laypeople, that is, monarchs and nobles. Emperors and an empress called the first eight councils, and the king of France pushed Pope Clement V into calling the Council of Vienne in 1311–12, while several monarchs, but especially the German monarch Sigismund, forced the supporters of the three contending popes to accede to the Council of Constance in 1414.

Why were monarchs so often involved in ecumenical councils? First, religion has an impact on people and not just on their private, spiritual lives but also on how they act in the public sphere. For example, based on their religious beliefs, people living in secular Western countries have monogamy as law. Fundamentalist Christians want to vet high school biology textbooks, while other religious groups, of both left and right, want to vet political policies and judicial nominations. At no period in history could political leaders ignore the religious views of their people.

Second, no one in the ancient and medieval eras believed in the separation of church and state, and in parts of the Catholic world this continued into the nineteenth and even the twentieth century. Believing themselves to have been chosen by God to rule, monarchs deemed it natural and appropriate to play a role in religious matters.

Third, in the Middle Ages and into the nineteenth century, the popes themselves ruled a sizeable portion of central Italy, sometimes as much as one-third of the country, so they were political as well as ecclesiastical leaders with continuing experience of the union of church and state. Furthermore, in accepting the role of monarchs in the church, the popes felt an obligation to oversee the moral behavior of monarchs in the exercise of their office. This meant that the popes routinely got involved in political matters outside of Italy, and it explains to the modern reader something puzzling about the medieval councils, namely, why they dealt so much with church-state issues and papal disputes with secular rulers.

The first ecumenical council met in the fourth century; the most recent one met in the twentieth century. Initially the councils met in an almost regular succession (325, 381, 431, 451), thus, fifty-six years between the first two, fifty years between the next two, and only twenty between the next two. The next four were separated by a century or more (553, 680, 787, 869–70). The seven medieval papal councils met frequently (1123, 1139, 1179, 1215, 1245, 1274, 1311), the greatest gap being a mere forty years, a single lifetime, and several bishops attended more than one council. The disorder of the fifteenth century provoked two councils only thirteen years apart (Constance, 1414–18; Basel-Ferrara-Florence, 1431–45), guaranteeing that some bishops attended both councils. Political pressure provoked Lateran V to meet from 1512 to 1517, while the Protestant Reformation necessitated Trent in 1545.

The longest gap between councils, 306 years, separates Trent from Vatican I, as the popes and the Vatican administrators governed the church without a council. Vatican I (1869–70), which gave the pope ordinary jurisdiction in every diocese, led many people to think that was the last of the councils, only to have John XXIII (1958–63) surprise the Catholic world by calling Vatican II (1962–65). There is thus no real pattern as to when or how often councils will meet. The situation of the church and the will of the pope determine that.

Nor does the length of a council provide any guide to its importance. One of the most productive councils, Lateran IV, met for only three sessions—November 11, 20, and 30 in 1215—and irrevocably and effectively changed the medieval church. Lateran V, on the other hand, met for five years (1512–17), ostensibly to deal with abuses, but did next to nothing to reform anything. Trent seems to have met for an interminable eighteen years (1545–63), but, in fact, it met in three sessions (1545–47, 1551–52, 1562–63), being frequently disrupted by political events and stretching over the pontificates of Paul III (1534–49), Julius III (1550–55), Marcellus II (1555), Paul IV (1555–59), and Pius IV (1559–65). In spite of these disruptions and changes of leadership, Trent accomplished a great deal both by responding to the Protestant challenge and by largely determining how Catholic reform would progress.

The number of participants also varied, but this too had little impact on the councils' productivity. "As few as a dozen members were in attendance at one point during Constantinople IV (869–870) and only seventeen during a particular session at Trent (1551–1552). These numbers stand in stark contrast to the 2,540 people clogging St. Peter's basilica during Vatican II's first session in 1962" (Bellitto, *General Councils*, 11).

Generalizing about the ecumenical councils can be a hazardous practice.

Mysteries and Heresies

Many of the councils, especially the first six, dealt with major doctrinal issues, such as the nature of the Trinity and the Person of Christ. Often those theologians whose views the councils rejected received the label "heretics." In the traditional view, this was appropriate since "everyone" knew the truth from the apostolic era onward, and these "heretics" rejected the common faith.

Modern scholars take a different approach. First, they emphasize that theologians deal with mysteries. In common parlance, a mystery means a puzzle of some kind that some brilliant scientist or detective will, with hard work and ingenious use of the little grey cells, eventually solve. But, in theology, the Greek word *mustérion* means something we cannot understand. Religion deals with the supernatural, that is, the *super naturam* in Latin, what is "beyond our nature" and thus impossible for us to understand.

When the Greek bishops at the early councils worked out the well-known trinitarian formula that the persons of the Trinity are three individual persons who share in the divine substance or essence, they did not "explain" the Trinity. That is simply impossible for humans because the divine being is beyond full human comprehension. What the bishops did do was to investigate the Scriptures and previous faith statements and creeds, and then they, as teachers of the church, devised a formula that they believed and hoped would explicate their *collective understanding* of the Trinity, not the very nature of the eternal Trinity.

A great medieval theologian, Anselm of Canterbury (ca. 1033–1109), gave theology its classic definition: *faith seeking understanding.* The theologian is a person of faith who believes in the Trinity and who *seeks* to understand it. No theologian can ever claim that her/his theology has explained the nature of the Trinity but rather that her/his theology has provided a rational explanation of Christian faith in the Trinity.

When we bear in mind that faith involves mysteries, we can understand that some theologians, trying to give shape and comprehension to those mysteries, would come up with formulas that the larger church would later reject. We should see them not always as heretics but sometimes as sincere Christians genuinely trying to make sense of their belief. Indeed, some "heretics" had distinguished careers as bishops; the fourth-century Apollinaris of Laodicea, ironically, had won fame as a fighter for orthodoxy. Some "heretics" died as martyrs, offering the ultimate witness for their faith, acts for which their critics rarely gave them any credit. At Vatican II, prominent theologians who had been silenced by the Vatican or their religious superiors for their supposedly unorthodox views played an important role in the formulation of some of the council's most important decrees.

The term "heterodoxy" means deviation from commonly accepted teaching, and that term better applies to many early theologies than heresy. But is there actual heresy? Absolutely. Heresy is a conscious deviation from a publicly stated doctrinal position of the church. Let me give an easy example. The church accepts the Gospel of Mark as inspired Scripture. Mark opens his gospel with "This is the Gospel of Jesus Christ, the Son of God." It would be heresy to deny that Jesus Christ *is* the Son of God, but it would not be heresy to speculate on *how* Jesus is the Son of God.

As we noted earlier, the church constantly involved itself in the affairs of the world, as it still does. Every council met within a particular historical framework, and we cannot understand a council outside that framework. On the other hand, a book on the councils cannot be a minisketch of church history. What we will do here is focus on the councils and try to illuminate their historical situations so that we can see each council against the backdrop of its era but without overburdening the historical record. In some cases, this approach presents no problems. For example, four medieval councils, the first four Lateran ones, all met in less than a century so their historical background is quite similar and can be relatively easy to follow. But more than three centuries span the gap between the closing of Trent and the opening of Vatican I, so our treatment of the historical background for Vatican I will necessarily be somewhat sketchy.

Finally, Vatican II presents some unique problems. First, there were in attendance more than two thousand bishops from around the world along with hundreds of *periti*, who produced a sizeable number of documents, making a thorough tracking of both people and writings beyond the scope of one chapter. Second, since Vatican II closed less than a half century ago, many Catholics remember the council in their own ways, and some participants, such as a young theologian named Joseph Ratzinger, are still alive and active in the church. Third, some of the effects of the council remain difficult to judge. For example, Vatican II introduced the vernacular liturgy to the Latin rite. The first generation of Catholics to grow up with *only* the vernacular liturgy, that is, those born in the 1960s, are just reaching middle age. Scholars need to examine their worship practices and patterns to see how they differ from those of generations raised in the Latin liturgy. Fourth, a literal mountain of material exists from and on this council. Before starting this chapter, I Googled Vatican II. Under a variety of headings ("Overview," "Documents"), some of which overlap, Google offers 11,296,000 web sites on the council. No doubt the number has grown since I wrote that sentence. In the face of an incomprehensible amount of material, this book will provide a historical sketch of the council and try to focus on what it did that was new and how it impacted the church. It will also be impossible in a book this size to go deeply into the various personalities of the council. In his masterful *What Happened at Vatican II*, John O'Malley provides a brief guide to the more prominent council participants; his list includes sixty-two names. A book can do that, but a chapter cannot. (For detailed but accessible accounts to this council, please consult O'Malley's volume and *A Brief History of Vatican II* by Giuseppe Alberigo; both are listed in the bibliography.) This text will provide a brief, historical account of that council.

And now, on to the councils.

CHAPTER ONE

The Trinitarian Councils

The Earliest Christians

In the Acts of the Apostles, the evangelist Luke reports how Jesus' disciples, both men and women, including Jesus' mother, got together and determined that Jesus' work on earth must be continued by the community, guided, as Luke says, by the Holy Spirit. But divine assistance did not make the task easy, and Luke shows us a community struggling not just against outsiders but also searching for its identity.

The earliest disciples were all pious Jews, and they saw their mission as only to the Jews, a strategy that enjoyed some remarkably large conversions but also engendered hostility with the Jerusalem authorities, who had favored Jesus' execution. Early on, problems surfaced between the Jewish-Christians of Palestine and converts from the Diaspora, that is, Jews living outside Palestine. The disciples successfully dealt with the problem, but it signaled that problems would occur as Christianity moved into a non-Palestinian environment.

But move it did, led by a diasporan Jew named Saul, better known as Paul, author of epistles and relentless missionary. Paul believed that the Holy Spirit motivated him to take Jesus' message to all people, not just to Jews in the Diaspora but also to Gentiles, an idea that puzzled and even repelled some of Jesus' Jewish followers. Opposition to Paul grew, and so the leaders of the Jerusalem church called a council, circa 50, to deal with the matter. To their credit, the Palestinian Jews agreed that the faith should be brought to all people, affirming both Paul and his work.

Paul and other, now anonymous, missionaries spread the faith throughout the cities of the eastern Mediterranean, along the way picking up a new name, "Christians" (followers of the *Chrístos*, the Messiah), a term first used of them in the Syrian city of Antioch, home to a large diasporan community.

Luke makes it clear that the missionaries often went to cities that already had sizeable Jewish populations who would be more receptive to the message. For instance, if a missionary told a pagan audience that Jesus is the Son of God, the pagans would naturally want to know, which god? When the Christian taught that Jesus fulfilled the prophecies of the Hebrew Bible, this would make little sense to pagans who looked to oracles, not books, to know the gods' will.

But the diasporan communities lay in Gentile lands, and more and more Gentiles entered the church. Demographic evidence for early Christianity is sketchy at best, but no later than 150 a majority of the Christians were Gentiles, as they have been ever since.

Christians in the Greco-Roman World

The movement into Gentile lands also meant that the Christians came into increasing contact with the Roman state and with Greco-Roman culture.

Popular images, especially in films, portray vicious Roman emperors avidly persecuting innocent Christians, but the reality differed considerably. The Romans tolerated a wide variety of religions within the empire, and they persecuted only when they believed a religion or its adherents might cause trouble, as, for example, the druids did in Britain. Otherwise the Roman attitude was "Peace and Taxes." The empire genuinely respected Judaism as a religion and made religious concessions to its adherents. Such tolerance did not reconcile the Jews to foreign domination, and they unsuccessfully revolted twice against the Romans in 66–70 and 132–35. The Romans harshly punished the rebels but made no attempt to eliminate Judaism as a religion.

The Romans initially tolerated Christianity. In the Acts of the Apostles Luke portrays the Roman proconsul in Corinth declining to get involved in a religious dispute between Paul and the Jews of that city, and several times Luke shows Roman officials saving Paul from angry pagan or Jewish mobs. This tradition continued.

But what about the persecutions? The first empire-wide persecution did not occur until 250; before that the persecutions were local and often caused by some unexpected event, such as a drought, for which the pagans blamed the Christians. Christian references to Jesus as Lord and as one who would come back to rule the world made pagans wonder if the Christians had political ambitions, while Christian liturgical terminology (eating Christ's body, drinking his blood) caused further suspicions. Significantly, for the first two centuries, all Christian literature to and from the Roman community was in Greek, suggesting a community largely of foreigners, which probably also augmented suspicions. But there were entire provinces (Spain, Britain) where no persecution was recorded before the empire-wide one of 250.

The best-known persecution, that of the emperor Nero (54–68) after the great fire in Rome in 64, involved only members of the Roman community, and Nero's successors did not persecute. Other persecutions broke out in North Africa, Egypt, and Gaul (modern France), but these did not form part of a continuous policy, just reaction to some local problem.

In fact, 99 percent of Christians lived and died in peace. Many became prominent locally, and some went well beyond that. In 258, when he initiated a short-lived persecution, the emperor Valerian (253–60) first removed all the Christians from the Roman senate, proof that Christians had reached that high level of Roman society. Diocletian (283–305) launched a persecution in 303, supposedly because Christian members of the imperial court crossed themselves to avoid blasphemy when the emperor was presiding over a pagan sacrifice. Furthermore, Diocletian could stand on the veranda of his palace and see a Christian church a short distance away.

Perhaps the best example of the Christian ability to fit into Roman society comes from Antioch. In 272 the church there was headed by Paul of Samosata, a luxury-loving, high-living bishop of questionable orthodoxy. Furious with their bishop, the members of the Antiochene community successfully appealed to a Roman court to get Paul deposed—Christians taking a Christian-versus-Christian dispute to a Roman court!

Although few endured persecution, all Christians had to live with the possibility of it, and many Romans never fully trusted them. There were martyrs, but, in general, Christians lived in peace in the empire.

In the long term, the Christian interaction with Greco-Roman culture had a much greater effect on the development of the faith. One consequence of this interaction is very visible—literally, very visible. The ancient Jews were aniconic, that is, their religion forbade them to make images of people, which is why we have images of great Babylonians, Egyptians, Greeks, and Romans, but of no Jews, not even David or Solomon. When Gentiles converted to Christianity, they had no reservations about art in religion, and so, in the late second century, Gentile artists produced the first Christian art. Having only pagan models to work from, they used those, and thus the earliest images of Jesus derive from images of Alexander the Great as the Jewish Jesus becomes a clean-shaven, toga-wearing Greek, while God the Father often looks like Zeus. Other Gentile customs and practices, which did not disagree with Christian teaching, entered the faith, just as the modern church, with its European heritage, opens itself up to practices from Catholics of the developing world.

But the most significant change, and one that echoed repeatedly in the ecumenical councils, was the adoption of Greek philosophy. Scholars long ago noted that the New Testament gives Jesus many titles, such as Savior, Lord, and High Priest, which connote action, but the New Testament authors rarely ask questions such as how could Jesus be both divine and human (the major concern of the third, fourth, fifth, and sixth ecumenical councils). Today Catholics know the church answers this question by teaching that Jesus is one *person* (Greek term) with two *natures* (Greek term), while in the Trinity the Son of God is *homoóusios* (consubstantial; Greek term) with the Father. The great theologians of antiquity made extensive use of Greek philosophers. For example, Augustine of Hippo (354–430) drew from Platonic philosophy; the medieval theologians did likewise, favoring Aristotle; in the modern era, the greatest Catholic theologian of the twentieth century, the German Karl Rahner, SJ (1904–84), drew from both Immanuel Kant and Martin Heidegger.

How early did the Christians embrace philosophy? The New Testament provides the occasional hint, but most scholars would point to the middle of the second century and a group of writers called the Apologists. Apologetics is the science of rationally defending one's position. The Apologists, all Gentile Christians, wanted to demonstrate that Christianity was not a disloyal religion of Near Eastern peasants, and so they strove to show the Greeks and Romans the truth about the faith. This marked the first time in history that Christian writers targeted non-Christians, and, naturally, the Apologists had to use arguments that would convince outsiders. To claim that Jesus fulfilled prophecies of the Hebrew Bible might impress Jews but had no meaning for pagan Gentiles for whom different arguments were needed. The best-known Apologist, a Palestinian named Justin, used philosophical terminology most effectively and paved the way for others to do likewise. (He died a martyr in Rome circa 165 and is known as Justin Martyr.)

By the time Nicea I convened in 325, the overwhelmingly Greek-speaking bishops there had accepted the notion that Greek philosophy could help in formulating Christian teaching.

Councils before Nicea

A council is a natural idea. People with responsibilities think it best to confer with others who have responsibilities. We may safely assume that Jesus' followers were having meetings to discuss pressing matters very shortly after his death, but the first council mentioned anywhere appears in chapter 15 of the Acts of the Apostles, where Luke recounts the Council of Jerusalem circa 50.

A great issue faced the Christians. Led by James, head of the Jerusalem community, they had focused on converting Jews, and most doubted whether they should spread the faith to Gentiles. The unquestioned champion of evangelizing the Gentiles was the apostle Paul. Basically, Paul presented his case; the assembled leaders, apparently all men, discussed what Paul had said; and James, speaking on behalf of the other leaders under the inspiration of the Holy Spirit (Acts 15:28), agreed that the missionaries could go to the Gentiles.

Luke tells us about this council in exactly one page of the biblical text. We know nothing of the discussions that must have ensued, but we can see that what the council decided became definitive. Or did it?

In his epistle to the Galatians, Paul mentions that after the council he was working among the Christians of Antioch. Peter the apostle was there, and he ate and mingled with the Gentile converts. But when representatives of the Jerusalem church arrived, they refused to eat with the Gentiles, and, to Paul's shock, Peter and even Paul's missionary companion Barnabas did likewise. Paul tells us that he rebuked Peter to his face. We do not know Peter's side of the story, and we must recall that Peter died a martyr among the Gentile Romans, so he clearly changed his attitude, but Paul's account gives the first example of a recurring problem in conciliar history: believers, even leaders, who were reluctant to accept conciliar decisions.

Evidence for councils mounts quickly. Bishops met in Asia Minor (modern Turkey) in the second century. By the end of that century, the North African Bishop of Rome, Victor I (189–98), convoked a council to deal with the thorny liturgical problem of determining the date of Easter, and he convinced other churches to meet in councils and agree with his position. The third century saw the bishops of North Africa meeting annually, when possible, to deal with matters challenging the church in that area. In 256 no fewer than eighty-seven African bishops attended a council in Carthage, a larger number than would attend some sessions of several ecumenical councils.

In the first two decades of the fourth century, just before ecumenical council Nicea I, we know of councils in Spain, Asia Minor, and Gaul. Two major elements of the ecumenical synods arose initially at these regional meetings. First, the metropolitans or chief bishops of the provinces presided at them. This practice did not apply universally, especially when bishops from mostly rural areas might get together, but it became common. The leaders were the bishops of Rome in Italy, of Carthage in North Africa, of

Arles in Gaul, of Alexandria in Egypt, and of Antioch in Syria. These bishops achieved this status not just because they were bishops of the largest cities in their provinces but because many of these churches were apostolic foundations, a prestigious point in an era and place where tradition counted heavily.

Very significantly, most of these apostolic sees lay in the East, where most apostolic missionary activity had occurred. In fact, only one metropolitan see in the West could claim an apostolic foundation, and that was Rome, which actually claimed a double apostolic foundation, namely, Peter and Paul. (In later centuries, the popes would focus primarily upon the Petrine foundation.) Except for North Africa, Rome's unique and impressive apostolic foundation usually made it the unquestioned leader among the Latin bishoprics. Roman bishops, when claiming authority over another see, did not cite the civic or secular importance of Rome but rather insisted they were writing with the authority of the apostle Peter.

The other major element that preceded Nicea was the actual conduct of the councils. To quote Leo Davis, SJ:

> There is evidence to show that the deliberative procedures of the Roman Senate left their mark on the collective deliberations of the Christian bishops. Bishops adopted for many of their councils the official senatorial formulae of convocation. Like the Senate the council was a deliberative assembly, each bishop having equal rights in its discussions. Like the imperial magistrate who presided over the Senate, the principal bishop first read out a program designed to keep discussion to the point at issue. The assembled bishops were then interrogated and each offered his *sententia*, his official response. A final vote was usually not necessary, for the *sententiae* most often issued in unanimity, the result of previous negotiation. The unanimous decision was circulated among the faithful in a synodal letter. Bishops then felt themselves bound to abide by the decisions thus promulgated. [The emperor] Constantine [who called Nicea] would later find the Church governed by procedures with which he was familiar. (*First Seven*, 23)

This acceptance of senatorial procedure was just one of many ways in which the governance of the empire impacted the church, which also utilized the empire's system of dividing regions into dioceses and provinces.

Constantine

Nicea I met because of two momentous events in Christian history: the advent of the first Christian emperor and the final reckoning of trinitarian theology.

Diocletian, the persecuting emperor, resigned his office in 305, having prepared an ordered transition for the government of the empire, which he had divided into two parts, East and West. But the transition failed because ambitious generals and politicians who were slighted in the transition decided to take matters into their own hands. In a few years the empire suffered from a massive civil war with seven claimants for the imperial throne.

One was Constantine, a pagan who worshiped the sun god. He had enjoyed success in the war, and in 312 he faced his greatest test, a battle outside Rome against the pagan general occupying the city. Just before the battle, he had either a vision or a dream (two accounts of the event survive) in which he saw either a cross or the Chi-Rho ☧, a symbol based on the first two Greek letters, Chi (*X*) and Rho (*P*), in the word *Chrístos*. Believing this to be a sign that the Christian god was on his side, Constantine had his soldiers put the Chi-Rho on their shields and then went on to win the decisive battle of the Milvian Bridge, which resulted in the death of the general opposing him.

In 313 Constantine and his ally Licinius met in northern Italy and issued the Edict of Milan, which gave Christians freedom of worship and restored to them much of their confiscated property. Using this newfound freedom, the Christians successfully evangelized in much of the empire.

But the bishops found themselves facing a totally new situation. Pagan emperors considered themselves responsible to the gods for the welfare of the empire. One persecutor, Decius (249–51), believed that by allowing the Christians to flourish, he had angered the gods and thus he had to persecute. Constantine inherited this religious obligation. With the welfare of the empire at stake, he could not afford to ignore religious matters, pagan or Christian. Still a pagan, he did not interfere in Christian doctrinal matters, but he made it clear to the bishops that he expected the churches to support order in the empire. When they did not, he was furious. A bitter dispute broke out in North Africa over who was the true bishop of Carthage. When the dispute led to disorder and even riots in 316, Constantine intervened with force. The shocked bishops watched a pagan emperor "solve" a Christian religious dispute. But there was more to come.

Circa 319 the emperor himself converted to Christianity. The impossible had happened—a Christian emperor! His example caused many aristocrats to convert, and the once despised and even persecuted church now enjoyed imperial favor. Yet with it came even more imperial involvement (= interference) in Christian affairs. When some Christian intellectuals, like the church historian Eusebius of Caesarea, began to claim that God had chosen Constantine to reign, the emperor moved from being interested politician to sacred figure, just as sacred, if not more so, than the bishops themselves. This secular-ruler-chosen-by-God theory would haunt the churches—Catholic, Orthodox, and Anglican—down to the twentieth century.

But before Constantine tried to control the churches, he had one other matter to settle. He resented having to share the empire with the pagan Licinius. The two had quarreled and even fought some desultory campaigns as early as 316, but then they made peace. But Licinius rightly feared his former ally's ambitions, and he also feared that his own Christian subjects were disloyal, preferring Constantine to him. He foolishly began a minor persecution, which provided his rival with an excuse to invade. Constantine defeated and imprisoned Licinius in 324 and then executed him and his son and heir in 325. The new Christian emperor now ruled all of Rome.

Christian support had helped Constantine, but he knew that many of the Roman pagans, especially the aristocracy, resented his newfound faith. To thwart them, on November 8, 324, he started work on a new capital city and, with wanton pride, named it after himself, Constantinople, "the *pólis* (city) of Constantine." He nurtured the city, aiding its growth and decreeing that no pagan temple could be built there; his would be a thoroughly Christian capital. Again to thwart the pagans in Italy, he created a new senate for the new capital, thus weakening the stature of the senate in Rome. He also adorned his new city with large civic and ecclesiastical buildings, a practice followed by his successors.

Constantinople would affect the church in a significant way, as we shall see when we study the later councils. Since the leading Christian metropolitans or patriarchs traced their ecclesiastical lineage back to the apostles, naturally the emperor wanted the bishop of his city to have equal prestige. His staff made a half-hearted attempt to find some first-century martyr from the general area to give Constantinople some apostolicity, but soon Constantine and his successors made it clear: as bishop of the church in the emperor's own city, the bishop of Constantinople had equal stature to those sees claiming apostolic foundations. Some apostolically founded churches could live with this, but not the major four—Alexandria, Antioch, Jerusalem, and Rome—who resented Constantinople's *nouveau riche* status. The seed Constantine planted in 324 would bear much bitter ecclesiastical fruit in the centuries to come.

Just a year after founding his new city, the emperor made his weight felt in the universal church: he called an ecumenical council.

Trinitarian Theology

The other momentous event standing behind Nicea was the culmination of trinitarian theology. We can easily see how disputes could arise about the Trinity, whose persons appear in the opening verses of the earliest piece of Christian literature, Paul's first epistle to the Thessalonians (1:1-5). From the Jews the Christians inherited a rigorous monotheism, evident in Paul's epistles and the gospels of Matthew, Mark, and Luke. But in the Gospel of John a belief hinted at in other parts of the New Testament now became manifest. The prologue to that gospel, written in Asia Minor circa 100, teaches that the Word of God is God and that this divine Word became incarnate in Jesus. Evidence for Christian belief in Jesus' divinity also appears in a pagan source, written sometime between 112 and 116. Pliny the Younger, Roman governor of western Asia Minor, said in a letter to the emperor that the local Christians got up at dawn, went to a riverbank, and sang hymns to Christ "as a god." This belief spread quickly, appearing in Alexandria by 200. Indeed, Egyptians would dominate the trinitarian discussion at Nicea I.

But if God the Father is a deity, and God the Son, incarnate in Jesus, is also a deity, have the Christians not compromised monotheism by believing in two gods? (For reasons still uncertain, the earliest trinitarian debates did not include the Holy Spirit.) The Christians did not, of course, believe that, but they had to explain the mystery of how to preserve monotheism while insisting that both God the Father and God the Son are divine. This task would be theology at its most fundamental.

The earliest Christian writers after the New Testament, the Apostolic Fathers of the late first and early second century, used phrases like "God incarnate" and "God in human form" to describe Christ, but they did not work out any systematic theology. The Apologists like Justin Martyr took the matter further, using the Greek concept of *lógos* or "word" of God—well known from John's gospel—to express the relation of Father and Son, that is, the Word emanated from the Father and became incarnate. Another Apologist, Athenagoras, actually used the word *triás*, which later became the common Greek word for "Trinity." But the Apologists basically taught an "economic" trinitarianism, that is, the one Father unfolded into two and then three, his Word (= Son) and his Wisdom (= Spirit), a theologically small step by later standards but real progress.

A conservative reaction quickly set in the West, that is, in Rome and North Africa. Fearful that elevating the status of the Son and Spirit would lead to polytheism, some Roman theologians created Monarchianism, a theological approach that emphasized the unity of the three to the point of denying the distinct existence of Son and Spirit. Some Monarchian theologians adopted modalism, that "Son" and "Spirit" are names for the different forms or "modes" of the Father's activity, for example, "Son" for his redemptive work, "Spirit" for his sanctifying work. Other Monarchians advocated adoptionism, the belief that Jesus was just a good man in whom God dwelt as a divine, vivifying power.

Other third-century theologians turned on the Monarchians and advocated a more advanced economic trinitarianism, still seeing God as unfolding from one into three, but these theologians, especially an African named Tertullian, greatly advanced trinitarian theology with useful terminology. Tertullian first used the Latin word *trinitas* (*tria*, "three," plus *unitas*, "unity"), from which would come the English word "Trinity." He also used words like *substantia* and *persona*, basically arguing that in the Trinity the three persons partook in the divine substance. This sounds like later orthodoxy, but Tertullian remained an economic trinitarian who also thought of the divine in materialist terms. But the terminology he created would greatly aid later Latin theologians.

Economic trinitarianism soon fell to subordinationism, the prevalent third-century view. A great Greek theologian, Origen of Alexandria, insisted that God the Father always had to be a father, that is, the Son's generation from the Father is eternal and not part of a gradual unfolding. Other theologians quickly followed Origen's lead, dooming economic trinitarianism. But Origen also believed in a hierarchical relationship in the Trinity, and he subordinated the Son to the Father and the Spirit to the Son.

The third century also revealed a serious tension in Greek and Latin approaches to the Trinity. The Greeks feared that the Latins put such emphasis upon the unity of the Trinity that the individuality of the persons could be lost. Conversely, the Latins feared that the Greeks put so much emphasis on the individuality of the persons that the oneness of the deity would be obscured. To this was added a serious terminological problem.

As anyone who has studied a foreign language knows, the words for the same object in two languages often do not match exactly. For a piece of furniture, that may be inconvenient, but for advanced theology, it could be devastating. Some Latins spoke of three "persons" and one "substance" in the Trinity, but the standard Greek equivalent of "person" was *hypóstasis*, which could also mean "substance." There was also another Greek word for "substance," namely, *ousía*. When Greeks spoke of three *hypóstases*, Latins often heard "three substances," raising fears that Greeks were compromising the unity of the Trinity. Clearly this situation could not endure forever. In the early fourth century, an Alexandrian priest named Arius (ca. 260–336) put an end to it.

Arius recognized the inherent weakness of subordinationism: can a divine being be subordinate? Clearly the answer was no, and Arius then drew a crucial conclusion: the Son of God is subordinate because he is not divine. The Word is a creature, that is, a created being. He existed long before us because God created the world through him; he has perfections we cannot dream of, but he did not share God's being or enjoy any of God's manifest perfections. In a crucial phrase for Arius and his followers, "there was when he (the Son) was not." Although damned in Christian tradition as a diabolical heresiarch, Arius deserves credit for getting to the real question: how can the Son and the Father both be divine?

Arius commanded much attention as a preacher, and his teachings spread. The bishop of Alexandria opposed him, but Arius found support among other bishops, especially in Palestine. Some Christians loathed Arius for what he taught; others loathed him because they had no answer to the questions he raised. The Arian controversy quickly divided Christians in the eastern Mediterranean, which infuriated the most important Christian of all: the emperor Constantine.

The First Council of Nicea

Emperor first and Christian second, Constantine was enraged that his newfound faith, which he hoped might unite the sprawling empire, was now dividing it. But the emperor came up with an imperial idea: a council of the entire *oikoumene*, the inhabited (Christian) world. As a divinely chosen emperor, he had the right—which no Christian questioned—to call such a council. He eventually decided upon the town of Nicea in modern northwestern Turkey, a short journey from his palace in Nicomedia. He sent a summons to all bishops to attend. In fact, not all bishops, especially Westerners, could attend. The aged Bishop of Rome, Sylvester I (314–35), sent two priests to represent him. In addition, the emperor's theological advisor was a Westerner, a Spaniard, Hosius of Cordova (ca. 260–357). As for the emperor's participation, he did not take part in the daily discussion nor did he vote on any issue. He considered it his task to make sure the council got the job done.

On May 20, 325, the overwhelmingly Greek-speaking council of more than three hundred bishops opened to a welcoming speech by the emperor, who arrived in state, a very public witness to the new status of Christianity. Bishops who had been maimed in Roman persecutions were kissed by the emperor, a gracious show of his appreciation for their suffering. But perhaps not completely gracious—at least two bishops came from beyond the imperial borders, living proof that the emperor's new religion extended beyond his political jurisdiction, a pointed demonstration of Christianity's range and significance. (And no account of the bishops at Nicea would be complete without mention of a charitable but barely-known bishop from the southwestern Asia Minor town of Myra: Nicholas, who as St. Nicholas, would evolve into Santa Claus and become the best known of all Christian saints.)

Regrettably, the acts of the council do not survive but only accounts given by those who were present. Theologians had been attacking Arius for some time, but he had brilliantly used diverse scriptural passages to support his teaching. The bishops had to create some formula that would answer him while simultaneously reflecting the faith of the church. Arius had some supporters at the council, who put forward the creeds of their local churches as sufficient for a doctrinal statement, but the rest of the bishops rejected these, settling instead on a creed used in a Palestinian church, possibly Jerusalem. But to that creed came a crucial addition.

The bishops had learned that Arius could accept any kind of scriptural formulation and give it his own interpretation, and he had also managed to accept various creeds in a similar way. The bishops needed a formula that would pin Arius down, but this approach faced formidable opposition from a sizeable number of conservative bishops who objected to using terms not found in Scripture. The more theologically advanced bishops recognized something had to be done, and help arrived from a surprising source.

Constantine wanted to know if the bishops would agree to the term *homooúsios*, a Greek version of the Latin *consubstantialis*, that is, that the Father and Son were consubstantial, sharing the same divine substance. The emperor was a sharp man but no theologian; scholars assume the term came from his theological advisor, Hosius of Cordova, although "consubstantial" did not have official status in the Latin churches. Although some bishops, such as those in union with the Alexandrians, would have been open to this, most bishops reacted with surprise or indignation, and for two reasons. First, the term does not appear in the Bible. This meant that the bishops would have to go outside of Scripture to find an adequate way to express their faith. Although this is normal today, this represented a step many hesitated to take. Second, *homooúsios* had a somewhat questionable history.

As we saw earlier, Greek terminology relating to person and substance allowed for different shades of meaning. *Homooúsios* could mean that Father, Son, and Holy Spirit partook in the same divine substance, but it could also mean that they were literally identical with no distinction among them. To many bishops, the Latin-speaking emperor and his Latin theological advisor were trying to force a Greek version of a Latin term that would in turn force the bishops to assent to Western Monarchianism.

But the controversial term had several advantages. First, more and more bishops were coming to realize that Arius could not be pinned down by relying only on Scripture and that an extrabiblical term that represented the essence of Scripture would suffice. Second, "consubstantial" was widely, if unofficially, used in the Latin West, and rejection of a Latin concept would impair church unity at a crucial time. Third, although the term had been created by second-century Christians called Gnostics, who were widely reviled as heretics, *homooúsios* had been used by orthodox Christians as well. Fourth, and most important, Arius could not accept the term.

The bishops accepted the imperial suggestion and adopted a statement of faith that said that the Father and Son are of one substance, that the Son was begotten of the Father and was not created, and that the Son was True God of True God. As would be typical of councils down to Vatican I, the bishops included anathemas (denunciations). They declared anathema the notions that there was a time when the Son did not exist, that he was created from nothing, and that he did not share the same substance with the Father. Arius and his supporters could not accept these. Constantine banished Arius to Illyria (modern Balkans), and two Arian bishops who refused to sign the council's statement were deposed. Victory for the "homoousians," as they were called, seemed complete, but events after the council would shatter that illusion.

Although best remembered for its trinitarian formulation, Nicea also did important pastoral work, passing what are typically called disciplinary decrees. None was more important than trying to standardize the reckoning of the date of Easter, a major problem since the second century. Considering it scandalous that some Christians celebrated the feast of the Resurrection on different days, the bishops ordered the churches using the traditional Jewish calendar to reckon the date by following the method used at Rome and Alexandria, apparently unaware that those two churches did not agree completely on the method of computation.

The bishops also attempted to settle two schisms, one in Egypt and one in Syria, and they also dealt with moderation and compassion with how to readmit to communion Christians who had lapsed during persecutions. Institutional issues also emerged. The bishops acknowledged the supremacy of Alexandria in Egypt and of Antioch in Syria; they also accepted Rome's supremacy in "the West" but did not spell out any formal geographical range. This basically acknowledged an existing situation since the three great bishoprics had already emerged as leaders. Jerusalem also obtained special status, but its bishop remained under the authority of the bishop of Caesarea, the Roman administrative capital in that area. Constantinople did not yet exist as a city (its solemn inauguration as a *pólis* occurred in 330) and subsequent councils would deal with its status. The bishops also handled lesser issues, such as forbidding a bishop to ordain as a cleric someone from another diocese. The general tendency was to impose more order on the daily life of the church.

Nicea also set a pattern for future councils by issuing decrees and canons. In general, decrees are dogmatic statements, proclaiming the faith of the church on a point of dogma, although some councils passed disciplinary decrees. Canons were ordinances, often brief, that included a penalty for ignoring or disobeying them. The penalty often took the form, "Let him be anathema," that is, cursed, but some canons had more specific penalties.

On June 19, 325, the bishops officially approved the council's decree on the Trinity. The emperor's theological advisor, Hosius, was the first to sign the decree, followed by two priests representing the Bishop of Rome. The Eastern bishops recognized the primacy of the Roman see as a double-apostolic foundation (Peter and Paul) and as the church of the imperial capital. Then, as now with the Orthodox churches, the Eastern bishops did not acknowledge any Roman jurisdictional authority over their churches.

The council continued until August 25, and the emperor invited the bishops to a sumptuous feast, which, understandably, none of them passed up.

A question that scholars still debate is the nature of the Nicene Creed. The evidence suggests that the bishops chose a baptismal creed from the church of Jerusalem and then revised it. As we shall see, what believers know as the Nicene Creed was actually drawn up at the next ecumenical council, Constantinople I, in 381. But we do know that the creed that Nicea produced did affirm that Father and Son are *homooúsios*, but the council did not pronounce on the Holy Spirit, merely noting, ". . . and [we believe] in the Holy Spirit."

Nicea's Historical and Ecclesial Significance

Historians consider Nicea's greatest significance as the establishment of a new, creative way for the church to deal with crises. The assembled bishops, speaking as a group, could now affirm what was Christian teaching on particular doctrinal points. Christians were no longer bound to twisting the Bible endlessly to prove a point. The bishops strove to keep to the biblical text but, failing that, strove to propound a teaching that respected the Bible and was consonant with it. For example, trinitarian references or allusions to Christ's divinity abound in the New Testament, and so the bishops claimed that their teaching drew out what the Bible did not say fully, but, at the same time, they recognized that they had indeed taught something new. Later generations would call this process the development of doctrine.

Did the Nicene bishops recognize what they had done? We cannot be sure, but Constantine was. After the council, he wrote to some bishops that he considered the judgment of three hundred bishops to be none other than the judgment of God.

After the Council

This initial ecumenical council foreshadowed elements of many others, one of which was a confused reaction following the council. Although, theologically speaking, the Holy Spirit guides the councils to their ultimate conclusions, historically speaking, after councils some participants often have second thoughts about what happened or are surprised at the reaction of others to the council's work. In fairness to Nicea I, it was the first ecumenical council and did not have the prestige and acceptance that came regularly to later councils, but the reaction to this initial council was genuinely traumatic.

The problem lay in *homooúsios*. The term proved too innovative for many conservative bishops, whose concern about its lack of a scriptural foundation had not abated, but the real problem was a fear that the term had Monarchian overtones. Nicea's opponents sensed this unease and slowly worked to discredit the council and its leaders. The politically minded and well-connected Arian bishop Eusebius of Nicomedia targeted three chief Nicenes: a bishop of Antioch who had made disparaging remarks about Constantine's mother (who had been his father's mistress); a bishop of Ancyra who had genuine modalist leanings; and Athanasius, an Alexandrian deacon who accompanied his bishop to Nicea and who now reigned as patriarch of the Egyptian city. The first two targets fell easily, but Athanasius proved a tougher one to hit. An autocratic ruler, he made many enemies, and his enemies had much ammunition to use against him, including telling Constantine that the Alexandrian bishop could, if he wished, halt the flow of grain from Egypt to the emperor's new capital, Constantinople. In 336, Athanasius went into exile in Trier, Germany, virtually the end of the empire for an Egyptian. So successful were Nicea's enemies that in 336 Constantine even agreed to the rehabilitation of Arius in Constantinople. Amazingly, the evening before the formal ceremony of rehabilitation, Arius died of an intestinal hemorrhage in a public toilet, which the Nicenes enthusiastically interpreted as a sign from God. When the emperor died in the following year, the Nicenes looked to a new day.

But that day did not arrive. Constantine's three sons—Constantine II, Constantius II, and Constans—divided the empire. But Constans warred against Constantine II, conquered, and executed him, so Constans, a Nicene, ruled in the West, while Constantius II, an Arian, ruled in the East. Given the great role of the supposed divinely appointed emperor in Roman society, it made a great difference who the emperor was. Generally, the Western bishops supported Nicea, and they supported the Eastern Nicenes. In 340 Pope Julius I (337–52) offered refuge to Athanasius, and the pope made it clear to the Eastern bishops that Rome supported Nicea. In the East, the bishops were divided. Some openly professed Arianism, but the greater number rejected this yet had no way to express their faith in such a way that responded to Arianism but did not commit to *homooúsios*, still thinking it to have Monarchian overtones.

Naturally, this situation distressed the bishops, who worked to rectify it through a series of councils, both regional and larger. But they could not avoid imperial intervention in their activities, and the Arian emperor Constantius had no qualms about meddling in the councils, with the result that the Eastern councils produced a wide variety of creeds that managed to please many and offend just as many. Furthermore, the Western bishops would accept nothing less than complete support for Nicea, and so they routinely rejected the Eastern creeds. A confused situation worsened in 350 when the Western Nicene emperor Constans lost his empire and his life to a usurper, whom Constantius in turn defeated and executed. Now one man ruled the empire, and he was an Arian.

But even an emperor's power had limits. Despite his strongest efforts, Constantius could not convince the people of Alexandria to abandon Athanasius, who frequently fled his see to avoid arrest, once escaping to the desert where he enjoyed the hospitality of the desert monks before his triumphal return to his episcopal city in 346. The emperor never abandoned his attempts to compromise Nicea, but Athanasius was slowly coming to the conclusion that he had to reach out to the bishops who had reservations about *homooúsios*.

Many Nicenes took a hard line toward dissidents, treating them as heretics. But, as is so often the case with the promiscuous use of that word, the bishops were not so much "heretics" as concerned about what the council had actually taught. Athanasius did not help things by making no distinction between *ousía* and *hypóstasis*, so that Greek-speaking bishops could conclude that Nicea taught that the Father, Son, and Spirit were actually just one person, not three. Furthermore, for a time after the council Athanasius himself rarely used the word *homooúsios*. Indeed, the leading Western Nicene theologian, Hilary of Poitiers (d. 367), had not heard of *homooúsios* and the Nicene Creed until after the year 350.

In what was becoming an uncertain theological environment, some Eastern bishops hoped to refute Arius and avoid Monarchianism by saying that in the Trinity, Father and Son are *hómoios*, that is, "like" one another. This term avoided several problems, but its general vagueness obviated its value. Far more acceptable was *homoioúsios*, that is, "alike in substance." As a way of opposing Arianism and avoiding *homooúsios*, this term enjoyed great popularity. Even Liberius of Rome (352–66), a supporter of Nicea, enjoyed communion with homoiousian bishops.

Athanasius now worked to make his theology clearer, but politics constantly weakened his attempts at reconciliation with other bishops. Constantius II arranged for council after council to find some formula to replace Nicea, only to be foiled by Western resistance and by Eastern Nicenes. When he died childless in 361, his only living male relative was Julian, known to history as Julian the Apostate because he had abandoned Christianity for paganism. For his own safety, he had kept his views private, but, as emperor, he tried to reinvigorate paganism. Athanasius again went into exile but assured his people that he would return soon. He did. Julian's reforms failed, and the emperor died in battle against the Persians in 363, after a reign of only twenty months. But from Julian comes the definitive observation on the post-Nicene battles: "Wild animals do not attack one another as fiercely as do these Christians."

After the brief (363–64) reign of an elderly Nicene, two emperors again shared rule, the Nicene Valentinian I (364–75) in the West and the Arian Valens (364–78) in the East. Occupied with barbarian invasions until 369, Valens could cause only limited problems for the Nicenes, and at this time Athanasius took up a new aspect of Nicene theology: the person of the Holy Spirit. What strikes modern believers about the Nicene Creed is the brief phrase "and in the Holy Spirit," an oddity after the more detailed descriptions of the Father and Son. As he so often did, Athanasius responded to the misunderstandings of Nicea.

Many bishops considered the Holy Spirit to be a lesser person in the Trinity and possibly not even fully divine. Athanasius realized that such a belief would weaken *homooúsios*, and so he made it clear that just as the Son shares the essence of the Father, so does the Spirit partake in the essence of the Son, that is, he was *homooúsios* with the Son. But, as Davis puts it, "Yet, according to the custom of the time, Athanasius did not call the Spirit God" (*First Seven*, 107).

Always remembered as the great defender of Nicea and as the most important of ancient trinitarian theologians, Athanasius was nevertheless not the man to bring the post-Nicene controversies to an end. He remained a polarizing figure, and his high-handed treatment of others, especially in his own diocese, made him widely resented. He had effectively created a strong alliance with Rome, but many Eastern bishops had reservations about Western theology, and, as papal claims grew in the fourth century, the Rome-Alexandria alliance did not endear Athanasius to bishops in the East. Fortunately for the church, three men emerged to secure Nicea's triumph.

Scholars refer to these three as the Cappadocians, because all came from the same area of eastern Asia Minor. They were Basil of Caesarea (330–79), his brother Gregory of Nyssa (ca. 335–ca. 395), and their friend Gregory Nazianzen (329–89). The Orthodox churches revere Basil as a great ecclesial statesman and a major theoretician of Orthodox monasticism, Gregory of Nyssa as a great mystic, and Gregory Nazianzen as a great theologian; indeed, in Orthodox tradition he is known simply as "Gregory the Theologian."

For our purposes, their greatness lies in their ability to see that the Nicenes and homoiousians were not far apart. They worked for decades to show that what Nicea teaches is that in the Trinity are one *ousía* and three hypostases, that is, to finally equate *ousía* with the Latin notion of substance and *hypóstasis* with the Latin notion of person. That one sentence sums up a great deal of complicated theology and complicated negotiating, but slowly and surely the Cappadocians showed their episcopal brethren that Nicea, still firmly supported in Egypt and the West, could be understood in a way that proclaimed genuine Christian teaching, did not violate biblical statements about the Trinity, and did not contain Monarchian sentiments. The Holy Spirit presented more of a problem because Basil, although suggesting the Spirit's divinity, never taught it openly. But Gregory of Nyssa took the Nicene Creed to its logical conclusion. Again, to quote Davis: "While confessing the unity of nature [in the Trinity], he [Gregory] insisted that the difference among the hypostases rises out of their mutual relationships. The Father is the Cause, the Son is of the Cause directly, the Holy Spirit of the Cause mediately. The Father had no origins; the Son is generated by the Father; the Holy Spirit proceeds from the Father through the Son" (*First Seven*, 113). But generation in the Trinity is eternal and implies no lessening of the divinity of Son and Spirit.

Although not every problem disappeared, finally theologians had cleared up Nicea's terminological inexactitude, and the Eastern bishops (excluding, of course, the confirmed Arians) could now accept Nicea. The struggles continued but not for much longer. The Arian emperor Valens died in battle against the Goths in 378. The Western emperor, a Nicene named Gratian (367–83), appointed a Spanish Nicene named Theodosius as emperor in Constantinople; he reigned as Theodosius I (379–95). Both Nicene emperors moved against the Arians, depriving them of churches, removing them from office, and finally outlawing Arianism. (In fact, this move did not eliminate Arianism, since Arian missionaries had successfully evangelized among the Germanic tribes north of the Danube, and when these tribes eventually conquered much of the Western empire, Arianism returned for some centuries, although it would never be the majority faith.)

Yet no one could ignore the troubles of preceding decades, and now on the throne of Constantine, Theodosius I decided to imitate his predecessor, and so he called a council to meet in Constantinople in 381 to put an official stamp on the end of Arianism.

The First Council of Constantinople

In addition to its dealing with trinitarian doctrine, this council also shows clearly the Catholic notion of the relation of the papacy to an ecumenical council. The emperor and his theological advisors invited 150 Eastern bishops. They did not inform Damasus of Rome, and the West was practically unrepresented. The popes of later ages did, however, accept Constantinople I as an ecumenical council for Catholics.

Regrettably for historians, the acts of the council do not survive, so the story must be put together by accounts provided by participants. One thing is evident: ecclesiastical politics played a great role, a harbinger of what would happen at future councils. The emperor had the bishop of Antioch appointed president of the council, but he died shortly after it began. In the meantime, the great theologian Gregory of Nazianzus had become bishop of Constantinople, having transferred from a smaller see, and the emperor now appointed him the council's new president. Since the ancient church often used the imagery of a bishop being wedded to his see (it was used in a canon at Nicea), many bishops had reservations about the legitimacy of Gregory's transfer and, in effect, his promotion, although the council initially approved of his presidency. But when the bishops from Egypt arrived, things changed. Accustomed to being the East's premier theologians and bishops, the Alexandrians resented the bishops of Constantinople who, in Alexandrian eyes, owed their prominence to a secular event, being bishops of the Eastern capital. Again the issue of the transfer arose. Gregory could have weathered the ensuing storm, but he was a theologian, not a politician, and he resigned the presidency of the council and his bishopric. Piqued by the treatment of his bishop, the emperor Theodosius I recommended (= ordered) the bishops to accept the appointment of "Nectarius, an elderly civil official from the imperial legal department. Though only a catechumen, he was hurried through baptism and ordained a bishop in his baptismal robes, two bishops being assigned to instruct him in his episcopal duties. The new bishop of Constantinople became the third president of the council" (Davis, *First Seven*, 120). Yet, despite this inauspicious beginning, the council did good work.

Most important, it confirmed the teaching of Nicea. The labors of the Cappadocians bore fruit. But, in a significant example of the development of doctrine, the bishops moved beyond the previous ecumenical council to affirm the full divinity of the Holy Spirit, causing a number of bishops from Macedonia to leave the council in protest of this "innovation." The creed of the council in its original form does survive, and many scholars think, as at Nicea, the bishops adopted an existing creed from a local church, in this case, from a Constantinopolitan baptismal creed. Other scholars wonder if there even was a creed, simply because no mention of such appears in church documents until 451. But Norman Tanner, an expert in creedal statements, speaks of the "creed of 381 . . . usually called the Nicene creed . . . since it was considered a development of the creed of 325, not something different from it. In scholarly circles, however, it is more accurately called the Nicene-Constantinopolitan creed . . . in order to distinguish the two" (*Councils*, 24–25). Some scholars consider the two creeds to be distinct (Kelly, *Creeds*, 304). The general consensus, however, is that the council did not draw up a creed but rather adopted one that could be harmonized with Nicea. We will thus speak of such a creed from Constantinople I, even though it does not appear in history until the Council of Chalcedon in 451.

In addition to affirming its predecessor and proclaiming the Holy Spirit as fully *homooúsios* with the Father and Son, Constantinople I also passed some canons, the largest number dealing with groups now deemed heretical by Nicene standards. The council warned bishops to restrict their ecclesiastical ventures to their own dioceses, proof that the earlier warning of Nicea was being widely ignored. But the most important canon turned out to be the third: "The Bishop of Constantinople shall have primacy of honor after the Bishop of Rome because Constantinople is the new Rome." This was genuinely revolutionary. Traditionally, the prestige of a see had depended upon its apostolic foundation (many Eastern sees had been founded by the apostle Paul) and its tradition of doctrinal orthodoxy. Now the secular status of the bishop's city became a determinant. To be sure, this was a primacy of honor, not jurisdiction, and it certainly did not allow the bishop of Constantinople to interfere in sees in Syria or Egypt, but the writing was on the wall—and Damasus of Rome read it very clearly.

By the late fourth century, the bishops of Rome enjoyed *de facto* leadership over the bishops of Italy, and the popes routinely extended their authority beyond Italy's borders. Papal authority never enjoyed much success in North Africa, but Spanish and Gallic bishops usually accepted it. Rome's authority rested upon its double apostolic foundation, although by the third century its bishops emphasized the Pauline base less and less, relying instead on the Petrine base, especially Christ's words to Peter in Matthew 16:18: "you are Peter, and upon this rock I will build my church." Indeed, by the late fourth century, the popes had begun to address other bishops as "my son" instead of "my brother." To be sure, the pope's authority certainly derived heavily from his being bishop of the Western capital, but the fourth-century popes had developed an extensive theology to justify their prominence in purely ecclesiastical terms.

Damasus recognized the danger in the third canon. If ecclesiastical prominence rested upon secular prominence, the day might come when Constantinople would outrank Rome in a secular sense (this did, in fact, happen in the sixth century) and thus would outrank Rome in an ecclesiastical sense. A council of Italian bishops in 382, quoting Matthew 16:18, affirmed that the Bishop of Rome "has obtained the primacy by the voice of our Lord and Savior in the gospel" and then cited the deaths of Peter and Paul in the Eternal City. Following Damasus's lead, the bishops of Rome have never accepted the third canon of Constantinople I. Actually, papal suspicion about the council remained deep. Felix II (483–92) did not acknowledge it; not till the time of Hormisdas (513–23) did Rome acknowledge this second ecumenical council.

The reception of the council in the East was little better. Many conservative Nicene bishops feared that by adding to the creed of 325, Constantinople I had somehow compromised the authority of Nicea. Furthermore, was it even an ecumenical council? Unlike Nicea, Constantinople I did not have an Athanasius to battle on its behalf. Yet, it had put an end to the Arian threat, and after 381 almost all bishops accepted the full divinity of the Holy Spirit. Furthermore, unlike Constantine, Theodosius did not abandon "his" council. Slowly but surely the two councils gained stature in the East.

But now the bishops had a far different problem to deal with.

CHAPTER TWO

The Christological Councils

The Christian Empire

The fourth century saw the conversion of Rome to Christianity, and, as historians wryly point out, the conversion of Christianity to Rome. No longer the apocalyptic Whore of Babylon, the Roman Empire was now accepted by Christians as the framework of their lives. Boundaries of church provinces generally coincided with those of the empire, and imperial organizational terms like "diocese" became part of church vocabulary. Even the humblest bishops became important secular figures, while the great bishops, such as those of Rome and Alexandria, became major players in imperial affairs. The reverse was also true. Roman nobility became interested in church affairs, and the emperors, as divinely appointed rulers, played a greater and greater role in church affairs. To be sure, bishops often questioned, resented, and challenged *how* the emperors carried out their roles, for example, in supporting movements bishops considered heretical, but no one questioned the *right* of the emperor to be involved.

The Christian empire hardly revived the Garden of Eden. The emperors assumed greater and greater powers, and the gaps between rich and poor as well as between the rich and working people, such as farmers, increased inordinately. Many local nobles tried to avoid the financially ruinous obligations of office, and the challenges of maintaining the extensive frontiers proved beyond the capabilities of even Rome's best generals. In 378 a tribe of German barbarians, the Visigoths, defeated and killed the Eastern Roman emperor Valens, thus opening up the Danube frontier to increased barbarian penetration. But the Eastern emperors managed to patch up the frontier, while things literally fell apart in the West. On New Year's Eve in 406, the frozen Rhine allowed hordes of other Germanic barbarians to cross into Roman Gaul. In 410 the Visigoths actually captured and sacked the city of

Rome. Fortunately for the Romans, they did not consolidate their conquests but moved on, eventually settling in Spain. The decline and fall of the Western empire had begun, and by the end of the fifth century it would be no more.

But ecclesiastical life in the empire did not reflect these ominous conditions. Large churches continued to spring up about the empire, a reflection of imperial and noble favor. Liturgies began to reflect imperial court ceremonies, such as the introduction of incense. Talented artists found work in the church, and genuinely glorious mosaics adorned the great buildings. Bishops became more prominent and wealthy. The bishop of Alexandria became one of the wealthiest men in the empire, while in Rome a pagan noble told Pope Damasus that he would be happy to convert if he could live like the bishops of Rome! Such examples should not obscure the fact that most clergy were hardworking men who labored under anything but luxurious conditions.

But ecclesiastical wealth did have a consequence. Centered in Egypt, the monastic movement had begun in the late third century. In the fourth century, many zealous Christians, offended by what they considered the growing Christian emphasis upon—and enjoyment of—wealth and power, fled to the deserts of the East and the forests of the West to become monks. These refugees included women and men, although the latter predominated. The monks became the new heroes, replacing the martyrs who, in a Christian empire, no longer existed. The martyrs had died once for the faith, but the monks died a little bit every day via rigorous fasting and discipline, a process known as mortification, literally, "to make dead." Ironically, in centuries to come, those who initially fled the institutional church would return to govern it, at least in the West.

But despite all the glory and publicity that the monks won, bishops still governed the church. And for all the empire's troubles in the fifth century, theological problems, especially in the East, did not go away. To these we now turn.

Christology

As the name suggests, Christology is the study of Christ or, more correctly, the theology of Christ. Unlike theology, which appears in all religious traditions, Christology is uniquely Christian, and it appears in the earliest Christian literature, the New Testament. These Scriptures dealt heavily with what Christ did, that is, his role as Savior, Redeemer, Messiah, High Priest, and sacrificial Lamb, among others. Much New Testament Christology emphasizes the work of the human Christ, but the Gospel of John, written circa 100, shows a growing belief in Christ's divinity. By the end of the second century, this belief had become universal.

But with it came obvious problems. How could someone be both human and divine? Would the divine not overwhelm the human and render it inconsequential? Would the human not taint or corrupt the divine? How did the two mix—was Jesus divine when he performed a miracle and human when he wept for Lazarus? And the question that trinitarian theology had to face: if Christ is divine and the Father is divine, would that not mean two gods, thus vitiating Christian monotheism?

The previous chapter shows how the early Christians dealt with the last question; this chapter will focus on the human and divine in Christ.

Our starting point may be surprising. Contrary to what we might expect, the problem lay not with Christ's divinity but with his humanity—that is, the ancient Christians found it easier to accept his divinity rather than his humanity, and so much of their theology focused on how to preserve his divinity from corruption or compromise with his humanity. Some genuinely ingenious theories appeared.

Docetism came first. Mostly Gentile converts, the Docetists believed that a spiritual being like God would be corrupted by contact with a fleshly body—an understandable assumption for Greeks—but how then could they explain the Jesus whom people had seen and spoken with? He had a body. Actually, no. He did not have a real body but only "seemed" to. The Greek word for "seem" is *dokéo*, hence, "Docetism." This theory seemed to work well as simple theories often do, but it had a serious weakness. If Jesus did not have a real body, then how could he have suffered, died, and risen from the dead? Docetism vitiated the redemption and had no theological future, although it certainly has modern followers among people who believe that Jesus was sort of a god in disguise and who cannot accept that Jesus had any human limitations, for example, that he might forget something. For all its shortcomings, Docetism tapped into a common Christian sentiment.

A group of second-century Christians called Gnostics had another idea. They did not reject Jesus' physicality, but they did have a low opinion of the body, recalling Plato's dictum that the body is the prison of the soul. For them, Jesus' lowly, miserable human flesh could not possibly have been worthy enough to effect the redemption of humanity from sin. Instead, Jesus redeemed the human race by the special and secret knowledge (Greek: *gnósis*) that he brought from heaven. The Gnostics enjoyed widespread acceptance in Egypt and influence in other areas, but most Christians had accepted the Jewish idea of the goodness of the material world (Gen 1:31), and Gnosticism also failed as a Christology.

One of Gnosticism's greatest opponents was an Alexandrian named Origen (ca. 185–254), who produced the first systematic theology, that is, the first treatise insisting that different branches of theology should be seen in relation to one another. Thus, our understanding of God influences our understanding of Christ, which in turn influences our view of what Christ's church should be. Origen pointed the way to the later third-century and fourth-century concerns about the Trinity, because until the Christians had settled the relation of the Father and Son in the Trinity, they could not effectively approach the question of the incarnate son. Christology per se did not disappear, but the great Christologies appeared in the late fourth and especially the fifth centuries.

One of the sadder stories of the christological debates involved Apollinaris of Laodicea (ca. 315–92). In 362, having become bishop, he sent two delegates to a council organized by his long-time friend Athanasius and held in Alexandria to promote Nicene fortunes. Significantly, Apollinaris shared Athanasius's tendency to equate *hypóstasis* and *ousía*. But, however orthodox his trinitarian theology, Apollinaris had questionable ideas about Christ. Accepting Christ's *hypóstasis* as the basis of his unity—this at a time when the Cappadocians were writing of three hypostases—Apollinaris followed what scholars call the Word-Flesh Christology. Apollinaris spoke of the one nature of the Logos (Word) made flesh, by which he meant the Logos, the Son of God, took on flesh to become incarnate. He did not mean that the Son of God "clothed" himself with human flesh. There was a real unity there. If there were a separation of Logos and flesh, how could Jesus have redeemed us since the death of his physical body would be useless if divine and human were separated? One could speak of Jesus' true humanity. Fearful of those who would disconnect the divine and human in Christ, Apollinaris offered this theology.

But, unfortunately, there was more. The Logos did not take on a human soul or human reason because he did not need them. A spiritual, divine being did not need a spiritual, human soul, and the Word of God had no need of human reason. The Word would vivify the human in all ways. There really was no fully human subject in Christ, but rather "One nature (*phýsis*) of the Logos made flesh."

Red flags went up all over the Christian world as theologians and bishops heard echoes of Docetism. Synods at Rome (377), Alexandria (378), and Antioch (379) condemned this theology. At the Council of Constantinople in 381, these condemnations received ecumenical confirmation. The council held to confirm the triumph of the Nicene cause condemned the teaching of one of the Nicene heroes, but, to their credit, the bishops there refrained from condemning Apollinaris by name. After the council, the emperor Theodosius issued several decrees banning the teaching of his theories. But condemnations and bans do not form a reply, and that awaited the work of Gregory Nazianzus.

Gregory argued that Word-Flesh Christology basically deprived Christ of his true humanity. He advanced several arguments, but the crucial one focused on soteriology, the theology of salvation. Adam and Eve sinned by using their reason and will to make a decision; how can Jesus redeem us unless he too has a human mind and will? And how could Jesus save our immortal souls if he did not have one himself? Gregory summed up his view in a telling phrase: what has not been assumed cannot be saved. If Jesus did not assume a full human nature, he could not have saved our human nature.

But, as with Nicea, terminology became a problem. Whereas Apollinaris spoke of one nature, meaning the fusion of the divine and human in Christ, the term could equally mean that the human disappeared into the divine. He also used the term "person" as well as *hypóstasis*. Gregory, having emerged from the Nicene controversies with an established theological vocabulary, argued that Jesus was one person with two natures, both of which maintained their integrity but were fully united. For all that, Gregory had his doubts about Jesus' complete humanity, unsure what to do with gospel passages that dealt with Jesus' ignorance—today accepted as part of his human development—or his cry of dereliction in the Garden of Gethsemane.

Other writers besides Gregory entered the lists against Apollinaris, but they did not advance the question much beyond what Gregory had to say. The full patristic Christology would await the fifth century.

Ecclesiastical Politics

We cannot separate the story of fifth-century Christology from ecclesiastical politics. The bishops of Rome made significant claims about their authority, and Eastern bishops did not challenge those, mostly because Rome was so far away and the popes had little influence in the East where the emperors at Constantinople did not want interference from a bishop in the Western empire. The real problem in the East was Constantinople.

Eastern bishops had traditionally made much of their sees' foundations, often going back to the apostolic age, long antedating the Christian empire. Now emperors, claiming divine right to rule, forcefully intervened in ecclesiastical affairs. Not surprisingly, the emperors often favored the bishops of their capitals. In the late fourth century, a Western emperor made it clear that the Italian bishops should look to Rome for leadership and refer problems to the pope. The Eastern emperors felt the same way, and they routinely advanced the prestige and status of the see of Constantinople. But whereas the bishops of Rome had no rivals in the West, in the East were the bishops of Alexandria.

The patriarchs of the great Egyptian city enjoyed almost unrivaled wealth. Among other revenues, they actually received a tax on all the salt used in Egypt, and they had no hesitations about using their wealth to gain their ends. Furthermore, they looked back to the ancient church's most distinguished theological tradition, a school of theology that included Origen and Athanasius and that had upheld Nicene orthodoxy. Monasticism had started in Egypt and continued to be very strong there, and the monks supported the patriarchs. Lastly, on any controverted issue, the bishops of Alexandria could call upon the support of one hundred other Egyptian bishops. To the Alexandrians the bishops of Constantinople were merely usurpers whose sole claim to ecclesiastical authority was their imperial location.

After the Council of Constantinople, Nectarius reigned as bishop in that city until 397. At his death, the emperor Arcadius (383–408) had a foolish idea that he considered inspired. He had the most famous preacher in the East, John of Antioch (known after the seventh century as John Chrysostom or "Golden Tongue"), forced into accepting the bishopric, ignoring a candidate promoted by Theophilus, patriarch of Alexandria (385–412). John's background as a monk and preacher provided no preparation for the snake pit of ecclesiastical politics in the imperial city. A personally righteous man, John was shocked at the behavior of some bishops, and he forced six bishops of Asia Minor out of office for simony, that is, for purchasing their offices. It was the right thing to do, to be sure, but the other bishops of Asia Minor resented a Constantinopolitan bishop's interference in their area. A monk himself, John received monastic refugees from Egypt who had complained of persecution by Theophilus. Appalled by the morals of the court, John openly criticized the font of these abuses, the empress Eudoxia, referring to her as Jezebel, the wicked woman par excellence in the Bible. Theophilus of Alexandria worked with her to get John exiled, going to Constantinople with twenty-nine Egyptian bishops, forming a council, getting the emperor to tell John to attend—which he did not do—and then deposing John from office at the Synod of the Oak in 403. Imperial pressure forced John to accept his deposition and go into exile, but on the day he left, an earthquake occurred. The populace interpreted this as divine anger at John's exile, and he returned to the city triumphantly, touting his victory over the new Pharaoh! But his victory was short-lived. Eudoxia had not changed her ways, and the righteous monk referred to her as Herodias, seeking the head of a new John (the Baptist). No earthquake saved John this time. He went into an exile so harsh that he died from its rigors in 407. Alexandria had triumphed over its hated rival.

But Theophilus's tactics produced a reaction. Pope Innocent I (401–17) did not accept the sentence of deposition and refused communion with those who engineered it. Theophilus died in 412, and in 414 the bishops of Antioch and Constantinople urged reconciliation upon the new bishop of Alexandria, Cyril (412–44), suggesting he posthumously rehabilitate John and put his name on the list of bishops of Constantinople that Alexandria recognized. A true successor to his uncle Theophilus and himself a participant at the Synod of the Oak, Cyril replied he would rather put Judas back in the company of the apostles.

In 425, the see of Constantinople became vacant, and the emperor Theodosius II (408–50), ignoring what happened to John Chrysostom, chose Nestorius, another monk from Antioch, to be bishop of Constantinople. Like his deposed predecessor, Nestorius had an uncompromising personality but with a particular animus toward heresy, at least as he perceived it. To his shock, he learned that most Christians in his city held a heretical view about Jesus' mother Mary. They venerated her as *Theotókos*, Greek for Mother of God.

Nestorius's reasoning ran thus: for all her wondrous qualities, Mary was a human being and thus could not be accurately referred to as the Mother of God, that is, of the omnipotent, omniscient, eternally existing deity. Mary could legitimately be called *Christotókos* or Mother of Christ. This makes sense logically, but, as we have seen, theology deals with mysteries of the faith, not logical propositions. Nestorius overlooked that many great theologians, probably back to the third century, had used the term *Theotókos*; these theologians included Athanasius and the three Cappadocians. A list like that would have made a prudent man hesitate and ask why they did so, but Nestorius had a strong sense of his own rightness and righteousness. He also arrogantly overlooked the pastoral dimension. *Theotókos* had been widely used liturgically, even in Constantinople, and was deeply popular among the people. When local monks protested his teaching, he had some of them arrested and scourged. His attack on the venerable title offended both theologians and the public.

Yet Nestorius did not have to worry about the multitudes he offended but rather just one man. Cyril of Alexandria combined his uncle's determination to weaken Constantinople with a brilliant theological mind. He genuinely believed that Nestorius had erred theologically, but he also saw a chance to again embarrass the imperial bishopric. Wary about looking too ambitious, Cyril sought an ally. Fortunately for him, Nestorius gave him one.

In 428 Nestorius sent some of his sermons to Celestine I of Rome (422–32), but he sent them in Greek, which the pope could not read. Celestine gave them to his deacon Leo (a future pope), who in turn gave them to a Gallic monk named John Cassian, who had lived in the East and knew Greek. Cassian quickly wrote a treatise opposing Nestorius's teaching. The Romans were convinced Nestorius taught heresy, while he thought the Romans did not know much theology.

Cyril moved quickly, first with a letter to Egyptian monks, warning them about Nestorius's theology. He knew that the Constantinopolitan bishop would see the letter, and Nestorius publicly criticized it. Cyril now wrote directly to Nestorius, challenging his views. In 430 he sent a second letter that outlined his own views and demanded that Nestorius subscribe to them. Cyril also sent a copy of the letter—in Latin—to Celestine along with a dossier of materials harmful to Nestorius. Acting on Cyril's information and renewing the traditional Rome-Alexandria alliance of Athanasius's day, Celestine called a Roman council, which condemned Nestorius's teaching and ordered him to abandon it. The pope asked Cyril to see that Rome's decision was carried out, a task the Alexandrian was delighted to accept.

What were the theological issues? In one sense, the perennial one of trying to reconcile Christ's divinity and humanity. Like many theologians from Antioch, Nestorius focused on the distinction between the human and divine, while Cyril, like most Alexandrians, focused on their unity. Nestorius clearly supported the full humanity and divinity of Christ, and he considered these to be two natures that retained their own existence in the one person of Christ. But Nestorius could not come up with a terminology for expressing their union, and he never really explained what constituted this one person.

Cyril insisted on the unity of divine and human to the point where he could say that the Word suffered for us, not because the divine suffered—an impossibility—but that the divine and human completed one another in the one person. For Cyril, "the Word had united to Himself in His own individuality (*hypóstasis*) in an ineffable and inconceivable manner, flesh animated with a rational soul, became Man and was called Son of Man" (quoted in Frend, *Saints and Sinners*, 152). This union meant that Mary could legitimately be called *Theotókos* since the divine Word was united with the man Jesus.

Today Cyril and Nestorius would debate their theologies in scholarly journals in which they would have to answer one another and respond to other theologians as well. But such a debate never occurred. Each wrote imperiously to the other, and a serious breach soon occurred. Armed with Roman support, Cyril called an Egyptian council, which informed Nestorius he would be deposed as bishop if he did not recant. In this Cyril followed the Roman line. But Cyril did not see Roman approval as definitive, and he promptly added to the Roman statement a series of twelve anathemas to which he demanded Nestorius must agree. The anathemas consisted largely of Antiochene theological views; Nestorius refused to accept them.

Resentful of Cyril's machinations, the emperor Theodosius stood by his bishop and decided to call an ecumenical council to meet in the Asia Minor town of Ephesus on June 7 of 431. There Cyril would be put in his place. Fearful of what might happen at a council, Nestorius's allies in Antioch asked him to accept the *Theotókos* and let the matter drop. He should have listened. As John Chrysostom had painfully learned, a monk was no match for an Alexandrian bishop in matters of ecclesiastical politics.

The Council of Ephesus

Nestorius arrived in Ephesus to a very hostile reception, being repeatedly and publicly denounced as an enemy of Jesus' mother. The local bishop, Memnon, closed the churches to him and his allies. So tense was the situation that Nestorius requested and received the protection of the imperial body-guard, led by Count Candidian, the emperor's representative at the council. Cyril arrived with fifty Egyptian bishops, some fanatic monks, and a bodyguard of waterfront thugs. When bishops arrived from Palestine on June 12, Cyril decided to open the council. Count Candidian told him not to do so because the Antiochenes and Romans had not yet arrived, but on June 22 Cyril simply opened the council without them. Nestorius refused to attend, and the majority of the 160 bishops there promptly condemned and deposed him while praising Cyril and Celestine of Rome. The people of Ephesus rejoiced that Mary had conquered Nestorius! But the rejoicing turned out to be premature.

On June 26, led by John of Antioch, the bishops of Syria arrived. They asked when the council would open, learned it had already been held, heard and rejected the results, and, on the same day, held a council of their own that condemned and deposed Cyril along with Memnon of Ephesus.

Less than a week later the Roman legates, two bishops and a priest, arrived, asked when the council would open, were informed that two coun-cils had already been held, and then promptly allied themselves with Cyril. To keep his Roman alliance intact, Cyril obligingly held another session of his council at which the Romans read from Celestine's decree. Delighted that the Romans agreed with them, Cyril and his supporters promptly called their council ecumenical since both East and West were in agreement.

But the most powerful voice had not yet been heard. The emperor, infuriated by the blatant, coarse politicizing, had Cyril and Nestorius arrested and brought to Constantinople. Nestorius made a dramatic gesture, offering to resign his bishopric if that would bring peace. To his surprise and disappointment, the emperor accepted his resignation. But the Antiochene bishops still represented and supported Nestorius's theology, so Cyril put his political skills to use. Dipping heavily into the wealth of his see, he sent gifts and bribes to members of the imperial family, important court officials, and even the emperor's favorite mistress. Eventually the emperor declared that he no longer wished to hear the name of Nestorius. He told the bishops to go home, although he wanted to keep Cyril under arrest. Too late. He had already fled back to his impregnable stronghold of Alexandria.

Ephesus was either a disgrace or a circus or some of both, but it did deal with theological issues, and later tradition would accept it, that is, the council (meetings) presided over by Cyril and of which the Roman church approved, as ecumenical. Rome expressed satisfaction at the results, if not with Cyril's methods of achieving them. Other Western bishops followed Rome's lead, but the situation in the East remained tense.

The Aftermath of the Council

Theodosius had reason to worry about what had happened. Again, an Alexandrian bishop had engineered the deposition of a Constantinopolitan bishop, the bishop of the imperial city. The bishops of Syria, a frontier province bordering Rome's traditional Persian enemy, were enraged at what the emperor had allowed to occur. But genuine Christian motives also surfaced. All sides believed in the unity of the church, and the council had virtually destroyed it. Many now wondered how to effect such unity. Even Cyril had second thoughts. His unscrupulous behavior had embarrassed some Egyptian bishops, and his Roman connection would do him no good if the other Eastern bishops rejected him. Something had to be done.

A centenarian Greek bishop named Acacius made the first move by corresponding with both sides, and, surprisingly, Cyril agreed to compromise. Using Acacius as an intermediary, Cyril wrote to the Syrian bishops, agreeing to work with them but insisting on the condemnation of Nestorius, which, to be sure, had been decreed by an ecumenical council. The Syrians hesitated but eventually agreed to Nestorius's condemnation. John of Antioch sent Cyril a profession of faith, which the Alexandrian accepted, calling it a further explanation of the faith of Nicea. They agreed that Mary had borne the flesh of the Word made flesh, but the divine Word could not be changed by human events. In 433 both bishops agreed to an Act of Union and then notified the emperor and the pope. Inevitably, hard-liners in both camps severely objected to the "sellout," but the desire for unity prevailed. Completely omitted from all these discussions was Nestorius, who from his exile in the Egyptian desert wrote a book entitled *The Bazaar of Heracleides*, which detailed his own life. The book needed a pseudonym because the emperor had ordered the burning of Nestorius's writings.

But the Act of Union could not quell the theological concerns about how the human and divine could be united in Christ. Speculation continued, although the second great christological council responded not to a theologian but to a poorly educated monk.

Eutyches (ca. 358–454) served as archimandrite or superior of a monastery of more than three hundred monks in Constantinople, where he enjoyed a great reputation as a spiritual advisor and greatly influenced his godson and the grand chamberlain of the court, the eunuch Chrysaphius. Eutyches admired the theology of Cyril of Alexandria, but he could not follow all of Cyril's nuances. The Alexandrian had accepted that Christ had two natures, but Eutyches concluded that this was so only before the Incarnation, but after that the two natures merged into one. As usual, language difficulties added to the problem, with Eutyches speaking of one *phýsis*, a word most Greek theologians used for "nature," but it could have the meaning of person, which is how Cyril used it. Favoring "an unbalanced emphasis on Christ's divinity" (Davis, *First Seven*, 173), Eutyches preached that the divine nature swallowed up the human after the Incarnation. His watchword became: "one nature, that of God made man, became flesh." Since many Greeks spoke openly of two natures, which for Eutyches meant two persons, the aged monk saw a revival of Nestorianism.

By 447, as his views became well known, other theologians began to write against him. These included prominent Antiochenes, who accused him of Apollinarianism (the elimination of the divine-human distinction); Eutyches' supporters in turn accused the critics of Nestorianism (denial of the divine-human union in Christ). This should have remained a theologians' debate, but politics entered in, as it usually did.

Hoping to settle the issue, Bishop Flavian of Constantinople (446–49) convoked the Home Synod, a meeting of the local bishops, which condemned Eutyches' teachings. By now the Alexandrian patriarch Dioscorus (444–51) had become involved, claiming that Eutyches' enemies were also enemies of the venerated Cyril. The monk and the Alexandrian bishop conspired to destroy Flavian. Eutyches protested Flavian's treatment of him to the emperor (still Theodosius II, who had called the council of Ephesus), and the emperor supported him.

Matters also reached Rome, where Leo I the Great (440–61), a good theologian himself, consulted other theologians, and the Latins charitably concluded that Eutyches had simply muddled things hopelessly and did not really understand the theological issues. But the emperor did not want to hear that. He called another ecumenical council to meet at Ephesus in 449 under the presidency of Dioscorus, not Flavian because of his opposition to Eutyches. Flavian soon realized that he, not Eutyches, was the council's target; again, an Alexandrian bishop would judge a bishop of Constantinople.

Pope Leo declined to attend, claiming it was improper for a pope to do so. By the fifth century the popes understood themselves to be judges of what others did and not just participants in a council, an attitude not shared in the East, where papal primacy remained one of honor. Leo sent four legates to the council who brought the *Tome to Flavian*, which explained the pope's own Christology. But Leo's earnest efforts would be valueless.

Dioscorus may not have matched Cyril's theological brilliance, but he did match his arrogance and ruthlessness. Before the council officially opened, he had all the bishops who had condemned Eutyches at the Constantinopolitan Home Synod excluded from the council. After the official reading of the emperor's letter of convocation, the papal legate Hilary (later Pope Hilary I, 461–68) requested the reading of Leo's *Tome*. Dioscorus put this off, and instead Eutyches arrived to give his profession of faith. Again, the papal legates requested a reading of the pope's letter; again, Dioscorus put them off. Next was the reading of the decrees of the Home Synod condemning Eutyches. The bishops denounced these and overwhelmingly (111 to 19) voted to rehabilitate Eutyches.

Now Dioscorus pulled a quick one. He asked the bishops if they all agreed with the creed of Nicea. All said yes, at which point he accused Flavian of Constantinople of violating it. An uproar ensued, Dioscorus called out for help, and into the council chamber came a mixture of imperial police and just plain thugs, who beat Flavian and threatened the legates. The council then went on to depose and condemn Flavian, who died a few days later as a consequence of the beating he endured. For the third time in less than a half century a bishop of Alexandria had engineered the deposition of a bishop of Constantinople.

Upon the return of his legates, the infuriated Leo convinced the Western emperor and his family to join him in writing to Theodosius to protest what had happened, but the Eastern emperor calmly assured the Westerners that all was fine. This did not placate the pope who gave the council its enduring name in the West, the *latrocinium* or Robber Council, but the Eastern situation remained unchanged.

Then, suddenly, everything changed.

In July of 450, when the emperor Theodosius was hunting, he fell from his horse and was accidentally killed. He had no son, so his sister Pulcheria succeeded to the throne. A supporter of Flavian, she promptly had the grand chamberlain and Eutyches' godson, the eunuch Chysaphius, executed, severely limiting Eutyches' influence at court. Knowing the people would not accept a woman ruler, Pulcheria married an ex-general named Marcian, and they ruled as emperor and empress. They had Eutyches confined to a monastery, arranged for a dignified funeral for Flavian's body, and established good relations with Leo. Across the Mediterranean, Dioscorus wondered what would happen. He did not have long to wait. The imperial couple announced a new council, the first but not the last time a woman would have a role in calling an ecumenical council.

The Council of Chalcedon

Pulcheria and Marcian chose Chalcedon as the site for the council. It lay just across the Bosphorus from Constantinople, thus giving the imperial couple easy access. Determined not to have a repetition of the *latrocinium*, Leo immediately contacted the imperial couple and argued for a council held in the West, but they disagreed, recognizing that this affair was primarily an Eastern one. Leo accepted their decision. He did, however, see to it that the Roman legate, the Sicilian bishop Paschasinus, became president of the council, thus thwarting in advance any attempt by Dioscorus to seize control. The Alexandrian did not give up—he even excommunicated Leo—but the tide was against him.

The Council of Chalcedon opened on October 8, 451, with a number of important court dignitaries present to guarantee imperial influence. Following Leo's instructions, the papal legates demanded Dioscorus be excluded. But papal power had limits in the East. The imperial court wanted and got a formal trial. Dioscorus listened to the reading of the acts of the *latrocinium* and of the Constantinopolitan Home Synod. Sensing the prevailing mood, Egyptian bishops in increasing numbers deserted Dioscorus. The imperial representatives declared the Alexandrian to be condemned, pending imperial approval of the sentence.

Two days later the bishops met again and ordered the reading of the decrees of the councils of Nicea and of Constantinople, the initial formal recognition of the latter as an ecumenical council. They also listened to documents from the Formula of Union between Cyril and John of Antioch and then to the *Tome* of Leo. The bishops vigorously approved these documents, thus marking the first time that a pope-theologian influenced the teachings of an ecumenical council. Three days later the council officially deposed Dioscorus as bishop of Alexandria, but, rather surprisingly, the bishops did not prepare a statement of faith.

On October 22 the imperial representatives made it clear that the emperor and empress wanted a statement of faith and that they would move the council to the West if they did not get one. The bishops promptly appointed a committee of twelve, including three papal legates, to prepare a statement. Relying upon the teachings of Cyril and Leo, the commission drew up and the council approved a statement that made the teaching as clear as a mystery of the faith could be. Christ was "begotten of the Father before the ages as touching the Godhead . . . born from the Virgin Mary, the *Theotókos*, as touching the manhood, one and the same Christ . . . to be acknowledged in two natures, without confusion, without change, without division, without separation . . . concurring in one Person" (Davis, *First Seven*, 186). The more common description: Christ is one person with two natures, one human and one divine.

Inevitably, this formula hardly satisfied everyone. Followers of Cyril still feared that the human and divine had been separated too much and that the hypostatic union of the divine and human in the one person had been insufficiently elaborated. Furthermore, the council, over the objections of the papal legates, again asserted the importance of Constantinople as the bishopric of the imperial city but went on to include a canon that said it had the same practical status as Rome, which still retained a primacy of honor. The legates could not get that canon changed, the emperor approved the decrees, and the council closed.

After the Council

Predictably, Leo refused to accept that the bishop of Constantinople had such great status because of the political importance of his city. He followed the Roman tradition of insisting that apostolic authority and not political importance had made Rome the chief see of the church, and so when Leo accepted the doctrinal decrees of Chalcedon in 453, he did not approve the canon that gave Constantinople this status.

Significant as this was for Rome, it was a minor irritant to the emperor for whom the real trouble lay in the East. The deposition of Dioscorus enraged many Egyptian Christians, and an anti-Chalcedonian reaction soon set in. Convinced that the sainted Cyril had taught that Christ had one nature, the Egyptians began a movement under that name, the Monophysite or "one-nature" church. Monophysitism spread rapidly throughout Egypt, and, to the surprise of many, in the sixth century entered Palestine and Syria as well, partly because of effective missionary work by the Monophysites and partly because many Eastern Christians wondered if Chalcedon had not compromised Christ's unity.

The story of Monophysitism's rise is a tangled one, but this is an outline. The emperor responded decisively, appointing a bishop named Proterius to replace the exiled Dioscorus in Alexandria. The population of the city never accepted him, and the emperor had to send troops to the city so the new patriarch could occupy his throne. Led by the priest Timothy, whose nickname was "the Cat," the Monophysites established their own theology, rejecting Eutyches but insisting on fidelity to Cyril. In 457 Timothy established himself as patriarch. The government quickly ousted "the Cat" and restored Proterius, who carelessly let himself be captured and torn to pieces by a fanatical mob. Urged on by Chalcedonian patriarchs of Constantinople, the imperial government realized that only force could keep a Chalcedonian patriarch in Alexandria, and so, after much bloodletting, Timothy "the Cat" was arrested and exiled. But Monophysitism remained strong and by the end of the century had become the national faith of Egypt as well as the cause of the next ecumenical council.

To those familiar only with modern ecumenical councils, these first councils represent a surprise, if not a scandal—violence, politics, imperial intervention, exile, betrayal, and all done in the name of religion. To be sure, there were also many good, honorable people involved, and all of them strove to realize the truth, to formulate as best they could the basic beliefs of the Christian faith, and, against considerable odds, they did so. And, as we shall see, later councils could match them in scandalous behavior.

Scholars almost universally consider these four to be the most important ecumenical councils, and for two reasons. First, they established an important method of elucidating doctrine when Scripture alone could not do so. Had they failed, the church would have been trapped by a sterile biblicism and unable to make use of the tools offered by secular learning, in this case, philosophy. Had the early church turned its back on such learning, some of the greatest names in theology over the centuries would never have written a word, nor would modern Christians have been able to use the advances of modern society to understand their faith, for example, applying the social sciences to ethical questions.

The second reason that these are considered to be the greatest councils is that Christianity teaches belief in one God, and Nicea I and Constantinople I established the basic Christian teaching about God. Furthermore, Christianity reveres Christ as both its founder and foundation, and Ephesus and Chalcedon established the basic teaching about Christ.

God and Christ. There are no more fundamental beliefs than these for Christians, and for the formulation of these beliefs, we must thank these confused, scandalous, combative but ultimately successful councils.

CHAPTER THREE

The Byzantine Councils

Between the close of Chalcedon and the opening of Constantinople II in 553, the Roman Empire in the West came to an end. Although it continued to exist in the East until 1453, historians generally refer to the Eastern Roman Empire as the Byzantine Empire. The next four ecumenical councils all involved the papacy and the Byzantine imperial house.

Western Christianity

Leo the Great died in 461 with the Western empire still intact, but every prescient person could see the future. For most of the fifth century barbarian tribes had been crisscrossing imperial territory, sometimes as wandering invaders but occasionally as permanent settlers such as the Angles and Saxons in Britain and the Franks in Gaul. The most ferocious of the barbarians was Attila, king of the Huns, a Mongolian people that had penetrated as far West as modern France. When the Huns arrived at the gates of Rome, Leo led a delegation to the Huns' camp and convinced Attila to turn away. (Later legend claimed that the Hunnish king had a vision of an angelic army standing behind Leo.) But when Attila, to satisfy his disappointed troops' demands for booty, pillaged and destroyed several northern Italian cities, Leo could do nothing. In 455, when a different barbarian people, the Vandals, arrived at Rome, the pope could not stop them, and they ravaged the city for three days and then moved on.

In 476, another barbarian king, tired of pretending that the Western empire still existed, deposed the last emperor, an infant named Romulus Augustus. Creating the fiction that they now ruled the entire empire, the Eastern emperors "appointed" barbarian kings to act as their "representatives," a title the barbarians accepted as a means of legitimating their rule in the eyes of Italian subjects, but the emperors had little or no power in Italy.

But the bishops of Rome remained major figures, proving the wisdom of their insistence that the importance of their see lay in its apostolic foundation and not in the secular importance of their city. To many Byzantines, the former imperial capital had been reduced to a frontier outpost in barbarian territory, but the word of its bishop still carried weight.

Yet problems abounded. The Ostrogoths, barbarian occupiers of Italy from the late fifth to the mid-sixth century, practiced Arianism, the heresy now discredited in Mediterranean lands but one that had reached the Goths via the missionary work of a fourth-century Arian bishop. The Ostrogothic kings feared that the popes wanted Italy restored to imperial rule for both political and religious reasons, and much distrust existed between the two. Ironically, just the reverse was also happening. Free of imperial interference in their affairs, the popes became increasingly independent of Constantinople and its endless theological difficulties. Gelasius I (492–96) distrusted "the Greeks, among whom heresies abound," and he enunciated what came to be called the Doctrine of the Two Swords, that is, that the emperor held the secular sword and the pope the spiritual one and that the spiritual one was superior to the secular one, and thus the emperor should defer to the pope in spiritual matters. Such an attitude was bound to cause trouble, and that trouble was not long in coming.

Winning Back the Monophysites

In imperial eyes, the bishops of Rome took a back seat to a very immediate problem, winning back the Monophysites who dominated much of Egypt and had spread into Syria. As Christians, the emperors believed that the church should be one, and part of their effort to win back the Monophysites had that laudable goal. But more to the point were political issues. The granary of the empire, Egypt played a major role in supplying much of the empire with food; it could not become a breakaway province. As for Syria, it guarded the Eastern frontier against Byzantium's only formidable enemy, the Persian Empire. Unrest in either, much less both, of these provinces spelled trouble.

At first the emperors resorted to force, but with no luck. They could have allowed the Monophysites to worship as they pleased, but that would have infuriated the Chalcedonians of the East. A compromise had to be found.

In 482, pushed by the emperor Zeno (476–91) and after conferences with some Monophysites, Acacius, bishop of Constantinople, drew up a document called the *Henoticon*, which avoided strict Chalcedonian terminology about natures but condemned both Nestorius and Eutyches, praised Cyril, and emphasized what the Chalcedonians and Monophysites had in common. Many Monophysites accepted the *Henoticon*, but Eastern Chalcedonians feared a sellout, and Pope Felix III (483–92) condemned the *Henoticon* and its author, provoking what the Romans called the Acacian Schism. But Zeno and his successor Anastasius (491–518) could afford Rome's wrath if that were the price of reunion in the East. Indeed, the emperor Anastasius went out of his way to accommodate the Monophysites.

Everything changed when Anastasius died childless in 518. To the throne in Constantinople came Justin I (518–27), a Latin-speaking Chalcedonian who wanted reunion with Rome. The pope, Hormisdas (514–23), exacted a high price, particularly the abandonment of the *Henoticon* and the condemnation of the memory of Acacius. But an agreement between Rome and Constantinople did not mean acceptance in Egypt and Syria, and the Monophysite troubles continued. Even the Chalcedonian emperor Justin I had to accede to some Monophysite demands in Egypt. To make matters worse, the Monophysites were splitting into factions, including groups that denounced the *Henoticon*, the very document designed to appease them. The religious and political discord persisted.

Justinian I (527–65)

The emperor Justin died childless, and his forty-five-year-old nephew Justinian succeeded him. The new emperor had enormous energy (he barely slept), boundless ambitions, a strong knowledge of theology, and a Monophysite wife.

The empress Theodora came from the lowest social rank, being the daughter of an animal trainer, and she actually had worked part-time as a prostitute. Yet she absolutely entranced Justinian, and, as even her worst enemies—and she had many—had to acknowledge, once married, she remained a loyal, steadfast, and supportive spouse. In 532 riots broke out in Constantinople, riots so severe that the emperor planned to flee the city. Theodora told him that he could go but that she would stay and die an empress in her palace. Emboldened by her courage, Justinian put down the riots, and her influence upon him was set for life.

Like all Byzantine emperors, Justinian worried about the Monophysites, but he had another great desire—to reimpose Roman rule in the West, in fact and not just in name, a difficult and very expensive prospect. Early successes in North Africa and some Mediterranean islands convinced him conquest would be easy, and he sent his best general, Belisarius, to invade Italy in the 530s, a campaign that would last for two decades. The Italians, resentful of Gothic dominance, initially welcomed the imperial armies, although their ardor waned as Byzantine officials, especially tax collectors, made their weight felt in Italy. The Italian bishops also welcomed the return of an orthodox ruler but, accustomed to Gothic noninterference in the church, they suddenly learned what it was like to be ruled by an emperor who considered himself head not only of the state but also of the church. Lesser Italian bishops could be intimidated into accepting the new state of affairs, but how would Rome react?

The emperor needed a pope who would go along with his new order in Italy. Now that imperial armies were advancing in Italy, liberating Rome from the Goths in 536, Justinian would impose his own candidate in the papal office. Where could he find one? He did not need to look very far. Theodora had already found one.

The Roman deacon Vigilius had accompanied Pope Agapitus (535–36) to Constantinople, where the pope excommunicated the Monophysite bishop and saw to the election of a Chalcedonian. While in the imperial city, Vigilius became a confidant of the Monophysite empress, who promised to help him become pope some day. Agapitus suddenly died in Constantinople, and Vigilius hastened back to Rome for the papal election. But he arrived too late. The clergy chose Silverius (536–37), the son of Pope Hormisdas and, significantly, pro-Gothic. When the Byzantine army occupied Rome, the general Belisarius summoned Silverius to a meeting, where he had soldiers rudely strip the pope of his episcopal garments and hustle him into exile in Asia Minor. Belisarius then arranged for the election of Vigilius.

When Silverius arrived at his place of exile, the horrified local bishop told Justinian that this was no way to treat the Bishop of Rome. Surprisingly, Justinian agreed and arranged for Silverius to return to Rome and face a new election. But Vigilius arranged to have him intercepted and exiled again, this time to an Italian prison island. Silverius died there less than a year later. Vigilius now reigned securely, and the imperial couple believed they had a pope they could control.

The invasion of the West was straining imperial resources, and Justinian realized that he could not carry it off successfully without pacifying the East; for example, troops being used to install and maintain Chalcedonian bishops could be better used against the Goths in Italy. But much of the East was Monophysite, and thus Justinian too fell prey to the siren song of reconciling the Monophysites without compromising Chalcedon.

This presented enormous difficulties, and Justinian did not shrink from them. First, he could not use the *Henoticon*. His predecessor, to whom he owed his rule, had condemned it, and he had supported his uncle Justin.

Second, Eastern Chalcedonians, especially monastic groups in the capital city, always watched carefully for any hint of a sellout. Third, the bishops of Rome and other Latin bishops had steadfastly denounced any approach that would compromise Chalcedon, and so Justinian had to find a way to convince the Latins that he was not sacrificing doctrine to pacify heretics. Obviously, Vigilius would be a major factor in achieving this.

Justinian realized that he had to have some formula of reconciliation. In fact, one had been circulating for decades. The Monophysites loathed a number of Chalcedonian theologians whom they considered to be Nestorians, willing to separate the divine and human Christ into two persons. Three Syrian theologians headed the list of those they hated: Theodore of Mopsuestia (d. 428), Ibas of Edessa (d. 457), and Theodoret of Cyrus (d. ca. 468). All had vigorously opposed the theological excesses of the Monophysites' patron saint, Cyril of Alexandria. Imperial advisors had toyed with the idea of condemning these three as Nestorians in hopes of appeasing the Monophysites, and now Justinian revived the idea.

The approach presented a major difficulty. All three had died in the peace of the church, that is, they were considered orthodox Christians at the times of their deaths. In fact, both Ibas and Theodoret had been deposed by the *latrocinium* of Dioscorus (Ephesus II in 449), only to be restored by the Council of Chalcedon two years later. By what right could they be posthumously condemned? But, Justinian asked, was it even necessary to condemn them? Would it not be possible just to condemn "Nestorian" passages from their writings?

This approach appears sleazy to the modern mind since we know that many people held views that later generations would reject; to cite an obvious example, the many past Christians who considered nothing immoral about slavery and even owned slaves. But the ancient and medieval worlds saw nothing wrong with ex post facto condemnations; for example, two years after Thomas Aquinas died in 1274, the bishop of Paris censored as heretical six propositions taught by the deceased Dominican theologian. Distasteful as postmortem condemnations might be, Justinian could effect them.

By 543 Justinian and his theological advisors, who loathed the three Antiochene theologians, recognized the difficulty of three posthumous condemnations. They decided not to condemn the persons of Theodoret and Ibas, the two theologians acknowledged at Chalcedon, but rather to condemn Theodoret's writings against some extreme partisans of Cyril and a letter of Ibas that Monophysites considered heretical. With Theodore of Mopsuestia, however, the condemnation would be of his person. The emperor ordered a compendium of the three theologians' writings to be drawn up; this document gave the controversy its name, the Three Chapters. He then published an edict condemning the Three Chapters and presented it to the Eastern bishops. Menas of Constantinople signed provisionally, saying he wanted to know what Rome thought. Some bishops signed conditionally; others accepted the document.

As the emperor suspected, the Latin bishops, especially in North Africa and northern Italy, believed he was compromising Chalcedon for the political purpose of winning over the Monophysites, and they refused to sign. Urged by his deacon Pelagius, who considered the imperial edict to be heretical, Vigilius vacillated. The infuriated emperor acted decisively, having Byzantine troops kidnap the pope in late 545 and take him to Sicily, where Justinian imprisoned him until 547 when the pope was taken to Constantinople.

Summoning up temporary courage, Vigilius excommunicated Menas of Constantinople for signing the edict, but ill-treatment wore him down and by June of 547, he restored communion with Menas and assured the imperial couple he would condemn the Three Chapters. In April of 548, still a prisoner, the pope issued his *Iudicatum*, a document that agreed to the condemnation of the Three Chapters but without compromising Chalcedon. In June of that year the empress Theodora died, but the pressure on Vigilius did not cease. The emperor was too committed to reconciling the Monophysites.

The situation in the West soon worsened. In 550 the African bishops excommunicated Vigilius. His own entourage in Constantinople raised such strong objections to his conduct that he had to excommunicate some of them. In December of 551 Vigilius fled from Constantinople to, of all places, the church in Chalcedon where the ecumenical council had been held. Imperial troops roughed him up there, but he got a safe conduct to return to Constantinople, where he learned that the emperor now sought to ratify the condemnation of the Three Chapters at an ecumenical council. Hoping to exercise some control over it, Vigilius urged the emperor to hold it in Italy, but Justinian had long since stopped caring what the pope thought. The council would be in Constantinople.

The Second Council of Constantinople

The council opened on May 5, 553. All but nine of the 151 bishops in attendance were Greek; the others came from North Africa, then under Byzantine rule. Justinian ignored Vigilius's requests to invite Italian bishops. An imperial emissary opened the council, reading a letter from the emperor that spoke of the four earlier ecumenical councils, thus providing the first mention at a later council of the ecumenical status of the others. The emissary also stated that the bishops were there to consider the case of the Three Chapters. To their credit, the bishops insisted that the pope be present and so sent an embassy to Vigilius, who pleaded illness and asked for time to recuperate. In subsequent sessions the bishops proclaimed their adherence to the faith of the first four councils and then condemned both the person and teachings of Theodore of Mopsuestia, some writings of Thedoret of Cyrrus, and the letter of Ibas. Vigilius now intervened with a statement of his own, drawn up by his deacon Pelagius, which condemned some teachings of Theodore but not his person nor the writings of the other two. Justinian refused to let the council see the papal document, declaring that the Three Chapters had already been condemned, and he imprisoned members of the pope's entourage. Cleverly, the emperor also showed the assembled bishops some writings of Vigilius, which made it clear that he had initially agreed to condemn the Three Chapters. In a final session, the bishops repeated their declaration, condemned the Three Chapters, and also condemned the theological writings of Origen (ca. 185–ca. 254), a pioneer in Greek theology who expressed views later deemed heretical. This condemnation led to a wholesale destruction of Origen's works, an irretrievable loss to theology. More than one modern scholar considers this to be the most important act the council took.

But, for contemporaries, the focus remained on the Three Chapters. Vigilius refused to accept the council and managed to hold out for six months. But, elderly and seriously ill, he declared that his advisors had misled him, and in February of 554 he accepted the decrees of the council. Justinian allowed him to return home, a long and arduous journey that the pope never finished. Vigilius died in Byzantine Sicily in June of 555.

His deacon Pelagius, while in prison, wrote treatises that showed that the decision of Constantinople II could be reconciled with Chalcedon, an important step that enabled the successors of Vigilius to accept this council as ecumenical and probably would have helped Vigilius had he lived to reach Rome. But in North Africa, even Byzantine rule could not prevent angry rejections of the council and the pope; in Italy, the northern bishops went into schism and were not reconciled to Rome until the seventh century. Opposition also appeared in Rome once Vigilius died, but Justinian moved quickly to impose the deacon Pelagius on the people as Pelagius I (556–61). Not surprisingly, this pope spent his brief pontificate trying to justify the condemnation of the Three Chapters and to win back the Latin bishops who had gone into schism. In many ways Pelagius was a superb pope, who energetically worked on poor relief, made the papal administration more effective, and revised and strengthened papal finances. His strong pontificate reconciled most Romans to him, but his acceptance outside of Rome was partial at best.

And what about the Monophysites for whose benefit this dreadful episode in church history had been carried out? Some accepted the Three Chapters, but most felt it was not enough. A century of seeing the emperor in Constantinople as an enemy would not go away immediately, and by this time the Monophysites themselves had divided into parties, bickering with one another, which made any general acceptance of Constantinople II impossible. The situation only worsened, and at times in many Eastern cities, including Alexandria, there were a Chalcedonian and a Monophysite bishop both resident. In a word, Constantinople II had failed to achieve its primary goal.

Justinian survived the council for a dozen years, dying in 565 at age eighty-two. He had done great, even remarkable, things during his long rule, but little of his work would survive him. The declining fortunes of the Byzantine Empire would produce the next ecumenical council.

Toward Constantinople III

The century and a quarter between the fifth and sixth ecumenical councils saw the Byzantine Empire in repeated and serious trouble. Just three years after Justinian's death, a swarm of Germanic barbarians, the Lombards, invaded Italy, conquering most of the peninsula. The Byzantines held onto Rome and a number of port cities, but much of Italy had passed into barbarian hands. Increasingly the popes made decisions without consulting the emperor's representatives in Italy, a process furthered by the increasing conversion of the Western barbarians (Franks, Anglo-Saxons, Irish, Spanish Visigoths) to Christianity. The popes had much to concern them in the West.

In the eastern Mediterranean, no successor worthy of Justinian appeared. The Monophysite problem plagued all the emperors. Persecution alternated with tolerance, and no emperor could take for granted the loyalty of his Monophysite subjects. Slavic tribes moved into the Balkan provinces, and the tremendous costs of the Italian war and now the Slavic invasions bankrupted the empire. In 610 a general named Heraclius led his army from Carthage in North Africa to Constantinople, deposed the reigning emperor, and took the title for himself.

Heraclius (610–41) faced enormous challenges. Under an ambitious new shah, the Persians attacked Byzantine territory, capturing Antioch and Jerusalem, from where they carried off the greatest relic in Christendom, the True Cross, in 614. The Persians went on to occupy Egypt and even to threaten the imperial capital. Heraclius rose to the challenge, working with Sergius, patriarch of Constantinople, to launch a holy war, a crusade, against the Persians. The emperor succeeded brilliantly, restoring Byzantine rule in the East and even capturing the Persian capital. In 630 he personally restored the True Cross to Jerusalem.

But the Persian war had shown Heraclius how important it was to pacify the frontier provinces, especially since the Persians, indifferent to the fractious nature of Eastern Christianity, had simply left the Monophysites alone. The emperor urged the patriarch Sergius to find some formula to reconcile the Monophysites without offending the Byzantine Chalcedonians and the Latin bishops of the West. No doubt the reader is sighing, déjà vu.

Sergius could not refer to "one nature," but he realized that the Monophysites wanted some formula that would emphasize the unity of divine and human in Christ. Reasoning that the human Christ could never act in a way different from that of the divine Word, Sergius spoke of one activity (*enérgeia* in Greek) or Monoenergism. Furthermore, Christ could not will contrary to the Word, so Sergius also spoke of one will (*thélesis* in Greek) or Monothelitism. In the course of time, the emphasis on Monoenergism would fade, and so this episode in church history is known as the Monothelite controversy.

Sergius succeeded in convincing some leading Monophysites to accept this formula, and he did not object when they understood Monoenergism as another way of saying Christ had one nature. But, as Davis puts it so well, "The life of an ecclesiastical politician is not an easy one, and Sergius's careful plans were soon upset" (*First Seven*, 265). A Palestinian monk named Sophronius considered this new approach to be backdoor Monophysitism. Sergius asked him to refrain from publicizing his doubts, which the obedient monk did, but when the Jerusalem clergy elected Sophronius to be bishop of that city, he felt he could no longer be quiet. In 634 a synod of Jerusalem clergy declared that Christ had two operations and two wills. This was serious opposition, but Sergius quickly countered it.

The Byzantines still ruled Rome, and the popes stayed in regular contact with Constantinople. Sergius wrote to Pope Honorius I (625–38), giving a vague explanation of the new teaching but insisting that it followed the teaching of Leo the Great. Most scholars believe that Honorius, an aristocrat who had an active pontificate filled with political challenges, did not fully understand the theological issue at stake. He affirmed that Christ had two natures but accepted that he had only one will. Armed with this papal support, Sergius energetically pushed his plans, publishing a doctrinal statement called the *Ecthesis*, which the emperor Heraclius approved in 638. Oddly enough, that year also saw the deaths of Sergius, Sophronius of Jerusalem, and Pope Honorius.

But also by that fateful year, the Byzantine Empire—indeed, Christianity itself—had changed forever.

Islam

The tribes of the Arabian Peninsula had practiced a crude form of paganism and had never managed to unite for any purpose for very long. But in the seventh century one of the great figures in religious history, the prophet Mohammed (570–632), changed all that. Like many religious reformers, Mohammed had a deep spirituality, a coherent teaching, organizational abilities, and a remarkable ability as a preacher. But beyond those, he was a marvelous conciliator. Not only did he win over most of the Arab tribes to submission (Arabic: *Islam*) to the one true God, Allah, he also united them politically. After his death in 632, his successors, who took the title Caliph, led campaigns against their age-old enemies, the Byzantines and the Persians.

The old Persian Empire disappeared forever, quickly conquered by Arab armies. Byzantium survived but at a very high price—the loss of major provinces in the Near East and North Africa. In 634 Arab armies invaded Syria. The Byzantine army that was sent to repel them suffered a catastrophic defeat in 636, and all of the Near East lay open to Arab armies. In 638 they captured Antioch. In that same year, they captured Jerusalem, surrendered to them by the dying bishop Sophronius. In 642 Alexandria, the moving force in so much of early Christianity, passed into Arab hands, surrendered to them by the bishop. Carthage in North Africa held out till 698. By the end of the seventh century, major centers of ancient Christianity had passed into Muslim hands.

The early Muslims did not persecute, and the Christians continued to worship, although they had to pay a tax that Muslims did not. Importantly, the Muslims did not care about divisions among the Christians, so the Monophysites worshiped freely, indifferent to what anyone in Constantinople thought. Fighting for their very existence, the Byzantines could not worry about reconciling the Monophysites. Monothelitism declined in importance for Heraclius.

But the Romans remained concerned about it. Pope John IV (640–42) rejected the *Ecthesis* of Sergius as heretical, and he made an attempt to vindicate what Honorius had done. Pope Theodore I (642–49), a Greek from Jerusalem who admired Sophronius, had no use for Monothelitism, and he broke off communion with a bishop of Constantinople who professed that doctrine. Martin I (649–53), a former papal legate to Constantinople who understood the issues, took an especially firm stand. In 649 he called a synod of Italian bishops that condemned Monothelitism. Present at the synod was a Byzantine theologian whom the pope admired, Maximus, who prepared the best theological assault on the new heresy.

But by now the Byzantines had stabilized the situation in the eastern Mediterranean, and the emperor Constans II (641–68), hopeful of winning back the Monophysite provinces from the Arabs, was in no mood for Roman dissent. In 653 an imperial emissary hauled Martin I out of his sickbed and forced him to journey to Constantinople, where he was tried and convicted on trumped-up charges of disloyalty. Condemned to death, the pope had his sentence commuted to banishment, but the harsh conditions of his exile brought about his death in 655. Constans II also had the theologian Maximus arrested and brought to the imperial city. He refused to accept Monothelitism and was banished until 661 when he was returned to the capital and questioned again. He refused to give in, and his captors cut off his tongue and his hand so that he could never again preach or write against Monothelitism. Maximus, who died in 662, earned the title "the Confessor," that is, one who suffers for the faith.

In 668, an imperial official assassinated the emperor Constans II, and his successor, Constantine IV (668–85) partly owed his throne to Pope Vitalian (657–72). Wanting to reconcile with the West, Constantine IV could not do so immediately because he had to deal with renewed Muslim attacks. Not until 678 could he focus on religious matters, and he contacted Rome about reconciliation. Pope Agatho (678–81), a Greek from Sicily, responded favorably to the imperial initiative but understandably insisted that Constantinople had to abandon Monothelitism. In 680 the pope sent legates to a council the emperor had called; the legates brought with them a letter from Agatho explaining the Latin position, which had been ratified by a council of 125 bishops.

The Third Council of Constantinople

Constantine IV had decided to turn the council into an ecumenical one, inviting bishops from all over the empire, including the Monothelite stronghold of Syria. The emperor appointed the papal legates as presidents of the council, although he personally took part in the first eleven sessions, effectively outranking all the bishops. Although the outcome was clear early on, the council stumbled along. It was essential that the bishops consult the works of the great orthodox theologians of the past, but they soon found themselves quoting the same author for directly opposite viewpoints. Archivists from the patriarchal library had to examine the competing texts to determine the authentic ones. That settled, the bishops moved on to the issue of Monothelitism.

Most opposed it, although the bishop of Antioch in Syria led a spirited defense of it, but to no avail. The assembled bishops confirmed that Christ had two wills, a human and divine one, and—glancing at Monoenergism—two operations, human and divine. They condemned Monothelitism and those bishops, living and dead, who supported it. The deceased bishops included several patriarchs of Constantinople but also Pope Honorius, a point that the Roman legates accepted. The council also accepted the letter of Pope Agatho as true to the teachings of Chalcedon, of Leo, and of the Monophysite hero Cyril of Alexandria.

This council also witnessed a genuinely weird event. A Monothelite priest claimed he could prove the truth of his theology by raising a man from the dead. He had a corpse brought into the council chamber, laid a Monothelite confession of faith on the body, and then prayed into the dead man's ear. Alas for the priest, the deceased remained so, and Monothelitism remained condemned. On September 16, 681, the sixth ecumenical council came to an end.

Pope Agatho had died before the end of the council, and Leo II (682–83) received and approved the decrees. It may seem surprising that he approved decrees that condemned Honorius, but traditionally the popes have understood his acceptance of Monothelitism to be a personal decision made by one who did not understand the issues at hand and not to be an official papal proclamation. Scholars generally agree.

Another question arises: after two centuries of trying to win back the Monophysites, why did the emperor Constantine IV abandon the cause? Probably because he realized that he could not win those provinces back from the Muslims. Indeed, Muslim power had done nothing but increase in the seventh century, and the emperor had to worry about Constantinople, which remained firmly Chalcedonian. To jeopardize his position in his remaining provinces as well as to give away any hope of ruling in the West for a lost cause was just absurd, and the emperor knew it. History proved him to be right. Not until the First Crusade (1095–99) by Latin armies did the Holy Land return to Christian hands, and even then only temporarily.

From Constantinople III to Nicea II

A century would pass before another council would meet. Enormous changes took place in Latin Christianity in that time. The ancient Latin churches could be found in two places, Western Europe and North Africa, the latter being home to hundreds of churches, important saints, and great theologians. But in the second half of the seventh century Arab armies overran North Africa, which has been Muslim ever since. Literally half of Latin Christianity ceased to exist. In 711 the Arab armies crossed into Spain, conquering 90 percent of that country. In 732 at Tours in central France the Arab armies met defeat at the hands of the Franks, commanded by Charles Martel ("The Hammer"), guaranteeing that Latin Christianity would continue to flourish in Western Europe.

By the end of the seventh century most of Europe west of the Rhine had been converted to Christianity. The addition of converted barbarians to the existing European Christian population at the very time that the Byzantine Empire had lost several provinces to the Arabs meant that the Latin bishops now spoke for about as many Christians as did the Greek bishops. The balance of ecclesiastical power had shifted westward.

The leaders of the Latin bishops, the popes, still lived in territory controlled by the Byzantines, and, although they remained loyal to the empire and strove to preserve imperial power in Italy, they got little reward for their efforts. The Byzantine emperors continued to think of the popes as important Western bishops but not as ones to whom they should listen. Byzantine policy both in the West and in the church rarely took papal views into consideration. The popes were expected just to obey imperial decisions. That approach might have worked better if the emperors had provided the popes with aid in time of crisis, but the precarious position of much of the East made that impossible. Consequently, the popes increasingly made decisions without consulting the empire.

The popes had long resented the emperors' willingness to tamper with doctrine in order to win back the Monophysites, but a political matter actually turned the popes away from Byzantium. In the seventh and early eighth centuries the Lombards, centered in northern Italy, had tried to dominate the entire peninsula, mostly at the expense of the remaining Byzantine territories but also of papal ones. The popes repeatedly asked the empire for help, but such help as was provided was sporadic and often ineffective.

The popes looked elsewhere for assistance, and Pope Zacharias (741–52), a Greek from Sicily, found it. The Frankish victor at Tours, Charles Martel was not a king but held the title "Mayor of the Palace," which made him the power behind the throne. In 750 his son Pepin held that office but, tired of the charade by which an incompetent king of a vapid dynasty officially held power, decided to become king himself. Because kings were sacred figures, he could not just kill the king. Pepin wrote to Zacharias and asked whether it was right that he who held no power should hold the title. Clearly

Pepin was planning a coup d'état, but the question raised the right issue. The pope responded that he who had the power in fact should have the power in name. Pepin promptly deposed the king, shut him up in a monastery so that he could produce no heirs, and then took the throne, grateful to the pope.

In 754, the new pope Stephen II requested Pepin's help against the Lombards, who in 751 had seized Ravenna, the Byzantine capital of Italy, and were menacing papal territories. Pepin complied. He defeated the Lombards in 755–56, but instead of returning the conquered Byzantine territories to the empire, he made the "Donation of Pepin" to the papacy, that is, land in central Italy that became the nucleus of the Papal States and made the popes significant Italian political rulers until the nineteenth century. The popes now relied upon the Franks for assistance against their Western enemies. Unfortunately for the popes, the Frankish rulers would soon follow the lead of the Byzantine emperors in ecclesiastical affairs.

The Byzantine emperors after the Third Council of Constantinople proved ineffective in resisting the Muslim threat, which yearly grew worse. In 717 a military man, a Syrian named Leo, seized the throne as Leo III (717–41), just in time to defend Constantinople from a year-long siege by Muslim forces. He literally saved the empire, and his grateful people never forgot that. This deep popular support allowed him and then his son to keep office in spite of their vicious and long-lasting attack on a major element of Christian religion, the icon.

Leo III considered icons to be idolatrous. To be sure, he was not the only one. Early Christians shared the Jewish opposition to portraying even human beings, much less divine or sacred figures, and icons came into use against learned opposition but with popular support. Theoretically, icons acted as symbols of a greater reality. Thus a portrait of Christ was not itself sacred, but it pointed beyond to the sacred person of Christ. But, unsurprisingly, the popular mind soon invested the icons themselves with power, often to an embarrassing degree. Icons spoke, they wept, they bled, and they performed miracles. Bishops warned about superstitious devotion to icons, but they recognized that some icons, by their prominence in a church and by the devotion they inspired, could take on a sacred character of their own. To use a modern example, an image of the Blessed Virgin in a beautiful stained glass window in a Gothic cathedral, an inspiration to centuries of believers, cannot be compared with a plastic "virgin" on sale in a discount store. And if making something physical to be sacred sounds unbiblical, recall the great Jewish devotion to the Promised Land and the ark of the covenant.

How to make the distinction? Theologians suggested that Christians could venerate icons but adore only that to which the icon pointed. This sensible distinction had been around for centuries before Leo III, but he wanted none of it. Icons were idolatrous, and as God's chosen emperor, he had to destroy idolatry. His campaign against icons is called the Iconoclastic Controversy.

Leo's campaign was long and involved, but it began in a startling way. The emperor ordered the removal of a famous and much-loved image of Christ above the bronze doors of the imperial palace. His soldiers went about cities, removing and sometimes destroying icons, a practice the Eastern churches would not see again until the Bolsheviks attacked Russian Orthodox churches. Some bishops heroically stood up to the emperor and paid the price for opposition; others followed the emperor's lead; the populace had doubts but saw Leo as their best defense against the Muslims and so put up with his campaign.

But Leo's writ did not run very far in the West. Pope Gregory II (715–31) quickly denounced iconoclasm in a strongly worded attack. His successor, Gregory III (731–41), a Greek-speaking Syrian, called a synod that denounced iconoclasm, provoking the emperor to remove some papal ecclesiastical territory and transfer to it the bishops of Constantinople. But Gregory III remained firm. Subsequent popes would follow his lead.

Opposition came from another place that Leo could not reach. From the safety of Muslim-controlled Syria, a Damascus Christian named John (675–749)—known as John Damascene—launched an important theological defense of icons. He did not win over the emperor, but he did provide iconodules (supporters of icons) a solid basis for venerating images.

Leo III died in 741, to be succeeded by his son Constantine V (741–75), who loathed icons more than his father did. But, like his father, Constantine was a brilliant commander who routed the Muslims both on sea and on land, and who carried the war into Muslim territory. He thus won the allegiance of the people and of the army, and the campaign against images continued. In 754 he called a council in a palace near Constantinople, where 338 bishops voted to support the emperor's position and actually declared their council to be ecumenical, something that neither the Orthodox nor Catholic churches have ever accepted.

Constantine V died in 775, and his son Leo IV reigned for only five years. At his death in 780, his wife Irene seized power in the name of her ten-year-old son Constantine VI. She venerated images and determined to overthrow the iconoclastic policy. She started effectively by opening negotiations with the Frankish king, Charlemagne (768–814), and with the pope, Hadrian I (772–95), knowing the Western Christians opposed iconoclasm.

(She also hoped to revive Byzantine political influence in the West.) But she ruled in Constantinople and needed a local bishop to support her. The bishop of the capital had just died, and she appointed an iconodule layman named Tarasius to replace him.

Irene and Hadrian agreed that an ecumenical council was needed to deal with the controversy, and so she called one to open in 786, thus making Nicea II the only council to be called solely by a woman, who attended the opening session.

The Second Council of Nicea

The Second Council of Nicea did not actually open in Nicea but in Constantinople on August 1, 786. Almost immediately a group of iconoclast soldiers burst in and tried to kill Tarasius, the bishop of Constantinople. The empress promptly adjourned the council, relocated it to Nicea, and rescheduled it for September 24, 787. The patriarch Tarasius opened the council, which consisted mostly of Greek bishops, although several Italian bishops, including two papal legates, were there. Although the outcome was a foregone conclusion, the assembled bishops debated biblical and patristic texts and then concluded that images "should be given due salutation and honor and reverence, not indeed that true worship of faith which pertains only to the divine nature" (Davis, *First Seven*, 310). The bishops also noted the traditional veneration that images had received among believers for centuries, and they acknowledged the value of images for teaching purposes, no small point at a time when more than 90 percent of the population was illiterate. The bishops also included some disciplinary canons dealing largely with monastic and clerical conduct.

The papal legates approved and signed the acts of the council, which gave it Roman recognition, but Pope Hadrian actually had to wait seven years to give the council his public approval. To shorten a very complicated tale, the Frankish king Charlemagne and his bishops, who could not read Greek, received a very defective Latin translation of the council's acts, so defective that the Franks thought the council had approved iconoclasm, the very reverse of what it had done. The Franks did not bother to check and confirm the accuracy of their translation, and they took some steps insulting both to the council and to Hadrian, who labored tirelessly to straighten things out. Only in 794 could the aged and worn-out pope give public affirmation of Nicea II; he died on Christmas Day the following year.

With an iconodule empress ruling in Constantinople, the situation in the East should have gotten better, but Irene's son Constantine VI wanted to rule on his own. With the army's help, he forced his mother out of the palace in 790, but Irene connived to return in 792, thanks to popular dissatisfaction with her son. Now an adult, Constantine had married, but shocked the church when he rejected his lawful wife and married his mistress. Had he been a successful general, he might have survived the scandal, but he was not. His mother seized power again and had her son blinded so that, as a disfigured person, he could never rule. Constantine died from his wounds in less than a week. Learning nothing from her previous expulsion, Irene again ruled aggressively, stirring up opposition and leading to a palace coup d'état, which dethroned her in 802. The new ruler exiled her to an island in the Aegean Sea. Irene survived there for only a year.

For a half century the Byzantine throne shifted back and forth among various claimants, some of whom were iconodules and some of whom were iconoclasts. Only in 843 could Methodius, patriarch of Constantinople, proclaim to the world that the Iconoclast Controversy had ended. As the many images in churches and private residences prove, iconoclasm has never returned.

From Nicea II to Constantinople IV

The Church of England and most Lutheran churches accept the first four councils as ecumenical; Orthodox churches accept the first seven. From this point we will study councils that only the Roman Catholic Church recognizes as ecumenical.

Between the seventh and eighth ecumenical councils the Latin Christian world changed significantly. In early Christianity, Latin speakers resided on both sides of the Mediterranean, but the Muslim conquest of North Africa proved to be final. The number of Christians there dwindled constantly, and by the ninth century Latin Christianity had effectively become Western European Christianity.

In 768 Pepin's son Charlemagne became king of the Franks, reigning until 814. When the Lombards began to oppress the papacy, Charlemagne invaded Italy, destroyed the Lombard state, and incorporated it into his kingdom in 773. This relieved Lombard pressure on the popes, but now a powerful new patron had become their neighbor. The popes quickly learned that Charlemagne, a devout man, had learned much from the Roman and Byzantine emperors and had decided that he would play a great role in church affairs, even to appointing bishops and abbots. The popes could only acquiesce.

Under Pope Leo III (795–816), the Frankish king's influence grew enormously. Leo came from southern Italy, and several Roman aristocrats, including relatives of his predecessor, Hadrian I, resented Leo. In 799 they instigated a mob to attack the pope and to attempt to blind him and cut out his tongue. Leo survived, but his enemies managed to depose him and lock him in a monastery. He escaped and fled to Charlemagne in Germany, followed quickly by representatives of his Roman enemies. The pious Charlemagne genuinely believed that no power on earth could judge the apostolic see, but, in spite of this, he did not automatically support Leo. Instead, he sent some of his own staff to Rome to investigate the situation, that is, the king would decide whether or not the pope would be restored. Charlemagne took his time deciding, not coming to Rome until December of 800. He decided in favor of Leo and ordered the execution of the pope's enemies, but Leo convinced him to commute the sentence to banishment. All Rome now knew that the pope owed his throne to the king.

On Christmas Day in 800 in Saint Peter's Basilica, Leo crowned Charlemagne emperor, had him acclaimed by the Roman populace, and then knelt before him, the only pope ever to do such a thing. Charlemagne accepted this new title, which infuriated the Byzantines, but he believed that with a woman (Irene) ruling in Constantinople, there was no legitimate emperor in the East. Diplomatic niceties aside, the Frankish king had an imperial title, and the Byzantines could do nothing about it.

At the time no one realized what a price both papacy and empire would pay for this act. Claiming the imperial title, successive Frankish and later German kings felt they had the right to intervene in Italy and in the church, while the popes repeatedly pointed out that, although these rulers could claim the title of king from their people, only a pope could crown someone as emperor. This church-state struggle would dominate much of medieval papal history, and it did not take long to begin.

Charlemagne died in 814, succeeded by his only living son, who had three sons of his own who soon fought over land and titles, ushering in a dynastic struggle that often put the title of emperor up for grabs to the strongest. The papacy often got involved in these struggles. But at the time of Constantinople IV, when Nicholas I (858–67) was pope, a temporary peace had settled on the West. This pope's problems would lie in the East, and, for once, they did not involve doctrinal controversy.

In the 840s a struggle had erupted in Constantinople between monks and the secular clergy, with the former believing they should be the dominant element. In 847, when the patriarch of the capital died, the emperor Michael III (840–67), later known as Michael the Drunkard, was a boy, and his mother Theodora acted as regent. She chose for patriarch Ignatius, a prominent monk and son of a former emperor, Michael I (811–13). A difficult man, Ignatius quarreled with local bishops and also with Rome. In 856 Bardas, brother of the empress, effected a coup d'état, and he exiled Theodora to a convent. She plotted to return in 858, but Bardas foiled his sister's plot, accused Ignatius of complicity, and deposed him. In his place Bardas put a layman named Photius, who, after a six-day "training course," became a priest.

Scion of a noble family, Photius was a great scholar, a famous bibliophile, and, as time would show, a remarkable survivor. The infuriated followers of the deposed Ignatius fought Photius's appointment from the beginning, and in 859 the "Ignatians" met in the church of the Hagia Sophia and declared Photius deposed. A schism had begun in the Eastern churches.

At this point Photius sent an announcement of his appointment and a statement of his orthodoxy to the Eastern bishops and also to Pope Nicholas, who had been struggling with the Byzantines about which church, Rome or Constantinople, had charge of the ecclesiastical provinces in the Balkans, especially since a pagan tribe, the Bulgars, had just settled there, and both sees wanted to evangelize them. Aware of the schism in the East, Nicholas sent legates to Constantinople to investigate the case of Ignatius. In 861 the legates took part in a local synod, which refused to reinstate Ignatius and also denied the papacy's rights in the Balkans. Convinced his legates had been duped, Nicholas kept Photius at bay, listened to agents sent by Ignatius, and in 863 presided over a Roman synod, which deposed Photius.

This remarkable step deserves explanation. By the ninth century the doctrine of papal primacy had grown significantly in Rome. The Byzantine bishops acknowledged papal primacy but considered it to be one of honor, not jurisdiction, and they did not recognize any Roman right to interfere in their decisions. The emperor decided who was bishop of Constantinople and did not need papal approval to do so. But in Rome the appointment of the bishop of the imperial capital was considered invalid without papal approval. The popes believed they could intervene in the East.

Politics complicated matters. The Byzantines still controlled some parts of Italy, and while the papacy's barbarian protectors, the Franks, could control the land, they had no navy. The Byzantine navy provided protection for the papacy against seaborne Muslim assaults. Furthermore, the emperor could prevent Rome from undertaking a mission to the Bulgars.

In 864 the Bulgar khan turned away Byzantine missionaries, insisting that he would appoint his own archbishop, to which the Byzantines could not agree. Sensing that this failure may have weakened Photius, Nicholas wrote to the emperor in 865, offering to negotiate but only if the decrees of the Roman synod of 863, that is, the one that deposed Photius, would be accepted in Constantinople. Michael III, ruling on his own since the assassination of Bardas in 865, stood by his bishop Photius, who in 867 took the drastic step of calling a synod and declaring the pope deposed. But Photius's triumph was short-lived.

Politics intervened yet again. A usurper, Basil the Macedonian, had Michael III killed and took the title of emperor for himself, becoming Basil I (867–86). He deposed Photius and reinstated Ignatius. (Since Byzantium was an absolute monarchy, we have no idea what the average Christian citizen thought of these ecclesiastical-political shenanigans.)

Basil I proved to be a shrewd man. Ignatius might have reclaimed the bishopric, but the emperor left in place many clerics appointed by Photius so as not to cause havoc in local churches. Recognizing that much of the trouble derived from papal intervention, the new emperor decided to improve relations with Rome, starting with a letter to Nicholas about the new situation. The letter, however, reached not Nicholas, who had died, but his successor, Hadrian II (867–72).

Basil wanted Rome to take an open approach to the question of the bishop of Constantinople, and he made both Ignatius and Photius send representatives to Rome in 869. But Hadrian II could not overlook Photius's synod of 867, which had declared Nicholas deposed. The new pope convened a Roman synod, which condemned and deposed Photius; it even declared priests ordained by him to be deposed. For Rome, the matter was settled. But the emperor saw things differently.

The Fourth Council of Constantinople

Basil realized that his people and bishops would not tolerate a Roman synod deciding who would be bishop of Constantinople, nor, of course, did he want the pope to make a decision traditionally made by emperors. He told Hadrian he was calling a council to settle matters. Hadrian agreed and sent two papal legates to preside over the council, which opened on October 5, 869. Ignoring papal demands, the emperor appointed one of his nobles to preside. The legates returned the favor by being absolutely inflexible in pushing Rome's demands, making it clear that peace with the papacy depended upon acceptance of them. The infuriated emperor shot back, insisting that Photius could not be condemned without a hearing. Photius appeared at the council but, with dramatic effect, refused to utter a word. Had he done so, he would have recognized the legitimacy of a council called with the express purpose of deposing him. Another bishop spoke on his behalf, but the papal legates demanded the council not to listen to him.

Finally, the council made it official: the bishops voted to depose Photius, and the emperor concurred. Ignatius became bishop once more.

But the emperor Basil had one more card to play. When Roman missionaries had gone to the Bulgar khan, he told them what he had told the Byzantines: that he wanted to appoint his own archbishop. Like the Byzantines, the Romans had no choice but to refuse. In 870 a Bulgar embassy arrived at the council to learn whether their fledgling church would be governed by Rome or Constantinople. To the chagrin of the papal legates, the Byzantines made sure that the council did not decide the question. After the council had closed (February 28, 870), the emperor decided the Bulgar church would be governed from Constantinople. The outraged legates could do nothing. After their return home, Pope Hadrian wrote to the emperor to complain, but Basil felt that the papacy had intervened enough in Byzantine affairs.

Relations between Hadrian and Ignatius were cool but peaceful. After the pope's death in 872, his successor, John VIII (872–82), worked for better relations with the empire, partly because he naturally regretted the poor relations between Christianity's two most important sees, but also because Muslim forces had occupied Sicily and parts of southern Italy, and were threatening Rome. Furthermore, no one in Rome could forget the raid of 846 when Muslim pirates had sacked Rome and plundered even Saint Peter's Basilica, stealing many of its treasures. John needed the Byzantine fleet for the safety of the Holy See. In 877 he sent an embassy to Ignatius.

When the papal envoys arrived in Constantinople and went to the episcopal palace, to their astonishment, they met not Ignatius but Photius!

Ignatius had held his bishopric until his death in 877, but in the time after the council, Photius had managed to return from exile, to win the emperor's favor, to become tutor to the emperor's sons, and upon Ignatius's death, to regain his bishopric. The legates wrote to Pope John about the new situation, adding the important detail that the clergy of the capital had unanimously accepted their sort of new bishop, who, of course, had been appointed by the emperor Basil. The subtext of the message was blunt: there would be no support in the court or the capital for any more action against Photius.

Pope John then came up with a good idea. He would not oppose Photius if he would just apologize for his previous misdeeds at some future synod. Having seen the consequences of provoking Rome, Photius agreed, and a synod met at Constantinople in 879. But the Eastern clergy would not tolerate a synod at which an imperial patriarch would apologize to Rome, and Photius did not publicly confess to anything. But he diplomatically allowed the legates to speak their piece, to insist upon Roman primacy, and even to claim that, in exercise of his primacy, Pope John VIII had reinstated Photius to his bishopric. For his part, Photius stressed his desire for goodwill and subtly added that he had not officially done anything in Bulgaria, but he did not renounce steps taken by others, such as the emperor.

John VIII ratified the decrees of the 879 council, and the Byzantine fleet pushed back the Muslim pirates, giving Rome some much-needed relief. But the pope did more. To quote Hans-Georg Beck, "John VIII recognized what (pope) Nicholas I was not prepared to admit, namely, that Rome was confronting not so much an individual adversary at Constantinople as the spirit of a church, which jealously guarded its old rights, genuine and imaginary, which was always basically prepared at any time, in spite of any discord, to make common cause against Rome" and that "Church unity could only be assured if the problems were solved in the spirit of Christian charity and less in the spirit of authoritative thought" (*History of the Church* iii, 187). The little-known Pope John VIII deserves far more recognition than historians have given him.

The papacy calls its first struggle against Photius the "Photian schism," but no second schism occurred. The two sees got along well until 886 when the new emperor, Leo VI (886–912), the bishop's former pupil, had him deposed. Photius retired to a monastery, where he lived peacefully until his death.

The papacy regards the 869–70 council as an ecumenical council, Constantinople IV. Many Orthodox clergy consider it an attempted humiliation of Constantinople by Rome, and some consider the 879 council in Constantinople ecumenical, although most deny that designation to any council later than Nicea II.

A significant period in the history of the councils had ended. Never again would a Byzantine emperor or empress call an ecumenical council. From this point, conciliar and papal history would be inextricably intertwined as the popes would call and preside over future ecumenical councils.

CHAPTER FOUR

The Papal Councils
of the Twelfth Century

More than a quarter of a millennium elapsed between the eighth and ninth ecumenical councils, Constantinople IV in 869–70 and Lateran I in 1123. Naturally much happened in both East and West, but we must concentrate on the latter.

By the late ninth century the empire created by Charlemagne lay in ruins, the prize of anyone strong enough to seize it. It eventually died a deserved death in 911. The situation of the empire reflected that of most of Western Europe in the ninth and tenth centuries, hammered by the attacks of the Saracens (African Muslims) in the South, the barbarian Magyars in the East, and, most dreaded of all, the Scandinavian Vikings who seemed to be everywhere—destroying, raping, pillaging. No central state could resist these invaders, and power passed more and more into the hands of local nobles, who could organize whatever defense might be available. To be sure, the besieged Western Christians occasionally won some significant battles, but the overall picture reflected universal concern and gloom.

The papacy did not escape from the general ruin. As landowners in central Italy, the popes had an important secular role, and their unquestioned religious role gave them much prestige, even in the secular world. Control of the papacy offered much to a noble family, and in the tenth century three great Roman families strove, with varying degrees of success, to put their own candidates, sometimes family members, into the papal office. Of course, if the candidate of another family secured the office, it could be years, even decades, before the other families had another chance to the papacy, so, with disappointing frequency, the nobles chose not to wait, arranging for depositions, mutilations, and even murders of popes. In some cases, the pope put in office by a noble family took his office seriously and chose to act as Bishop of Rome rather than as agent of his family, only to discover that the family would simply replace him with someone else. The tenth century represents the lowest point in papal history.

But, regardless of the unworthiness of several of its occupants, the papal office had great significance for the Western church, and many good people wanted things to change. The rulers of Germany took the lead in effecting such change.

In the tenth-century political struggles in Germany, one man, Otto I the Great (936–73), emerged as a true king. The fractious German dukes resented his leadership, but the Magyar invasions forced them to unite against a common enemy. When Otto routed the Magyars in 955, his prestige grew enormously, and the dukes reluctantly acknowledged his overlordship.

From 955 to 964 the most scandalous of all the popes ruled Rome, John XII, illegitimate son of a powerful Roman noble, who assumed office at eighteen and at twenty-seven died, according to contemporary Roman gossip, in the arms of one of his mistresses. Roman monks accused him of committing crimes that he had invented himself (!); more sober accounts also acknowledge his appalling debauchery. He was not a politician, and soon an ambitious Italian prince, Berengar of Ivrea, began attacking the Papal States. John appealed to Otto for help.

Realizing that the title "king of Germany" was essentially a national, even tribal, one, Otto longed for the imperial title, which only a pope could give him, and so he welcomed John's ambassadors. Otto offered to protect the pope, restore his lands, and not interfere in the governance of the city of Rome. John's ambassadors found these terms agreeable, and in 961 Otto invaded Italy, restored papal sovereignty in the stolen lands, and went to Rome. On February 2, 962, John XII crowned Otto emperor of the Romans, thus creating the Holy Roman Empire, which would survive until its extinction by Napoleon Bonaparte in 1806. Otto showed his gratitude not only by restoring the lands Berengar had taken but by adding to them, so that the Papal States now comprised almost two-thirds of Italy. Otto took his new title and left Rome to finish off Berengar.

John XII soon worried that he had acquired not a protector but an overlord. If he owed his continued occupancy of the papacy to Otto, how could he disobey him? John soon plotted against the emperor, who returned to Rome in the fall of 963, and called a synod that deposed John and replaced him with Leo VIII (963–65). Otto then left Rome, John raised a revolt against Leo, and Otto returned but John avoided imperial retribution by dying of a stroke.

What neither John nor Otto could have known was that they established a basic element in imperial-papal relations that would last for centuries.

Otto, by law and tradition, was king of the Germans, and no pope could appoint a ruler of Germany. On the other hand, Otto required John to crown him emperor of the Romans, that is, German law and tradition could make a king but only the pope could make that king an emperor. But once that king became emperor, he believed that he could routinely intervene in church affairs.

Otto's successors soon manifested this attitude, imposing popes on the Romans, such as Silvester II (999–1003), a French bishop whom Otto III (983–1002) chose at the advice of a French abbot. The Roman families had to live with the imperial choices, but their power in the city continued until the reign of Henry II (1002–24).

A genuinely pious man (he was canonized in 1046), Henry worked to get good bishops in the empire, and he insisted the bishops improve the morals of the lower clergy. He supported the papacy, and he had Benedict III (1012–24) work with him on church reform. Henry demonstrated that a pious, conscientious lay ruler could use his great power to effect reform in the church, a lesson not lost on contemporaries. But this raised two problems. First, the lay ruler owed his primary allegiance to his kingdom. What would happen if the interests of the church and kingdom differed? Second, a pious ruler might reform the church, but what would happen if a power-seeking ruler made appointments or decisions not in the interests of the church?

In 1045 another reforming emperor, Henry III (1039–56), visited Italy where a schism had broken out with three claimants to the papacy. On his own authority Henry called a synod at the Italian city of Sutri, where he sat in judgment on the "popes" and declared all three unworthy. He then appointed a German bishop to be Clement II (1046–47), followed by three other reformers. These four popes chose the names of popes of the early church (Leo, Damasus, Victor) to indicate their desire to return to the supposed early golden era of early Christianity. They focused on reform of the individual, that is, that the Church would improve if good men became bishops and abbots; Leo IX (1054–59) deposed a number of French bishops for simony. Nicholas II (1058–61), hoping to stop simony, initiated structural reform by decreeing that henceforth the cardinal bishops (suburban Roman bishops with liturgical functions) would elect the popes.

(Another event of Leo's pontificate was the schism between Eastern and Western churches, a schism not healed until the reign of Paul VI [1963–78]. A short-tempered patriarch of Constantinople, Michael Cerularius, resented several Latin liturgical practices, some theological points, and especially the infiltration of Latin rites into Byzantine territories in southern Italy. Leo sent a deputation to deal with these matters, but Humbert, the cardinal heading the delegation, was as hardheaded as Cerularius. Unknown to both sides, Leo died on April 19, before the struggle between the two men began. Patriarch and legate could agree on nothing, and on July 16, 1054, Humbert laid on the altar of the Hagia Sophia an excommunication of the patriarch and his advisors. Eight days later, at a synod convoked in Constantinople by the Byzantine emperor, the patriarch excommunicated the papal legates and their advisors. At the time, no one considered this a final break; relations between the two churches continued. Only later did historians refer to this dispute as a schism and then the Great Schism. This event would eventually impact ecumenical councils but not until Lyons II in 1274.)

Gregory VII (1073–85) was a Roman deacon who had worked for twenty years with reforming popes before assuming the papal office. He correctly realized that lay rulers, no matter how personally moral and pious, subjected the church to lay rule, which in turn compromised the church. If a king wanted a bishop to appoint the monarch's younger brother as abbot of a monastery, could a bishop who owed his office to the king really refuse, even if the younger brother were unworthy to be an abbot? Gregory realized that reform had to be structural as well as personal, and he took on an important issue to start his campaign.

Bishops were both ecclesiastical and secular rulers appointed by the king. At their installation ceremonies, the bishops received the insignia of office from the king—significantly, both secular and ecclesiastical insignia, the latter including the ring and crozier, a process known as investiture. Since this occurred at a public ceremony, Gregory realized that the people saw, in effect, the monarch creating bishops, so he chose investiture as the issue upon which he would challenge lay dominance, hence the name Investiture Controversy. The pope initiated his struggle against the emperor Henry IV, (1056–1106), who had begun his rule at the age of six and had only recently attained his majority, that is, his right to rule without a regent.

Henry rejected the pope's claim to remove his right of investiture, and the German bishops—all appointed by emperors—supported him, even claiming to depose the pope. Gregory responded by deposing the emperor, a daring gambit that succeeded because the restless German dukes resented their youthful ruler and used the papal deposition to claim that Henry no longer held office. To stem off rebellion, Henry made an ignominious reconciliation with the pope, who lifted the deposition. When he regained full power, Henry again denied the pope's claim, was again deposed, but this time no rebellion broke out. Henry invaded Italy; Gregory fled to the Normans in southern Italy, who sheltered him, supposedly as a guest, although they refused to let him leave. He died in Norman territory in 1085. His attempt to weaken lay power over the church had been a practical failure. Why?

First, most medieval people, including most clerics, believed monarchs to be sacred figures, who had the right to intervene in religious affairs. Second, Gregory's papal predecessors had focused on individual reform and had accepted the prevailing situation. Third, many rulers were simply too strong for the pope to face down; for example, in England William I the Conqueror made it clear that he would appoint bishops with no outside interference. Fourth, and most important, the bishops had all been appointed by monarchs, that is, the system had worked for them, and they had much to lose if it were changed.

Even on the theoretical level Gregory had failed, but that was because his almost mystical views of papal authority were far too advanced for the eleventh century. He believed that only the pope could depose or reinstate bishops; that he could transfer them to different dioceses; that he could ordain a cleric in any church he wished, regardless of what the local bishop thought; that he could evaluate the decisions of everyone in the church but no one could judge his decisions. In fact, over the centuries, the popes would gain all of these powers and more and would do so with the general acceptance of the bishops and rulers, but in his own era, Gregory looked like a power-hungry tyrant who ignored the traditional rights of princes and bishops. Yet Gregory had raised a fundamental issue that his successors could not ignore: how much control should lay rulers have in the church?

Forcing the issue had produced only conflict; clearly some kind of compromise was needed. Urban II (1088–99), best known for calling the First Crusade in 1095, "fully [assented] to Gregory's principles, but elastically adapting their implantation to the present situation, . . . led the reform papacy out of the narrow pass and toward victory" (Jedin, *Councils*, 386).

Urban recognized that the rulers could not be forced into giving up such an essential element of their power, but he also recognized that Henry IV had done a marvelous job of showing Catholic Europe the harm that untrammeled lay power could do. Henry's troops had occupied Rome, he had installed an antipope whom he forced the Roman people to accept but whom no one outside of Henry's power recognized, and he had caused turmoil in the German churches. The pope decided to approach the rulers.

He took intelligent initial steps. Gregory had concluded that bishops installed by their rulers were not true bishops and thus no one ordained by them was truly a priest. Unless he found evidence of simony, Urban usually let the installation and ordinations stand, thus avoiding fights with the rulers and causing the people to fear that improperly ordained priests could not offer valid Masses. But he did not successfully settle the investiture issue.

His successor, Pope Paschal II (1099–1118), came up with what would be the ultimate solution. In both England and France, the local bishops convinced the king to accept a compromise. The king could invest the bishop with the insignia of his temporal power, and as a secular magnate, the bishop would owe allegiance to the king. The king would not, however, invest the bishop with the insignia of his ecclesiastical office. Inevitably, the agreement had numerous associated technicalities, but this was the basis, and, as Friedrich Kempf says, "Paschal was wise enough to tolerate the two compromises that had been reached without his direct participation" (*History of the Church* iii, 394), something Gregory VII would never have done. These events occurred between 1102 and 1107.

Now Paschal had to deal with Germany, where Henry V (1106–25) had replaced his father as emperor. He indicated a desire for reconciliation, but, at heart, he was Henry IV's son. Paschal said he could not accept investiture as practiced in Germany but the king could give the bishops temporal insignia. Henry agreed, and in 1111 he went to Rome to be crowned emperor. During the coronation ceremony, Paschal read out the agreement that had been reached, which outraged secular and ecclesiastical princes, who both thought that their side had conceded too much. Watching the agreement collapse, Henry promptly arrested the pope and several cardinals, transported them outside Rome, and eventually forced Paschal to crown him emperor and to recognize his rite of investiture. On the surface, Henry had won, but Christian Europe had no toleration for this type of brutal domination of the church. After gaining his freedom, Paschal again insisted that secular rulers could not invest bishops. Yet he could not take on Henry again. Local events in Rome, where a noble family had managed to gain considerable power, led to a revolt and Paschal's withdrawal from the city in 1117; he died in 1118.

His short-lived successor, Gelasius II (1118–19), could do nothing about investiture, but the next pope, a French nobleman who took the name Callistus II (1119–24), settled the matter once and for all with an ecumenical council.

Henry V was tiring of the struggle. In 1122 imperial and papal negotiators hammered out the Concordat of Worms, named for the German city where they met. The emperor renounced the right to invest bishops with their rings and croziers but kept the right to invest them with their secular powers.

The popes had worked the same basic arrangements with the monarchs of England, France, and Germany, along with lesser princes, and, although the royal willingness to go along with the agreement wavered on occasion, the papacy had won a major victory. These agreements acknowledged that lay princes did not have an untrammeled right to treat the church as just one more element in their domains. They had acknowledged that the bishops had independent stature as ecclesiastical princes. As the papacy grew stronger and stronger throughout the twelfth century, the bishops looked more and more to Rome. Every bishop found himself with two masters, a drastic change from the traditional ways.

The First Lateran Council

Callistus wisely decided to call a council to ratify the new arrangement. The Roman Catholic Church recognizes this council as ecumenical, the first one called directly by a pope and not by a Roman emperor or a Byzantine monarch. The Concordat of Worms had basically ended the investiture struggle, at least on the theoretical level. On the practical level, some monarchs and nobles still tried to interfere with the ecclesiastical installation of bishops, but, overall, such practices were doomed. Yet Callistus was wise enough to want to get the agreement confirmed by a council, so he called one to meet at the Lateran cathedral, the pope's cathedral in Rome. (Modern Vatican City is an independent state, but, as Bishop of Rome, the pope must have a cathedral church in the city, and the basilica of Saint John Lateran serves that purpose.) Unfortunately for the historian, the acts (the authentic minutes) of the council do not survive, although much can be reconstructed from reports of participants.

The council opened on March 18, 1123, and closed either on March 27 or April 6; it probably numbered about three hundred participants. The pope called it to ratify the Concordat of Worms, which the council did. The assembled council fathers also passed a number of disciplinary decrees, extending the Truce of God (nobles agreed not to fight on certain religious feast days), granting to Crusaders an indulgence from the temporal penalties (purgatory) accruing to their sins, protecting the families and goods of Crusaders as well as of pilgrims, and minor issues relating to ordinations. A notable feature of this council was the pope's reliance on bishops rather than monks to handle diocesan matters. This may seem obvious today, but in the twelfth century monasteries had surprisingly wide leverage among the populace, and conflicts between bishops and monasteries were not uncommon.

The council brought some peace to Western Christendom, but nothing could bring peace to the city of Rome.

The Second Lateran Council

In the eleventh century the Roman aristocratic families, particularly the Pierleoni and the Frangipani, had regained considerable influence and had become involved with the papacy. The papacy's chancellor, Cardinal Aimeric, supported the reform movement but he feared that the traditional reform party, the Old Gregorians (named for Gregory VII), favored confrontation with the monarchs rather than cooperation. When Callistus II died, Aimeric and the Frangipani saw to it that the cardinals chose an Italian bishop who took the name Honorius II (1124–30). He favored the reform movement, and he supported the new religious orders, such as the Cistercians, who worked for reform. The pope also got along with most European monarchs, but he feared the rise of the Normans in southern Italy. Unable to dislodge them or even push them back, Honorius made peace with the Normans.

Honorius lived in Rome for his entire pontificate, but when he fell ill early in 1130, Cardinal Aimeric had him moved into a monastery within Frangipani territory in Rome. Aimeric convened a representative group of cardinals, both new reformers and Old Gregorians, and prepared for an immediate conclave when the pope died. But when Honorius passed away during the night of February 13–14, the Old Gregorians were underrepresented. Aimeric did not wait, and the next morning his group of cardinals promptly elected a Roman deacon who took the name Innocent II (1130–43).

This secretive move alienated many Romans, and Cardinal Peter Pierleoni and his family rejected the election and called a conclave of their own, at which Cardinal Pierleoni became Anacletus II (1130–38). Two papal elections in Rome in a single day had produced a schism.

The Pierleoni moved more quickly than their enemies, and they secured the city for Anacletus and his followers. Because the Pierleoni were of Jewish origin, although Christian for seventy-five years, Anacletus became known as "the pope from the ghetto." Sensing the changed mood of the Romans, the Frangipani abandoned Innocent and recognized Anacletus. Innocent had to flee Italy and soon arrived in France.

In France the refugee pope won the support of the greatest churchman of the day, Bernard of Clairvaux, a famous abbot, preacher, and spiritual writer. Bernard's assistance enabled Innocent to win the recognition of the kings of France and England as well as lesser monarchs and aristocrats. Innocent also gained the support of Lothar, king of the Germans. In 1133, with a German army, Innocent returned to Rome and crowned Lothar emperor (1133–37), but Anacletus maintained himself in the Pierleoni stronghold (around modern Vatican City), and when the emperor returned to Germany, Innocent again had to flee the city.

Anacletus looked for support outside Rome but found it mostly limited to northern Italy, although he did put together a short-lived alliance with the Normans of Sicily.

The schism continued until the death of Anacletus on January 25, 1138. His supporters promptly elected a successor, an Italian cardinal who took the name Victor IV, but he soon realized the impossibility of his position and, prompted by Bernard of Clairvaux, he resigned his office and accepted a pardon from Innocent.

Although triumphant, Innocent rightly feared that Anacletus's supporters might try something new, and he determined to wipe out all that the antipope, as Anacletus is now considered by the Vatican, had done. Innocent called a council, Lateran II, which opened on April 4, 1139. One hundred bishops attended, including a few from the Crusader states, the Latin kingdoms the Crusaders had established in Palestine. The official acts of the council do not survive, but scholars know that Innocent denied legitimacy to any of Anacletus's acts. This surprised and shocked many people. Schisms quickly become very messy. Each pope consecrates bishops who ordain priests, and these appointments can number into the hundreds. At the end of a schism, the victor often let stand many of his opponent's appointments, unless there was good reason not to, for example, if a bishop used simony to get an appointment. But Innocent would have none of that. He wanted it clear that Anacletus was never a true pope, and thus none of his appointments was valid.

The council met only three times and closed before the month of April was out. In addition to putting an end to the schism, the bishops pushed forward some reform proposals, extending the celibacy requirement to include subdeacons and deacons as well as priests. Innocent reigned peacefully until his death in 1143.

Toward Lateran III

In the twelfth century, the size and scope of the papacy grew considerably. Scholars speak of a twelfth-century Renaissance, and the papacy took advantage of that, becoming early supporters of a new educational institution, the university. The popes also promoted the study and practice of canon law, so that in dispute with lay lords and other bishops, the popes often had the best and most reliable legal knowledge at hand. The successful conclusion to the Investiture Controversy guaranteed that the popes played a role in choosing bishops, so less and less were the bishops the sole appointees of the lay lords and thus owing them their primary allegiance. The monarchs did not always accept this, as Thomas Becket, archbishop of Canterbury, learned when he defied the Norman Henry II of England, but generally the situation improved for the popes.

But a significant problem arose in the twelfth century. As the papacy became more active, as bishops, minor clerics, and even lay disputants looked to the popes for decisions on controverted issues, papal government had to grow to meet the demands. The popes created new offices and thus new officials. The bureaucracy increased, and though efficient compared to those of the lay lords, it was painfully slow and filled with appeals to ever higher officials, sometimes even to the pope himself. Twelfth-century popes complained about the amount of business they had, and, inevitably, the cardinals more and more chose popes who would be able to deal with the growing government.

A second significant problem accompanied the growth of the papal government, and that was the cost. If a bishop in Scotland was disputing with the canons of his cathedral and both appealed to Rome, the papacy might send an ambassador to deal with the problem. Since the ambassador traveled for months, brought assistants, and usually needed several weeks to reach a decision, the considerable cost of the trip for his party as well as for their stay in Scotland had to be borne by someone, usually the litigants. But if Rome did not send someone, then the disputants themselves often had to travel to Rome, to maintain lodgings there, and to engage lawyers to represent them at the papal court. All of that also cost a great deal of money.

Furthermore, the popes continued to come from the ranks of the aristocrats and thus lived like aristocrats, and as the popes became increasingly important, their courts and persons had to reflect this new status. It did not take long for Roman wits to mock (anonymously) these costly new developments. On city walls one could read this anagram: "The root of all evils is avarice," which in Latin read: *Radix Omnium Malorum Avaritia*, producing the acronym *ROMA*.

But the reaction against the new developments often took on very serious overtones. Some Christians considered the church to have been totally corrupted, and so they rejected the institutional church and formed groups of their own that strove to recover apostolic poverty; other groups saw the perceived corruption as a sign of the imminent end of the world, and they turned to apocalyptic speculations. Never a threat to the church at large, these groups troubled many individual regions and survived, in one form or another, to the Reformation. The twelfth-century popes had much on their plates.

But the immediate problems facing the popes were familiar ones: how to deal with the citizens of Rome and with the German emperors. Although the Roman aristocratic families continued to hold power, the city's people occasionally formed communes as a direct challenge to papal power. For example, Eugenius III (1145–53) could not enter Rome until ten months after his election, and even then the people turned him out within a month. But in 1153 the newly elected German emperor, Frederick I Barbarossa (1152–90), offered the pope protection against the people in return for Eugenius's promise to crown Frederick emperor in Rome.

Anastasius IV (1153–54) managed to stay in Rome during his brief pontificate and had few dealings with Barbarossa, but his successor, Hadrian IV (1154–59), to date the only English pope, requested and received the emperor's help against the commune (1155). Yet relations between the two remained cool, although Hadrian did crown Barbarossa emperor of the Romans. It fell to the next pope, Alexander III (1159–81), to deal with the emperor, a task that required an ecumenical council.

Barbarossa wished to restore the empire as it was in the times of Charlemagne and Otto the Great, and to do so he needed to dominate the church in his lands, which included lands in Italy and even some bordering on the Papal States. He got his chance with the conclave of 1159. Pro-imperial cardinals worked for the emperor's candidate, but a sizeable majority chose Hadrian's designated successor, who took the name Alexander III and was consecrated on September 20. Exactly two weeks later, Barbarossa had his own failed candidate consecrated pope, taking the name Victor IV (1159–64). Alexander promptly excommunicated Victor (and Barbarossa as well) in 1160, and the Vatican considers Victor to be an antipope.

In fact, Victor, an Italian cardinal, was a personally good man with a long and distinguished record of service to the papacy. But he was—and was widely considered to be—Barbarossa's pawn in a struggle to reassert imperial power over the German church and even over the papacy. Few bishops or rulers outside of Germany ever recognized Victor.

But Frederick Barbarossa had great power and a large army. The rulers who supported Alexander offered him little help, and Frederick treated Victor as if he were a legitimate pope. When Victor died, his "cardinals" chose a successor, Paschal III (1164–68), proof that Barbarossa intended to maintain the schism. In 1167 the imperial army occupied Rome, where Paschal was formally enthroned as pope.

But even in Germany support for the emperor's "popes" was waning, and in a surprise move, Frederick in 1167 suggested that both "popes" resign and a new election be held, proof that he knew his schism was doomed. When Paschal died, his supporters chose a successor, Callistus III (1168–78), but Frederick withheld recognition from him, since by now he wished to reconcile with Alexander. The emperor had concluded that he could not win over other rulers to his "popes," not even Henry II of England, who resented Alexander's support for Thomas Becket when that archbishop of Canterbury defied the king. The popes played too great a role in Western Europe for the monarchs and nobility to allow the German emperor to choose them.

To the surprise of almost everyone, Callistus III held out for a decade but finally surrendered to Alexander, who graciously gave him an appointment in the church. Some schismatic hard-liners elected one more "pope," Innocent IV (1179–80), but Europe considered this election a farce. Alexander had Innocent arrested and then confined for life to a monastery.

Alexander III had triumphed over his schismatic rivals, but the strife had taken a toll. The schism had used up time, energy, and money, and Alexander feared that many other matters had received insufficient attention or had even gone unattended. Furthermore, the schism had challenged his authority and called into question the very validity of papal elections. The pope concluded that the best way to settle the schism and get things back on track would be an ecumenical council. In 1179 he called Lateran III.

The Third Lateran Council

The origins of Lateran III can be found in an 1177 meeting between pope and emperor. Frederick Barbarossa realized that his "popes" were losing support, and so he resorted to force, invading northern Italy. With papal support, the northern Italian cities banded against Frederick and soundly defeated him. Yet Frederick refused to withdraw from Italy, and emperor and pope opened negotiations, concluding them in Venice in 1177. After years of confusion and strife, many elements entered the discussion, but, most important, Barbarossa recognized Alexander as lawful pope, while Alexander lifted his excommunication of Barbarossa and recognized him as emperor and his son Henry as King of the Romans, signaling papal recognition of Henry as a future emperor. Both rulers had suffered much, but both emerged from the treaty negotiations with their offices intact. Furthermore, both recognized the need to straighten out ecclesiastical affairs, and so the peace treaty signed at Venice spoke of "the council about to be summoned." Fortunately for Alexander, the emperor returned to Germany in late 1177, allowing the pope to plan the council largely on his own terms.

Lateran III opened on March 5, 1179. As with its two predecessors, the formal acts of the council have not survived, but scholars do know that only three sessions were held (March 5, 14, and 19), making this one of the shortest and most efficient councils.

It was also one of the most impressive. Approximately three hundred bishops attended, representing all of Europe, including faraway Scotland and Ireland. Seven bishops from the Crusader States spoke for the European Catholics of the Middle East. Bishops from states hostile to one another were there. Lateran III illustrates a point often overlooked about the councils: in the Middle Ages and Renaissance, the ecumenical councils represented the largest gatherings of Western peoples anywhere. Where else would Christians from Scandinavia meet Christians from Sicily? Where else would Christians from Ireland meet Christians from the Near East, since both of them came from literally the far ends of the Western Christian world? We should not picture the councils as mini-United Nations. They did not include rulers, and they focused only on ecclesiastical matters, but they were the most geographically diverse gatherings of the era.

The council issued twenty-seven canons, with Canon 1 holding pride of place. German emperors had managed to raise up antipopes almost with impunity, partly as a result of uncertain election procedures for popes. By the eleventh century many people believed that the vote for the pope should be unanimous, a pious expectation that rarely materialized. Instead, it practically invited schism because a single negative vote could become grounds for challenging a pope's legitimacy. Medieval Christians recognized that unanimity bordered on impossibility, and so they were willing to accept the cardinals' choices, but Alexander wanted to settle this matter once and for all. Canon 1 firmly restricted the election of the pope to the college of cardinals, and only a two-thirds vote would suffice to choose a new pope. Anyone who did not accept a pope elected in that way incurred automatic excommunication; any consecrations, ordinations, or sacraments conferred by a pope not elected in this way (e.g., one chosen by a lay ruler) were deemed invalid. Lateran III set the procedure for papal elections for the next ten centuries.

Consequent to that canon, the council invalidated the ordinations made by Barbarossa's antipopes; staying with this theme of ordination requirements, the council declared that a bishop must be at least thirty years old, of legitimate birth, and have the requisite qualities for office, the last requirement unfortunately being vague enough for monarchs and nobles to insist that their candidates could meet all the requirements.

The twelfth century saw the rise of several new religious orders, such as the Cistercians. These orders were transnational, that is, they spanned several countries, and the grand masters of those orders had great influence. Often the members of the orders looked to their grand master or to the pope, but local bishops often felt that the priests of the orders, who administered sacraments in their dioceses, paid little attention to them. The council emphasized the bishops' authority in their dioceses.

Problems of clerical discipline and behavior occupied much of the council, including one that seems almost humorous today. To quote Hughes: "One never-ceasing complaint is that bishops' official visitations tend to be ruinously expensive for the places they visit. Their trains—officials, guards, servants—is now cut down: archbishops to a maximum of forty to fifty horses [that is, knights and retainers], according to the country and its resources, cardinals twenty-five, bishops twenty to thirty, archdeacons seven; deans are told to be contented with two. No hunting, no hawks and falcons" (*Crisis*, 180). Since almost all the medieval bishops were aristocrats, they traveled in style, and one can imagine the financial impact on some poor, rural diocese when a noble bishop, who was a cousin of the king, arrived with a retinue of knights, retainers, servants, hunting dogs, and falcons!

But ecclesiastical extravagance had a more serious consequence. In the early church, heresies often focused on doctrine. The twelfth century witnessed the appearance of social heresies, that is, groups of people, often poor, who contrasted the luxurious lives of the hierarchy (but not of the parish priests, who lived as badly as the people) and claimed that the bishops had turned away from the apostolic poverty of the New Testament. These groups often contained unlettered people, who never understood the Bible well and quickly fell into heresy, but they represented the views of many medieval Christians.

Monasteries could not provide the required help since monks were not supposed to involve themselves in the affairs of the dioceses. What the church needed was a reform movement that would deal with these social heresies, and such a movement would arise in the next century, but in the meantime the dissident groups grew in size and strength, especially the Cathars (the pure ones) in southern France. The council excommunicated the Cathars and urged actions against them.

Unfortunately the council struck a very negative note regarding the Jews, approving a canon that declared that in all lawsuits the testimony of a Christian would count for more than that of a Jew. Those who accepted a Jew's testimony over that of a Christian risked excommunication. Whatever the intention, this virtually invited Christian nobles to cheat Jews, knowing that the Jews could never get just treatment in a court. This attitude toward the Jews, like that toward the Cathars, offends the modern mind and, of course, has no sanction in the contemporary Catholic Church, but this was quite standard for the Middle Ages.

Aside from these unfortunate matters, Alexander III had called a large, successful council. In just three sessions, this pope had dealt with most of the problems facing him, especially those arising from the schism, along with a papal election reform to prevent future schisms. Barbarossa continued to rule and to believe that the emperor had more rights in the church than the pope was willing to grant, and, less openly, other monarchs and nobles persisted in pushing their own agendas. Bishops still acted like aristocrats, money squabbles and scandals plagued the church, and the problems raised by the Cathars lay in wait, but Alexander could hardly have been expected to deal with everything. After all, he had spent his entire pontificate challenged by antipopes, and, thanks to Frederick's support of these antipopes, the pope had spent little time in Rome, literally wandering about France and Italy. Alexander had no stable court and no access to the church records that were kept in Rome, which in turn considerably hampered his conducting of the daily business of the church. Although historians do not consider him a great pope, he was a good pope who struggled against great odds.

CHAPTER FIVE

The Papal Councils
of the Thirteenth Century

Toward Lateran IV: Pope Innocent III

The story of Lateran IV, the most important medieval council, is the story of Pope Innocent III. Historians consider him a great pope, but few modern believers would give him that appellation. He actively involved himself in politics and not just in the Papal States but in all of Italy, France, England, Spain, Portugal, and especially the Holy Roman Empire. He never hesitated to use spiritual weapons, such as excommunication and interdicts for an entire country, to achieve his goals. He strongly supported the Crusades, approving of one and planning for another. He had no belief in freedom of religion and readily used coercion against those he deemed heretics. He differed so much from modern popes who eschew religious conflicts, who respect religious freedom, and who move people by prayer and example. How, then, can historians consider Innocent III to have been a great pope?

Innocent was a man of his world. We must recall that until 1870 the popes ruled a sizeable portion of central Italy, and the Papal States required a firm administrator. In those days, coronation ceremonies for rulers often involved a bishop, or sometimes the pope, anointing a ruler who then vowed to support the church, that is, rulers expected the hierarchy to be involved in politics. Byzantines and Muslims routinely used coercion against supposed heretics, and when they warred against one another, they often invoked a holy war. Innocent's attitude reflected the universal attitude of the age. This does not, of course, justify those attitudes, and at some point people must move beyond the confines of their era (as when Christian churches condemned slavery in the nineteenth century), but we will not understand Innocent by placing him in a twenty-first-century framework.

After the death of Alexander III, five popes enjoyed short reigns and had to deal with the usual problems—monarchs who agreed to respect the church and constantly worked to dominate it in their own countries. The most significant church-state event occurred in 1186 when Barbarossa's son Henry married Constance, daughter and niece of Norman kings of Sicily and heiress to that kingdom, which included much of southern Italy. The marriage guaranteed that Henry VI (1191–97) and his successors would rule lands in both northern and southern Italy and possibly have the papacy in a geographical vise.

Other problems persisted. The Roman populace continued to make demands upon the popes, who often had to live outside the Holy City to avoid political troubles. Occasionally members of the great Roman families aided and abetted the popular troublemakers.

In the East, the Crusaders' situation had severely deteriorated. In 1187 the Muslim leader Saladin had routed the Crusaders in battle and captured Jerusalem, along with many other Crusader cities. The Third Crusade (1189–92) set out to rectify things, led by three kings: Frederick Barbarossa, Philip II Augustus of France, and Richard I the Lion-Hearted from England. Barbarossa drowned in a river in Asia Minor, which caused many of his troops to return home (and simultaneously removed the papacy's strongest enemy). Philip made it to the Holy Land but became severely ill with dysentery and so returned home in 1191. Richard the Lion-Hearted won several impressive victories, but Muslim leader Saladin kept Jerusalem, although agreeing to allow Christian pilgrims access to the city. The future of the Crusader states was not promising.

Then there were everyday problems: clerical drunkenness, incontinence, maintaining of concubines, maladministration of the sacraments, elaborate clothing, poor preaching, and financial abuses of all kinds, including simony. Special problems pertained to monks: abbots encroaching on the bishop's responsibilities. Many popes had faced these problems, but Innocent was the man to do something about them.

On January 8, 1198, the aged (ninety-two) and increasingly ill Celestine III died. That very day, on the second ballot, the cardinals chose Lothar of Segni, a cardinal deacon, as Pope Innocent III. He was ordained a priest on February 21 and consecrated pope the next day at the age of thirty-seven. J. N. D. Kelly calls him "a man born to rule," and says that he "united exceptional gifts of intellect and character with determination, flexibility, rare skill in handling men, and also humanness" (*Popes*, 186).

A brief look at Innocent's papacy will set the stage for the council of 1215.

The perilous situation of Jerusalem provoked Innocent to call the disastrous Fourth Crusade of 1201–1204. French nobles led the Crusade, but things became complicated when their army arrived in Venice in 1201 without sufficient funds to pay the Venetians for transport to Constantinople. The Venetians offered a deal. Resentful of the commercial success of the Christian town of Zara on the eastern shore of the Adriatic, which was governed by the Catholic king of Hungary, the Venetians told the Crusaders that if they conquered Zara and handed it over to Venice, they could have passage to the East. The Crusaders agreed; Innocent threatened everyone concerned with excommunication for attacking a Catholic city; the Venetians and Crusaders ignored him and captured Zara.

This was bad enough, but things soon got worse. A dispossessed Byzantine prince, styling himself Alexis IV, contacted the Crusaders and offered them a huge sum of money and assistance for their invasion of Palestine if they helped him to gain the Byzantine throne. The Crusaders accepted the offer and sailed to Constantinople, arriving in the spring of 1203. They soon defeated the city's defenders but did not enter the city, contenting themselves with putting Alexis IV on the throne. But he proved to be an ineffectual leader with no popular support, and angry citizens murdered him, thus depriving the Crusaders of the funds and the assistance that Alexis had promised them. Frustrated and angry, on April 12 of 1204, they stormed and captured Constantinople amidst much violence. The French soldiers looked for loot and women (including nuns), the Venetians wanted to establish trading stations that would exclude their Italian seafaring rivals, and ecclesiastics of both parties stole relics from the Byzantine churches. This astonishing act poisoned Roman Catholic-Orthodox relations for eight centuries.

The Crusaders did not move on to Palestine but instead established a Latin kingdom based in the imperial city. Innocent was furious but could do nothing. Hoping for a possible reconciliation of Rome and Constantinople, he recognized the state and agreed to a Latin patriarch in Constantinople. This Latin state lasted until 1261 when the Greeks recaptured it, but mortal damage had been done to Byzantium, which never regained its previous stature.

Never one to be daunted by failure, Innocent clung to the crusade ideal, and at Lateran IV, he would urge a new crusade.

Heresy likewise occupied much of Innocent's time. The Cathars were a dualist heresy, that is, they divided creation into the spiritual and material, and then denounced the material as corrupt, contrary to much biblical teaching. But the Cathars' dualism was not the only problem. They strongly criticized the wealth and lifestyle of the hierarchy, and their own contrasting simple, even rigorous, lives won them much admiration among the believers of southern France, part of northern Italy, and part of northeastern Spain. The Cathars proved to be effective preachers and won over many people in the burgeoning towns of the High Middle Ages.

Although he condemned Catharism as treason against God in 1199, Innocent tried a combination of peaceful gestures and threats to win them over. In 1208 his legate to them was murdered, apparently by Cathars, and Innocent called for a crusade against them. The French king had no interest in it, but many northern French knights rushed to the colors. The northern French invasion of the South is known as the Albigensian Crusade, from the town of Albi, which was a Cathar stronghold. The "crusaders" won a series of victories, marked by vicious slaughter. In a town of mixed Cathar and Catholic population, the Crusaders' general Simon de Montfort told his soldiers: "Kill them all, God will know his own." As with the Fourth Crusade, Innocent did not wish the Albigensian Crusade to become what it did, but he cannot be totally absolved of guilt from what happened. After Innocent's death, de Montfort was killed in battle, and the French king moved in to pick up the pieces, considerably expanding the size of his kingdom, which—as we shall see—allowed the French monarchs to be the most potent enemies of the later medieval popes.

Heresy, too, would preoccupy Innocent at Lateran IV.

The Cathars succeeded with the people because of the low level of preaching and the low level of clerical conduct. Innocent approved the formation of the Order of Friars Minor or Franciscans, after he met Francis of Assisi and was duly impressed. The pope also urged the Spaniard Dominic de Guzman, later founder of the Dominicans, to combat the preaching of the Cathars with their effective preaching style.

At Lateran IV, the state of religious life would be a major concern for the pope.

Yet historians focus most on Innocent's dealings with Europe's monarchs and nobility. "The emphasis on the role of the priest and the claim of the pope to depose an unworthy emperor were two aspects of Gregory VII's pontificate that had a marked influence on Innocent. . . . Innocent was in no doubt as to the proper roles of kings and emperors. They were there to assist the papacy in its work of extending the Christian religion and maintaining a just society" (Sayers, *Innocent III*, 43, 45). If the monarchs and nobles claimed to be Christian rulers in a Christian state, who would determine if they were indeed acting like Christians and deserved their thrones? Only the pope could make such a judgment. And who would judge if the pope were doing his job as he should? No one; the pope is beyond human judgment. This was not a new view in papal circles, but Innocent was the first pope to make it stick.

He raised the papacy's profile in other ways. For example, popes had early on styled themselves the "Vicar of St. Peter." From the Gregorian period, some had tried the more exalted phrase "Vicar of Christ." Innocent, however, always used the latter title and made it so accepted that all of his successors have used it.

The pope had little trouble asserting his authority against smaller states like Portugal, and he had little success asserting it against a well-organized, strong state like France, but the touchstone for church-state relations remained the German empire. By chance, the emperor Henry VI had died in 1197, the year before Innocent's accession, leaving his infant son Frederick under the care of his mother Constance of Sicily. But the thirteenth century was a difficult era for a woman to rule, and the German nobles quickly manifested their restlessness and resentment of a woman as regent for the infant emperor-to-be. Constance needed a man to help her, and she turned to Innocent, "acknowledged him as her overlord, surrendering to him the state's traditional rights over the church, and on her death (28 Nov. 1198) arranged for him to be regent and guardian of her infant son Frederick II (emperor 1220–1250)" (Kelly, *Popes*, 187). But a man still had to rule, and the German nobility quickly divided between two candidates for regent during Frederick's minority. The pope backed one of them, but the other refused to give up his claims, and for most of Innocent's reign the Germans saw him as a partisan rather than as a pope judiciously assessing the merits of two claimants to a Christian kingdom. Even when the pope's candidate eventually won the title, he promptly ignored most of the pope's requests. For the popes, the empire continued to be a quagmire.

Yet Innocent enjoyed unparalleled success in England. In 1208 he imposed an interdict that forbade all public worship and administration of sacraments, and in 1209 he excommunicated King John (1199–1216) for not accepting the pope's choice for archbishop of Canterbury. These steps considerably weakened the king's authority. The English barons moved to weaken royal authority even further, and in 1213, to protect himself from them, John submitted to Innocent, acknowledging that he held England as a papal fief, that is, the pope was the country's true overlord and the king served at the pope's sufferance and paid the pope tribute. In 1215 the united barons replied with the Magna Carta ("Great Charter"), which limited royal power, expanded that of the nobility, and introduced the rule of law, for example, the right of *habeas corpus* in trials. The politically weakened John had to sign, but the infuriated Innocent promptly condemned the Magna

Carta since he, not the king, had final authority in England. Innocent died before the issue could be settled. (The British Museum displays a copy of the Magna Carta alongside a copy of the papal document condemning it.)

Lateran IV would speak of the monarchs' obligations to the church.

The Fourth Lateran Council

The year of the Magna Carta was also the year of Lateran IV, which opened on November 1, when Innocent—aged only fifty-five—had less than a year to live. The council would form the summit of his achievements. The invitation to attend went to more than four hundred bishops from every ecclesiastical province in Europe, including those from farthest west (Scotland, Ireland) and east (Hungary, Poland). Bishops also attended from the Crusader states and the infant Latin kingdom of Constantinople. To these were added more than eight hundred abbots and other religious superiors as well as representatives from European countries; some minor rulers came in person. Never before had the catholicity of Roman Catholicism been on such display.

Innocent dominated the council's three sessions (November 11, 20, and 30), not just by asserting his office but by the force of his personality, his gift for organization, his deep commitment to the faithful, and his belief that the pope acting in concert with the bishops could truly reform the church. In one sense, he was correct, and some of the council's reforms were long-lasting, but his death on July 16 of 1216 deprived the church of the council's prime mover and weakened its efficacy.

Once again, the acts of an ecumenical council have not survived, but scholars do have the council's seventy-one canons, which were decided upon in only three sessions, proof of the preparatory work the pope had done, and these canons reflect Innocent's concerns.

Consonant with Innocent's belief that true doctrine precedes all else, the first canon contains a creed, a basic statement of the Catholic faith against current heresies and an emphasis on the need for membership in the church to win eternal salvation. Next come two canons against specific heresies and for the obligation of lay lords to assist the church in maintaining orthodoxy, even by the use of force.

The fourth canon rebukes the Greeks for their perceived patronizing attitude toward Latins. As Tanner points out, for the Fourth Crusade's capture and sacking of Constantinople, "there is no remorse or apology" (*Councils*, 57). Tanner suggests the less civilized West had an "inferiority complex" toward Byzantium.

The fifth to sixty-sixth canons concern the life of the church and emphasize order and ethics. The canons cover such things as the nature of provincial councils, the appointment of teachers, reproving the immorality (drunkenness, incontinence, greed) of the clergy—and not just of the lower clergy. Bishops also find themselves being warned to change their behavior, especially to stop acting like the aristocrats most of them were. The council forbade the establishment of new religious orders, the bishops believing that too many already existed; this canon did not have much effect. It also forbade the display of relics that had not been authenticated by the Roman see. The council was less concerned about superstition than about avarice since the faithful had to make a donation to touch or even see a relic, which was thought to have spiritual powers.

But regulations can do just so much; the spiritual life counts for so much more. Canon 21 has had the greatest impact on Catholic life: "All the faithful of either sex . . . should individually confess all their sins in a faithful manner to their own priest at least once a year, and let them take care to do what they can to perform the penance imposed on them. Let them reverently receive the sacrament of the eucharist at least at Easter" (Tanner, *Decrees*, 245). Enshrined in Catholic tradition as two of the commandments of the church, these injunctions urged the faithful to take advantage of the grace and spiritual benefits available to them through the only sacraments that can be received on a regular basis.

No matter how forward-looking Lateran IV was in some areas, in others it sadly reflected medieval attitudes. Canons 67 to 70 rebuke the Jews for "savagely" oppressing Christians by lending money to them at usurious rates, forbid Jews to hold public office, and, a premonition of the twentieth century, insist that Jews wear distinctive clothing so that no one will mistake them for Christians. Not until Vatican II (1962–65) would a council praise the faith of God's chosen people.

The canons finish with a project dear to Innocent's heart: the crusade. In spite of the disaster of the Fourth Crusade, the pope never lost his conviction that armed liberation of the Holy Land from Muslims was a desirable goal. But his crusade never occurred. The princes had strong reservations about it, and Innocent died while on a trip to northern Italy to win support for a crusade.

Clearly the success of Lateran IV's decrees would depend upon the energy and will of the popes and bishops entrusted with carrying them out, a process significantly weakened by Innocent's death so soon after the council. Inevitably, some decrees enjoyed success while some did not, but, thanks to Innocent, the Catholic Church stood firmly behind reform and not just reform from above, that is, from Rome. Lateran IV expected bishops, priests, monarchs, abbots, and even individual believers to take part in reform, although always under papal leadership.

In 1216, the year of Innocent's death, his ward Frederick had become an adult and reigned as king of Sicily from his mother's inheritance and as king of Germany from his father's inheritance. Little could Innocent have guessed that his ward would single-handedly be responsible for the next ecumenical council.

Toward Lyons I

As the son of both a German and a Sicilian monarch, Frederick stood to inherit both kingdoms. Since the kingdom of Sicily included much of southern Italy and had a two hundred-mile border with the Papal States, and since the German empire either ruled or intervened in much of northern Italy, Innocent realized that if this boy ruled both kingdoms, he would have the Papal States in a vise. The pope arranged for his coronation as king of Sicily in 1198 when Frederick was four but kept him out of German affairs since Innocent supported his own candidate for the German throne. But the pope had a falling out with this candidate and so Innocent supported Frederick for the German throne, crowning him king in 1215, but only after getting Frederick to agree to cede the kingdom of Sicily to the Holy See and to go on a crusade. In 1220 Innocent's successor, Honorius III (1216–27), crowned him Frederick II, Holy Roman Emperor, and also crowned his son Henry King of the Romans, that is, the emperor-to-be.

Frederick quickly reneged on his agreement to give up Sicily, his true home. He did not like Germany and after his coronation did not return to the country until 1236. The Sicilian court sparkled with diversity. Jewish, Greek, and Muslim, as well as Western Christian, intellectuals helped to establish the court as a center of the arts and sciences, and the earliest Italian vernacular poetry was created there. Frederick established a university which survives today, the Università Federico II. He also had a menagerie with exotic animals such as giraffes and elephants, and he kept a private harem. A most irregular medieval Christian ruler!

In 1227 Pope Gregory IX (1227–41) insisted Frederick fulfill his crusade vow. In fact, the emperor had been preparing for it, albeit in an unconventional way. He arranged for a proxy marriage (his first wife now deceased) with the heiress to the Latin kingdom of Jerusalem and then promptly plotted to dispossess his new father-in-law, the king. Frederick set out for the Holy Land, but illness forced his immediate return. Gregory did not believe the emperor was ill and summarily excommunicated him for abandoning the crusade. Frederick now displayed his chief weapon in what would become his struggle against the papacy, namely, his blithe disregard for ecclesiastical sanctions. Innocent had used excommunication and interdict as weapons, but they only work if their targets fear them. Frederick simply ignored them.

Still excommunicated, he set off again for the Holy Land in 1228 without consulting the pope. Upon his arrival, he realized that the local Muslim ruler faced many Muslim enemies and did not want to have to fight a Christian army as well. Frederick promptly negotiated the handover of Jerusalem, Nazareth, and Bethlehem to Christians but with a guarantee that Muslims in those cities could worship freely. He also arranged a ten-year truce with the local Muslims. Finally, since the local bishop would not crown an excommunicate, Frederick crowned himself king of Jerusalem. His was the most successful crusade since the first one (1095–99), and Frederick and his army were home exactly one year after they left. The infuriating excommunicate had done what Richard the Lion-Hearted had failed to do.

In 1231 Gregory IX lifted the excommunication of the emperor, but soon Frederick involved himself in Italian politics, routinely siding with the opponents of the pope, who excommunicated him again in 1239. By now Gregory had had enough of the recalcitrant monarch, and so he called an ecumenical council to meet in Rome in May of 1241. One hundred bishops and two papal cardinal-legates set sail from Genoa to go to Rome, but Frederick's mainland Italian allies, the Pisans, intercepted them and interned them all. The council never met, and the pope died in August of that year, with the bishops and cardinal-legates still imprisoned by Frederick and the Pisans.

The new pope, Celestine IV (1241), died within two weeks of his election. For two years the cardinals refused to meet until Frederick freed their two imprisoned colleagues. As a goodwill gesture, he did so, and the newly freed cardinal-legates attended the conclave that elected Innocent IV (1243–54), a canon lawyer, an inveterate enemy of Frederick, and the pope who would call the next ecumenical council.

Innocent believed that popes had the right to rule Western Christendom in the secular as well as the religious sphere, an attitude that would make reconciliation impossible with an emperor intent on ruling or ignoring the church. A reconciliation between emperor and pope was attempted in 1244 but came to nothing. Later that year Innocent fled in disguise from Rome, sailed to Genoa, and then went on to the French city of Lyons, where he would reside for six years, safe from Frederick's power. From there he called an ecumenical council to meet in June of 1245 to deal with the problems that Frederick was causing the church.

The First Council of Lyons

Lyons I was not a large council. Only 150 bishops attended, and it held just three sessions, on June 26, July 5 and 17 of 1245. When Frederick challenged its ecumenical nature because so few bishops were there, Innocent tartly pointed out it would be considerably larger if the emperor would free the one hundred imprisoned bishops.

Innocent opened the council by announcing its schema, dealing with what he called the five wounds of the church. These were (1) reform of the clergy, (2) a new crusade to win back Jerusalem (when Frederick's truce ended, the Muslims took back the city), (3) the danger posed to the Latin Empire of Constantinople by the resurgent Greeks, (4) the movement of Mongols into Eastern Europe, and (5) Frederick II's persecution of the church. So comparatively unimportant were the first four wounds that the German Catholic historian Hans Wolter can dispose of them in three sentences: "The Council promoted reform by its clarification of juridical, especially procedural problems, its tightening of administrative controls, chiefly in regard to an improvement of monastic economic management, and its more precise definition of the powers of papal legates. It tried to meet the Mongol peril by its call for intensive measures of defense. Ecclesiastical taxes were prescribed for the safety of the Latin Empire, while in regard to the crusade, the desires of Lateran IV were renewed, but, significantly, no concrete planning was attempted" (*History of the Church* iv, 196–97). Then the council could deal with the real reason it had been called.

The council's official documents begin with Innocent's deposition of Frederick. Having been prepared by a canon lawyer and the pope's advisors, it makes many legal points, detailing the patience of the popes and their attempts at reconciliation, Frederick's abuse of their offers, his illegal behavior, a list of those whom he had bilked or cheated, his unjust attacks on church land and property, and his breaking of agreements. Within the legalese, Innocent still found a way to accuse Frederick of heresy, perjury, theft, sacrilege, violation of the peace, kidnapping, and cruelty. The document ends by branding him "an outcast and deprived by our Lord of every honour and dignity (his royal titles) . . . We absolve from their oath forever all those who are bound to him by an oath of loyalty, firmly forbidding by our apostolic authority anyone in the future to obey or heed him as emperor or king, and decreeing that anyone who henceforth offers advice, help or favour to him as to an emperor or king, automatically incurs excommunication" (Tanner, *Decrees*, I, 283).

Following the deposition were twenty-two canons, dealing largely with legal and procedural issues.

After Lyons I

The council dealt a great blow to Frederick, but the man widely known as the *Stupor Mundi* ("Wonder of the World") proved himself to be as resilient as ever. He lost ground in Germany, especially when two great archbishops there turned against him, but he retained his authority in the southern part of the country. His Italian position deteriorated severely; in 1248 a papalist army defeated his mainland forces. Frederick retired to Sicily but kept up the struggle on the mainland. In 1250 a large papalist army moved against the Sicilian kingdom, but Frederick's forces destroyed it and even gained back some Italian territory for the emperor. Still defiant and still reigning, Frederick died in December of 1250 and was buried in the cathedral of Palermo.

Eight years after Frederick's death, his sons and successors—and thus his family line (the Hohenstaufen)—had perished in battle against a new enemy, a French prince and younger brother of King Louis IX, named Charles of Anjou, to whom both Innocent IV and Urban IV (1261–64) had offered the crown of Sicily on condition that he would rule the country as a papal fief. Charles did indeed take the kingdom of Sicily in 1266 and then, ignoring his agreement with the popes, went on to dominate much of Italy.

Toward Lyons II

The ambitions of Charles of Anjou went far beyond Sicily and Italy. In 1261 the Byzantines, led by the emperor Michael VIII (1259–82), recaptured Constantinople and drove out the Latin ruler. For commercial reasons, the West had much sympathy for the restoration of the Latin Empire, and Charles of Anjou saw himself as just the person to achieve this. The emperor Michael feared such an attack and hoped that if the Byzantine and Roman churches were reunited, the papacy would help forestall an invasion by Charles. Michael knew that the Byzantine church would have to agree to papal supremacy, and he was willing to do so to protect his empire. When he contacted Pope Clement IV (1265–68), a Frenchman who supported Charles of Anjou, the pope set very harsh terms for reunion, specifically, the full submission of the Byzantines to papal authority. Since Michael had hoped to negotiate, the character of the papal response obviated any hope of union. As so often in the Middle Ages, politics and religion clashed.

When Pope Clement died in November of 1268, politics quickly reared its head again. The cardinals wrangled for almost three years until September of 1271, during which time Charles of Anjou increased his power, while the traditional antipapal forces in Italy went unchecked. When the cardinals finally abandoned politics, they elected a holy man, Blessed Gregory X (1271–76). Gregory had a long career as a diplomat, had studied theology in Paris, and then found his vocation as a Crusader. At the time of his election he was in the Syrian seaport of Acre, one of the last remaining Latin strongholds in the Holy Land. He left for Rome, promising never to forget the Holy Land, and he kept his promise.

Crowned pope on March 27, 1272, less than three weeks later he issued invitations to a general council to be held in Lyons, site of the last council and well beyond the influence of Charles of Anjou, as soon as preparations could be made. The council opened on May 7, 1274. One of the more significant nonevents, so to speak, occurred before the council. As a student in Paris, Gregory had met the great theologian Thomas Aquinas, whom he invited to Lyons II. Thomas died on March 7, 1274, while journeying to the council. One of church history's great "what ifs?" is how one of the greatest theologians who ever lived would have influenced the council.

The Second Council of Lyons

All of the more than three hundred bishops invited to the council knew that the status of the Holy Land would be a main issue, but Gregory had two others in mind, both influenced by his experience in the Near East. He had encountered the Byzantines there, and although he realized that the Byzantine emperor Michael VIII wanted papal support to keep Charles of Anjou at bay, the pope truly believed that a reunion of Rome and Constantinople would work on the ecclesiastical and even spiritual levels. While he was still in Syria he had negotiated with Michael VIII, and now in Rome he made reunion with the Byzantines a second focus of the council.

His experience of the arduous state of Christianity in the Crusader States and of the stringent demands made upon the clergy there made him cynical about the wealth and luxurious lifestyles of the aristocratic bishops of the West. Every medieval council spoke of ecclesiastical reform, but Gregory had no fear of calling his fellow bishops to order. In his opening speech at the council, the pope "said bluntly, that it was bishops who were bringing the

Church to ruin. . . . and he gave them warning that he was about to take severe action in the manner of their reformation" (Hughes, *Crisis*, 209).

The council met for three months, from May 7 to July 17, 1274, in a total of six sessions. The first council document focused on the need for a new crusade and the obligation of Christian princes and ecclesiastics to support it, even with new taxes to be laid upon them if necessary.

The next document dealt with faith in the Trinity. The earliest trinitarian professions of faith spoke of the Holy Spirit's procession "from the Father." In the sixth century the Spanish church added the phrase "and from the Son"; in Latin, *Filioque*. The Franks picked this up and added to their creeds. The popes originally opposed it, but by 1000 the *Filioque* had been added to the creed as said in Rome. Photius, the cause of ecumenical council Constantinople IV, strongly opposed this addition, and the Byzantine churches followed his lead. But Gregory X insisted that Michael VIII and the Byzantines accept the *Filioque* along with Roman primacy if they wished union with the West. The Greek envoys sent by Michael to the council accepted both conditions, and at the council's fourth session, Gregory joyfully proclaimed a reunion of the Greek and Latin churches. But the Byzantine hierarchy strongly opposed any reunion with the Catholics, and the emperor's plans foundered quickly when his ambassadors returned to Constantinople to find almost no ecclesiastical or popular support for reunion. Lingering resentment of the Fourth Crusades and recently overthrown Latin Empire was too strong. The reunion promptly collapsed.

The other decrees dealt with matters of ecclesiastical order. One cited how long lawsuits drag on, probably a reflection of the endlessly mounting legal appeals made to Rome from churches all over Western Europe. Another insisted something be done about the emergence of new religious orders, demonstrating that Lateran IV's prohibition on new orders had been compromised, if not ignored. Many decrees dealt with legal matters, but one decree impacted the papacy into the modern era.

The three years' wrangling over the election of a new pope had scandalized Europe and aided the papacy's enemies; Gregory wanted to make sure this would never happen again. The council passed a decree requiring the cardinals to meet no less than ten days after a death of the pope to elect a new one. The cardinals were to be locked up in a room with a key, thus "conclave" from the Latin words for "with," *cum*, and for "key," *clavis*. Except for servants to meet the cardinals' immediate needs, no one was allowed to make contact with them, and anyone who did would be excommunicated. If the cardinals did not choose a pope within three days, then for the next five days their meals would be limited to one course at lunch and one at dinner. If after these eight days, they still had not chosen a pope, their nourishment would consist of bread, water, and wine, and they would forfeit their ecclesiastical revenues while conclave went on. Authorities in the city where the conclave takes place (note the assumption that it will not automatically be in Rome) will see to it that these regulations are carried out. The shrewd pope had realized that, given their opulent lifestyle, the cardinals would not be eager to draw out the process.

Gregory gave the decrees of the council the force of law on November 1, 1274, but only after he had emended some of the decrees' wording. This initiated a process still in effect, namely, the necessity of the pope's approving the final wording of a council's decrees in order for them to be valid and binding; it also acknowledged the pope's right to emend conciliar decrees as he sees fit.

Gregory seemed to have accomplished a great deal, but his two chief aims never achieved fulfillment. The Byzantine emperor might have agreed to reunion, but the Greek clergy and people did not; the reunion fell through. As for the crusade, the ideal survived until the end of the Middle Ages, but the willingness of European monarchs to embark on one was fading fast. The Muslims controlled almost all the Holy Land and had proved themselves to be formidable foes. The Western monarchs objected to the length and cost of the crusades in both men and money for what often proved to be meager results. Gregory died in January of 1276. Had he lived longer he might have been able to organize a crusade, but, in fact, nothing came of the council's request, even though two of Gregory's successors, John XXI (1276–77) and Nicholas III (1277–80), continued to promote it. In 1291 the Muslim armies captured the remaining crusader stronghold in the Holy Land, and remaining Europeans were either killed, enslaved, or fled to Cyprus or Europe. The crusades to the Holy Land had ended. Future popes would try to revive them, but never again would a Christian army attempt to win back the holy places.

CHAPTER SIX

Schism and Conciliarism

Toward the Council of Vienne

In the papal election of 1292, representatives of two great Italian aristocratic families, the Orsini and the Colonna, struggled to elect their candidates, but to no avail. After more than two years of wrangling, in July of 1294 the cardinals chose a living saint, Pietro del Morrone, an eighty-five-year-old hermit famous for his rigorous spiritual life. He took the name Celestine V. Many in Italy hailed him as the "Angel Pope," that is, a pope who would inaugurate a new age on earth. Never had the cardinals chosen a pope more saintly—or more unqualified.

This octogenarian hermit had no talent or experience to govern the papal bureaucracy, financial offices, or diplomatic corps, to say nothing of negotiating with Europe's rapacious monarchs or even overseeing the day-to-day running of the church. Celestine had the honesty and humility to realize his lack of qualifications for the papal office, and he consulted with a prominent cardinal, Benedetto Gaetani, about whether a pope could resign. Gaetani assured him that this was so, and Celestine resigned the papal office on December 13, 1294, barely five months after assuming it.

To replace him, the cardinals chose Benedetto Gaetani, the very man who had assured Celestine he could resign. He took the name Pope Boniface VIII (1294–1303). Son of a noble Italian family, Boniface had extensive diplomatic experience, a brilliant mind, endless energy, and a determination to make the papacy the decisive force in European politics.

But he had to deal with first things first. Boniface realized that his enemies might use Celestine V against him, especially to question the legitimacy of his election, so he made sure that the ex-pope spent his remaining two years in a firm but comfortable detention. Immediately rumors began of mistreatment; these rumors would haunt Boniface later.

The Crusades had ended in 1291, and Boniface discovered the European rulers did not share his interest in reviving them. Instead, they had turned their attention to warring with one another, which precipitated the first great crisis of his reign. England and France were fighting one another, and each, without papal approval, had taxed the clergy heavily to support the struggle. In 1296 Boniface ordered a stop to this in a bull (a papal document with a weight—*bulla* in Latin—with a ribbon affixed to the document and weight) entitled *Clericis laicos*, which opened with the words "Antiquity teaches us that laymen are to a high degree hostile to the clergy," a far from diplomatic approach.

The English vacillated, but the French king, Philip IV (1285–1314), struck back quickly and effectively, banning the export of funds from France to Rome. The papacy depended heavily on French money, and Philip's action threatened Boniface with bankruptcy. The pope had to back down.

Boniface did not realize what kind of enemy he was up against. Philip, like Frederick II of Sicily, felt no debt to the papacy for his rule. On the contrary, since he provided the church in France with protection and services, he believed that the French clergy should serve the state's interests, a view that would grow increasingly in the Middle Ages down through the Renaissance and culminate in the reign of Louis XIV (1642–1715), who dominated the French church.

Boniface blatantly practiced nepotism, enriching and empowering the Gaetani family to the fierce chagrin of the Colonna family, which generally allied itself with the French. Boniface now had powerful Italian enemies as well as French ones. But the pope had a brilliant insight. Recognizing the immense spiritual prestige of his office, in 1300 he proclaimed the first Holy Year, offering indulgences to Romans and to pilgrims who flocked to the city. Whatever the pope's political status, his spiritual status enjoyed new heights, but, sadly, he did not recognize its importance nor did he focus on his spiritual role.

The pope turned again to politics in the following year. In another conflict with the French, Boniface emphasized papal supremacy over secular monarchs. In a response the pope could not have anticipated, the French unleashed a propaganda war, denouncing the pope and mocking his writings. The enraged Boniface responded in 1302 with his most famous writing, the bull *Unam Sanctam*, which reaffirmed a traditional belief that, for eternal salvation, every human person must be subject to the Roman pontiff, an affirmation of papal power that was, in fact, diminishing quickly.

In spite of the bull, the pope sought reconciliation with the French, but the unreconcilable King Philip now had a new plan: to kidnap the pope and bring him to Paris for trial on a number of charges, several of which had been drawn up by the Colonna family. Boniface, in residence at his palace in Anagni, rejected the charges and excommunicated Philip. Then a combined force of French troops and Colonna mercenaries confronted the pope in Anagni on September 7, 1303. When Boniface said he would rather die than go to France, one of the Colonna family stepped forward with a sword to oblige him, but the French leader of the raid prevented that, fearing the consequences of murdering a pope. Then, suddenly, the populace of Anagni rushed the palace to defend Boniface. The French and Colonna had to flee, and it appeared the pope had been saved. But the trauma of the attack and the realization that he could never be the pope he wished to be wore Boniface down, and he died in Rome less than six weeks after the attack.

The cardinals quickly chose a Dominican theologian to be Benedict XI (1303–4). A weak man, he enjoyed the company of only brother Dominicans, and he created but three cardinals, all from the order. Astonishingly, he absolved the Colonna family and the French king from guilt for what happened at Anagni. But continued difficulties with both of them caused him to rethink his actions; however, before he could do anything, he died on July 7, 1304. Since he died after eating a meal, rumors sprung up that the French or Colonna had poisoned him, but he actually died from acute dysentery.

The ensuing conclave elected the pope who would call the Council of Vienne. Some cardinals wanted a pope who would protect the name and legacy of Boniface VIII, while others wanted a pope who could work with the French and end the tension. Neither faction's candidate received the necessary votes, so the cardinals decided to look outside the conclave. Both groups thought they had found the right man.

The cardinals chose a French bishop from Normandy (which made him technically an English citizen). He took the name Clement V (1305–14). He had supported Boniface VIII, but his experience as a diplomat made him anxious to settle things with Philip IV. Furthermore, he suffered from an internal cancer that often prevented him from carrying out his public duties and weakened him generally. This good but fragile man offered no match to the ruthless and calculating French king. This weakness showed up immediately when he changed his intended place of coronation to a place that Philip preferred.

Significantly, Clement had no desire to go to Rome. The fractious urban political groups had often kept the popes from the Eternal City, and Clement, as a foreigner, feared he would be more unwelcome than most. He restlessly moved the papal court around southern France, finally settling in 1309 in papally-owned French territory centered on the city of Avignon. Clement and his successors would keep the papacy in Avignon for almost seventy years.

Clement also remade the college of cardinals. In 1305 he created ten new cardinals, nine of them French. Subsequent creations of cardinals by Avignon popes reinforced the French domination of the college. Other appointments would be to Italians, Spaniards, and Englishmen, but none of the seven French popes at Avignon ever named a German to be cardinal, effectively keeping France's traditional continental enemy from having influence in the highest reaches of papal government. These French popes and cardinals often tried to accommodate the French monarchs.

Initially what Philip wanted from Clement was a council that would condemn the memory of Boniface VIII, thus vitiating the late pope's strictures against the king. Soon, however, Philip came up with a new idea for the council.

An aggressive monarch, Philip spent much money on foreign wars, and he soon found the treasury empty. But he had discovered another source for funds. The now-defunct Crusades in the Holy Land had seen the emergence of military-religious orders, that is, orders of knights and soldiers who took religious vows to defend the Holy Land. They were among the most effective warriors in the crusading armies. The best known of these groups were the Knights of the Temple, usually called the Templars. In addition to being warriors, the Templars also served as bankers, with their bank in Jerusalem being the most important financial center for many Crusader States. With the end of the Crusades, the surviving Templars returned to Europe to their religious houses, and they brought much of their money with them. Philip wanted the Templar gold.

As he had done with Boniface VIII, Philip unleashed a propaganda war against the Templars, accusing them of heresy, sodomy, idolatry, and satanism. When the king felt that he had sufficiently damaged the Templars' reputation, on October 13, 1307, he had every Templar in France arrested. Under torture, many of them admitted to the crimes of which they were accused. Using this "evidence," Philip demanded that Clement condemn and dissolve the order; in this way, Philip could avail himself of the Templars' wealth. At first the pope doubted the Templars' guilt, but since in that era torture was routinely used to gather information and confessions, he slowly moved toward accepting their guilt, in spite of the fact that other European monarchs in whose lands there were also Templar houses had not found fault with the knights.

Although a weak man, Clement was still pope. He kept Philip at bay on both issues (Boniface VIII and the Templars), but eventually he agreed to handle these matters via an ecumenical council. He announced the council on August 12, 1308, but various delays and negotiations occurred, and the council did not open until October 16, 1311, in the French city of Vienne.

The Council of Vienne

Contrary to previous councils, this one did not include all the bishops because, knowing the incendiary nature of the topics under consideration, Clement decided to invite only a select number of bishops, 231 in all. He drew up his list of participants and then submitted it to the French king, who crossed off the names of 66 bishops he could not be sure of. Although the exact number of bishops in attendance is uncertain, it was probably between 165 and 180.

But when the bishops got to the council, they found that they had little to do. Clement announced that the council would deal with three issues: the Templars, the reconquest of the Holy Land, and church reform; the last two were standard items for all medieval councils. Most bishops knew that the monarchs had little inclination for a new crusade, especially since by then the Muslims had spent twenty years strengthening their defenses against any new invasion. The treatment of the Templars, on the other hand, was a hot-button, immediate issue, but Clement announced that he had formed a commission to examine the issue and, rather surprisingly, he announced no date for the second session. The bishops would have to wait until he decided to call them into session again.

In December the commission initially favored allowing the Templars to send representatives to the council, but Clement did not pass this knowledge on to the bishops, who were discussing the possibility of a new crusade. King Philip arrived in the vicinity of Vienne in January of 1312 and in March visited the city. Soon after that the commission for the Templars revised its decision to invite knights' representatives, possibly because Philip threatened to bring up again his desire for a condemnation of Boniface VIII. On April 3 occurred one of the most astonishing sessions ever held at an ecumenical council. Hughes provides a brief but telling account:

> It [the session] began with yet another procedural novelty—the Pope forbade any member of the council to speak, under pain of excommunication. There was then read his bull, *Vox in excelso*, suppressing the order [of the Templars]. The Pope gave no judgment about the crimes alleged—the question, Guilty or innocent?, was ignored. The bull explained that Clement V was acting, not as a judge at a trial, but as an administrator in the fullness of his apostolic authority. (*Crisis*, 225)

Exactly one month later Clement informed the bishops about the disposition of the Templar's properties, most going to another military order, the Knights Hospitallers, although Philip did manage to acquire a sizeable chunk for himself. Three days later, May 6, 1312, Clement adjourned the council.

Often overlooked is that the council passed a sizeable number of disciplinary decrees, trying to stem corruption, regulate matters between bishops and religious orders, repress heresy, and many other matters that had been discussed at previous councils and would reappear at future ones, at least until the Council of Trent dealt effectively with reform in the sixteenth century. Yet Clement and his Avignon successors took little action on these recommendations.

The treatment of the Templars was a disgrace; the crusade planning came to nothing, but at least Clement had managed to avoid the open condemnation of his predecessor Boniface VIII. This council marked a victory for Philip, and Clement had certainly demonstrated his power over the bishops, but neither lived long enough to benefit much from their efforts. Both died in 1314.

The Avignon Papacy and the Great Western Schism

The next six popes after Clement stayed in France, even building a palace at Avignon. The Avignon papacy, as it is known, has an undeservedly bad reputation for luxurious living and endless greed. Several of the popes lived very abstemious lives, and one, Urban V (1362–70), has been named a Blessed by the Catholic Church. Clement VI (1342–52), however, openly opted for extravagance of every kind, and he provided the basis for Avignon's nickname, "the Babylon of the West." But, when all is considered, we must conclude that the Avignon papacy severely harmed the church.

All seven Avignon popes were French, and although they often disagreed with the French kings, Catholic Europe perceived them as supporters of France, a serious disability for men called upon to govern a universal church.

When we recall that the popes ruled a state in Italy, we can see how Avignon's reputation for greed arose. Popes resident in Italy, even popes resident in Rome, had difficulty preserving the Papal States from feuding Italian nobles and territorially hungry French, German, and Spanish invaders, and all this cost a great deal. The popes could barely govern the Papal States from Avignon and often relied upon mercenaries to protect their territory. Furthermore, the almost endless fighting took many innocent lives and damaged the States' economy. Much of the money that the Avignon popes diligently collected went to preserve the Papal States.

But most serious of all was Avignon's symbolic status. For all its difficulties, Rome was the Holy City, the center of an international ecclesiastical institution, and a place for which even foreign invaders had shown respect. By contrast, Avignon looked like a provincial French city inhabited by

French popes often in league with the French monarchy. It presented a terrible image.

As the fourteenth century progressed, Catholic Europe began to fear that Avignon would become the permanent papal residence. From kings to saints cries went up for the popes to return to Rome. Urban V heeded them and returned to Rome in 1367, but political troubles in the States and in the city itself convinced him to return to Avignon in 1370. His successor, Gregory XI (1370–78), returned to Rome in 1377 and became quickly disillusioned by the constant warfare, some of the most vicious carried out by papal mercenaries led by Cardinal Robert of Geneva. Whether Gregory debated a return to Avignon, historians will never know because the pope died in Rome on March 27, 1378.

A conclave of immense importance occurred. The Roman populace feared the papacy would return to Avignon, and large crowds gathered outside the papal palace, chanting for the cardinals to elect a Roman or at least an Italian. The crowd's attitude became increasingly threatening. The mostly French electors could not agree on a candidate among the cardinals, so they went outside the sacred college and elected an Italian, Bartolomeo Prignano, archbishop of Bari in southern Italy. They sent word to him, but before he arrived, a mob broke into the conclave, and the frightened cardinals lied to them, saying that an elderly Roman cardinal had been elected pope. While this was going on, Prignano successfully made his way to Rome.

The new pope took the name Urban VI (1378–89). He was a commoner who had held various papal posts, and the aristocratic cardinals thought they could control him. Soon, however, Urban proved himself to be a volatile tyrant, not above threatening the cardinals—even grabbing and shaking them—if they did not obey him immediately. Soon the cardinals were threatening Urban, who did not back down. Convinced they had made a mistake, the French cardinals left Rome and, joined by three Italian cardinals, declared that they had elected Urban under fear of the mob and that this fear invalidated his election. Declaring him deposed, they elected Robert of Geneva, the cruel mercenary leader of the papal army, as Pope Clement VII (1378–94). The new pope and his cardinals then returned to Avignon. The Great Western Schism had begun.

The schism stunned Catholic Europe. Schisms were hardly new, but previous dissident claimants to the papacy had been created by monarchs such as Frederick Barbarossa. Now Europe confronted two popes, each elected by the same group of cardinals and each claiming the headship of the church. (The modern popes consider the Roman popes to be their predecessors and the other claimants to be antipopes.)

To their credit, the French and their Spanish allies did not immediately accept the Avignon pope. They carefully considered the issues for some months but finally supported him. France's main enemies, Germany and England, lined up behind the Roman pope, while England's enemy Scotland supported the Avignon claimant. Most but hardly all of the Italian states supported the Roman claimant.

It did not take long for the secular rulers to realize what a golden gift the cardinals had given to them. Merely by threatening to switch allegiance from one pope to another, they were able to wring concessions—many financial—from the one they supported. Not surprisingly, the popes often had little choice but to accede to the rulers' demands.

Whatever the rulers thought, other people genuinely lived in fear. Medieval Christians believed that they needed the sacraments for salvation, and the sacraments could only be consecrated by legitimate priests, who in turn were ordained by legitimate bishops, who were appointed by the legitimate pope. Many people feared the spiritual consequences of the schism. Indeed, it got so confusing to the faithful at large that a Spanish bishop mentioned no name but instead publicly prayed *pro illo qui est verus papa*, "for him who is the true pope."

The rulers eventually realized that this appalling situation could not go on, and so they worked with theologians and canon lawyers to find a solution. What challenged all possible solutions was the belief in the pope's "plentitude of power," that is, that the pope had supreme power in the church. Yet here was a situation in which papal power could literally do nothing. Something had to be done, but what?

(To use a modern analogy, suppose a pope fell into a coma, and his doctors could not predict when or even if he would come out of it; papal power cannot solve that problem. Or, suppose the pope's physicians diagnosed him with Alzheimer's disease; should he continue to exercise his office? But, if he will not resign, who has the authority or the right to tell him to?)

Several possibilities existed to end the schism. First, both popes could resign, and their combined cardinals could elect a new pope. But both popes considered themselves legitimately elected and refused to resign. Second, one pope could resign, but that ran into the same obstacle as the first solution. Third, when one pope died, his cardinals could elect the other pope to be their pope, but when the Roman Urban VI died, his cardinals promptly elected a new pope, Boniface IX (1389–1404).

But another remedy lay at hand; in fact, it had lain about for almost two centuries.

Codes of law always allow for all sorts of possibilities, no matter how seemingly minute or absurd or unlikely. In the early thirteenth century canon lawyers had speculated about what to do if a pope fell into heresy. Slowly but surely some canon lawyers constructed the view that the pope does not have absolute rule over the church because the power of the church is greater than his. They speculated that the ultimate power in the church resided in the ecumenical council. These few sentences summarize decades of very complex developments. The superiority of the council to the pope is the conciliar theory; its practical application is conciliarism.

Within months of the schism's beginning, speculation arose about a council, but a problem also arose: who would call it? Calling a council was a prerogative of a pope, and neither pope would call a council if he thought the council would have more power than he did.

But the legalities had to give way to the realities. When Clement VII died in 1394, the Avignon cardinals elected a Spaniard who took the name Benedict XIII (1394–1417). When the schism persisted into the new century, the Roman cardinals elected their third and fourth popes (Innocent VI, 1404–6, and Gregory XII, 1406–15). Both Gregory and Benedict proclaimed their willingness to resign if a solution to the schism could be found, but, of course, neither one did. But seeing the growing dissatisfaction with the schism among believers, the two popes negotiated with one another for a few months, but with no result. The notion of a council increasingly gained support.

Pushed by the rulers and the nobility, in 1409 the cardinals of both popes largely deserted them and met in the Italian city of Pisa, where they proclaimed the need to go above the popes' heads to a general council, citing the consequences of the schism for this clear violation of canon law. With some major exceptions (Germany, the Spanish kingdoms) Catholic Europe supported them. The Council of Pisa opened on March 25, 1409, with twenty-four cardinals, eighty bishops and archbishops, one hundred deputies of bishops who could not attend, abbots and generals of religious orders, and representatives of the secular powers.

The assembled bishops heard charges against the two reigning popes (perpetuating the schism, perjury), accepted the charges, and on June 5 voted to depose both popes. Then the Avignonese and Roman cardinals met together in conclave and elected the archbishop of Milan to be Pope Alexander V (1409–10). The schism was over!

Well, not exactly.

The other two popes naturally refused to recognize the validity of the council and thus of their own depositions. Each managed to hold on to a shrinking number of supporters, Benedict XIII in Spain and Gregory XII in southern Italy. Now, instead of two popes, there were three.

When Alexander V died after less than a year in office, his cardinals elected a new pope, an Italian cardinal who took the name John XXIII (1410–15), continuing the now threefold schism.

(Readers may be surprised to see the name John XXIII. Was this not the name of the pope from 1958 to 1963? Since the later popes did not recognize the legitimacy of the Avignonese and Pisan popes, the first pope after the schism to use a name that one of them did also used the same number. The Roman Clement VII reigned from 1523 to 1534; Benedict XIII from 1724 to 1730; and, of course, John XXIII. Significantly, the Pisan Alexander V was so widely accepted as pope, that in 1492, when a pope wished to take that name, he styled himself Alexander VI (1492–1503). Thus in the Vatican's reckoning of legitimate popes, there is an Alexander IV and an Alexander VI but no Alexander V.)

Three popes proved to be more than even the Germans, who had held aloof from the Council of Pisa, could stand. Led by their king and later emperor Sigismund (1411–37), they supported a new council, and the German king brought the council into being.

Sigismund realized that he could not succeed without the support of the Pisan pope John XXIII, who had the largest following of the three popes. John had successfully established himself in Italy, even driving Gregory XII from Rome. But papal and Italian politics fluctuated violently, and soon John found himself on the defensive and in need of secular help. Sigismund provided it for a price.

The German king forced the Pisan pope to call a council to meet in November of 1414 in the Swiss town of Constance, safely removed from Italian politics, French influence, and Spanish ambitions. Reluctantly John XXIII agreed, not aware that what Sigismund really wanted was the resignation of all three popes and the election of a new one who would be universally recognized. Sigismund's hard work and careful planning won over the French, English, Germans, and most of the Italians, and although the Spaniards did not support the council (the Avignonese pope was Spanish), they did not oppose it. This landmark council opened on time.

The Council of Constance

Constance attracted a huge throng of ecclesiastics, over three hundred cardinals and bishops from all three obediences, about three hundred theologians (who would have a great role to play), many lower clergy, as well as many representatives of lay lords with great trains of servants. Also attracted, as contemporary chroniclers wryly noted, were hordes of pickpockets, moneylenders, prostitutes, gamblers, and other unsavory types, there to take advantage of the great crowd of approximately twenty thousand people who literally invaded a town of ten thousand.

No council had ever met like this one, and so no tried-and-true procedure existed. Normally the bishops would be led by the pope, but there were three popes, all of dubious legitimacy. Furthermore, the Italian bishops outnumbered all the other bishops combined, and they strongly supported John XXIII, as did the French. The English and Germans would not accept this, so a compromise formula was drawn up. The University of Paris had formed student groups based upon nations, such as the German and English nations, with smaller groups joined to larger ones, for example, the Irish and Scots with the English. The council leaders agreed to follow that procedure and to form four nations—English, French, German, and Italian—and the college of cardinals would be the equivalent of a fifth nation for purposes of voting. When it came time to choose a pope, the representatives of the nations would meet separately and decide for whom they would vote, and they would then cast their one vote in the conciliar equivalent of the conclave, giving the college of cardinals only one vote in five. Many cardinals resented this diminution of their stature, but most of Catholic Europe blamed the cardinals for the schism, and they had no choice but to submit.

The council leaders decided to get rid of the three contesting popes, either by securing their resignations or by deposition. John XXIII, who had called the council, promptly decided to subvert it by fleeing. His flight indeed caused much consternation, but the German king Sigismund promptly stepped in, personally calming down the various council factions. His men then captured John and brought him back to Constance for trial. The embattled pope faced numerous charges, such as simony, perjury, misgovernment, and even lying to his parents. On May 29, 1415, the council declared John deposed. He accepted the deposition and was confined in the custody of a German nobleman until shortly before his death in 1419, when he returned to Italy to occupy a bishopric generously given to him by the reigning pope, Martin V (1417–31).

The Avignonese pope proved a tougher nut to crack. As a Spaniard, Benedict XIII enjoyed widespread support on the Iberian Peninsula. The lay lords at Constance wisely chose to ignore Benedict and instead to work on his Spanish supporters. Negotiations lasted for two years before all the Spanish realms joined the council to form another "nation." On July 26, 1417, the council deposed Benedict XIII. He did not submit but withdrew to an impregnable fortress on a Spanish peninsula where he "reigned" as pope, lording it over his cardinals (he created four of them), courtiers, and servants until his death in 1423.

The end of Benedict's pontificate involved two ludicrous stories, both worth telling.

First, realizing the council would depose him, Benedict argued that only the cardinals should vote for the popes, and then correctly pointed out that none of the cardinals created since the schism began in 1378 had a universally accepted legitimacy. The only cardinals universally accepted were those created by Gregory XI, the last Avignon pope, and only those cardinals could choose a universally recognized pope. As it happened, only one of those cardinals was still alive, and that was . . . Benedict! He said that he alone had the right to vote for the new pope, and he promised not to vote for himself. His legalist mind chose to ignore four decades of history, and the council fathers told him not to be ridiculous.

Second, after Benedict's death, three of his four cardinals were in his palace, and so they chose a new "pope," Clement VIII, who reigned in the palace until 1429, when he resigned and accepted a bishopric graciously offered to him by Martin V. But one of Benedict's cardinals was away when the others chose Clement in 1423, and when he returned, he was infuriated that the vote had been taken without him, and so in 1425, on his own, he chose another pope, Benedict XIV, thus provoking a "schism" in this ridiculous little papal court. Benedict XIV simply disappears from history after 1425.

The modern popes consider the Roman line to be authentic, and so for them Gregory XII alone had the right to call the council, and without him the council could not claim authenticity as an ecumenical one. By 1414 Gregory's obedience had shrunk away, and he knew the council would never leave him in office. Facing reality, he told the council leaders that he would abdicate, but only if he were allowed to call the council into session. He could not accept the authority of a council called by John XXIII, whom Gregory considered to be an antipope (also the Vatican view). The council leaders accepted his request. On July 14, 1415, Gregory's representative convoked the council. That being done, a cardinal informed the council of Gregory's resignation from the papacy. Sensibly, the council ratified the acts of Gregory's pontificate and assigned him a bishopric in Italy, which he held till his death on October 18, 1417, before the council had chosen its pope.

Gregory's convoking of the council gave it legitimacy for the later popes, but a larger problem exists. John XXIII had initially convoked the council. His flight left the council without a pope, thus questioning its legitimacy. On April 6, 1415, the council justified its existence by passing a truly revolutionary decree entitled *Haec Sancta* from its opening words: "This holy council of Constance . . . declares . . . that lawfully coming together in the Holy Spirit, being a general council and representing the Catholic Church, it holds authority directly from Christ, which authority everyone of whatever status or dignity, even the papal, is bound to obey in those matters concerning the faith, the ending of the schism, and the reformation of the Church in head and members."

This is conciliarism at its most basic. The council asserts that it meets under the guidance of the Holy Spirit, that it represents the Catholic Church and thus has the supreme authority in the church, and that its authority derives from Christ and even the popes must obey the council. Yet obviously the papacy today has the authority to call, dominate, and dismiss councils. What happened?

What happened historically we will soon see, but the doctrinal and canonical elements remain much debated. Some scholars contend that *Haec Sancta* represents nothing more than the council's self-justification for deposing John XXIII, who had convoked the council, and therefore the decree has no binding power for subsequent popes and councils. Others contend that since the popes have accepted the line of popes descending from Martin V, who was elected by the council, all the council's acts have validity. Yet others point out that if a council meets without a pope, the council has deliberately excluded the most important bishop of all and one whose close relation to the council is unquestioned. But no scholar doubts that Constance meant what it said because in 1417, before choosing a new pope, the council passed a second monumental decree, *Frequens*, which asserted that the new pope must call another council five years after Constance closes, then another one seven years after that, and then a council every ten years so that there would be, in effect, a council in every pontificate. The leaders of Constance truly wished to change the governmental structure of the church.

On November 11, 1417, the representatives of the nations chose a new pope, an Italian bishop who took the name Martin V. The pope came from the very influential Roman family, the Colonna (whose representative had once offered to kill Boniface VIII), yet he turned out to be the only pope from this family. Never again would a pope be chosen in the way Martin was.

Contemporary chroniclers recorded the enormous rejoicing in Constance that the church now had a new pope whose legitimacy could not be questioned. This represented quite a triumph for Sigismund and the other leaders who had kept the disparate assembly together for all that time. As pope,

Martin took the leadership of the council, and the assembled bishops recognized his authority. The schism had finally ended.

While the council focused on ending the schism, it also had to deal with the problem of heresy in Eastern Europe. The English theologian John Wycliffe (ca. 1330–84) had formulated an ecclesiology that distinguished the eternal, ideal church from its "material" manifestation, which included much abuse and corruption. He went on to say that prelates not in the state of grace could not legitimately hold office and could be deposed by secular authority. Wycliffe's views earned condemnations from the English hierarchy and from more than one pope, but he managed to live in peace until his death.

When a political marriage sent a Czech princess to England in 1382, Wycliffe's teachings migrated to Bohemia in Eastern Europe, where they attracted the attention of Jan Hus (ca. 1372–1415), a Czech priest. Although loyal Catholics, the Czechs resented German imperialism—and especially German attempts to control Bohemian silver mines—and they felt that Western church leaders, mostly Italian and French, supported the foreigners. Hus began preaching in Czech on the degenerate morals of the clergy and began to advocate some of Wycliffe's ideas about the hierarchy. The Englishman remained a rather quiet professor throughout his life, but the Czech, also a professor, quickly found himself a national hero. Hus also found himself being condemned as a heretic by both the Pisan and Roman popes (one of the few things on which they agreed). In 1411 the Pisan pope John XXIII excommunicated him. Removed from his teaching post, Hus took refuge with sympathetic Bohemian nobles.

Not considering himself a heretic, Hus requested a hearing from the Council of Constance, a risky step since many Western bishops and theologians had already condemned him. To protect himself, Hus requested and received a safe-conduct guarantee from King Sigismund, the moving force behind the council. But the safe conduct proved useless. The council fathers had Hus arrested and imprisoned, and they ignored Sigismund's protests against this. The council tried him, found him guilty of heresy, and had him burned at the stake in Constance on July 6, 1415. A year later, one of his associates, Jerome of Prague, met the same fate.

Hus's execution made him a martyr and a national hero. The University of Prague declared him to be a martyr and made the day of his execution his feast day. In his name, an anti-German rebellion began, which grew into the so-called Hussite Wars (1420–34), during which the Czechs adopted some practices, such as a vernacular liturgy and communion under both forms, that would reappear during the Protestant Reformation. Eventually the Czechs returned to the Catholic fold, but their nationalism never died down.

Constance had ended the schism and dealt with heresy, but it never got to its third objective, the reform of the church. The English and Germans blamed Martin V for this, but the nobility and hierarchy of both those countries had shown little interest in reform if it required giving up their privileges. The council did, however, pass a number of reform proposals.

One of the most important and unique councils of Catholic history came to an end on April 23, 1418. But many of those going home told one another, "I will see you in five years at the next council."

After the Council

Martin V faced challenges that no other pope had faced. For forty years Catholic Europe had been without a universally recognized pope. A generation of Catholics had come and gone in that time. Papal prestige was low because lay lords had not hesitated to bargain with and even threaten the popes of the three obediences, and most common people had simply learned to live without knowledge of the true occupant of the See of Peter. Furthermore, the papacy was broke.

Two-thirds of papal income came from the Papal States, and two-thirds of papal expenses went to the States. Disorder reigned in much of Italy, so much so that Martin could not take up residence in Rome until a full two years after the council had closed. Fortunately, he had considerable diplomatic skills and negotiated wherever possible, yet he was also willing to use the papal armies to assert his authority. In general, he succeeded. He kept the Spanish rulers of the kingdom of Naples out of the Papal States, and he ruled Rome successfully. Indeed, the always turbulent Romans appreciated Martin's efforts to rebuild the rundown city by employing first-rate artists and architects to restore both ecclesiastical and public buildings. Only when he controlled the States could the pope be sure of a steady income.

But he needed more. Papal government had to be reestablished, and that would cost a lot. At Constance, many bishops had complained about all the money that had flowed into the coffers at Avignon, and council leaders urged the pope to reform papal finances so that they exercised a smaller burden on the churches. But Martin could not afford to lose the funds that papal taxes and fees brought in, and so he simply put off financial reform and, in fact, never got around to it.

The disorder of papal Italy made Martin very wary about whom he could trust, and so he relied upon the branches of his family, the Colonna. In a burst of rampant nepotism, he turned papal offices and even papal lands over to various family members, who became rich in the process, and, of course, this antagonized the other noble Italian families whom the pope excluded from his largesse.

But nothing cast as great a shadow over his pontificate as the conciliar decree *Frequens*. Martin V did not support conciliarism. He wanted to act as previous popes had and not have to worry about getting approval for his actions; like previous popes, he wanted to be a man who could be judged by no one else. But this was a new era.

A Roman tradition says Martin shuddered every time he heard the word "council." But the fact was that a council had chosen him as pope, and to attack conciliar power would call into question the legitimacy of his own election. Furthermore, Catholic Europe had seen the Council of Constance solve a problem that the papacy simply could not solve, and it had seen Constance give great power to the rest of Christendom and not just the papacy. Many Catholics, including rulers and bishops, favored conciliarism, and so Martin obliged and obeyed the decree.

Frequens had called for a council five years after Constance, so Martin convoked a council to meet in Pavia, Italy, in 1423, but, when the plague appeared in Pavia, he quickly transferred the council to Siena. Few bishops attended, and after some months Martin disbanded the council, but not before the council fathers had set the time and place of the next council for the Swiss city of Basel in 1431. The great powers of Europe did not protest the closing of the Council of Siena, and the pope now had seven years before he had to call the next council. Martin planned to use that time to strengthen papal government.

As the seventh year approached, Martin concluded it was too dangerous not to call the next council, and so he did. It was to meet at Basel in Switzerland in 1431. On February 20 of that year, before the council opened, Martin died. His successor, the former monk Eugenius IV (1431–47), would deal with the Council of Basel, which, like Constance, would transform the church.

The Council of Basel-Ferrara-Florence-Rome

The new pope resented councils and did not accept the conciliar theory, but Catholic Europe expected a council and Martin V had called one, so Eugenius went along, sending Cardinal Julian Cesarini, a supporter of conciliarism, to open the council and preside over it. But Cesarini was in Germany, and so he sent a deputy to open the council on July 23, 1431. By the time Cesarini got to Basel, conciliar attendance was very poor, and no formal session had yet been held. Eugenius watched events in Basel very carefully. He recalled how Martin V had successfully dissolved the Council of Siena, and he contemplated a similar move. But Martin was a supreme diplomat, which Eugenius was not. On November 12 he prepared a bull that dissolved the council. But before the document reached Basel, the council had held its first formal session on December 14. When the council fathers received the bull of dissolution, they rejected it in the second formal session on February 14, 1432. The struggle had begun.

Eugenius quickly found himself in an untenable position. Only six of his twenty-one cardinals supported dissolution of the council. Most of the secular states wanted a council, including the Duke of Milan, whose armies constantly invaded the northern parts of the Papal States. The pope looked for compromise, but the time for that had passed. To his aid came Sigismund, the architect of the Council of Constance, who promised to restrain and moderate the activities of Basel, but he joined the other secular powers, fearful of a new schism, in urging the pope to give in. On December 15, 1433, Eugenius withdrew the bull of dissolution. The council would go on.

(Part of Eugenius's willingness to compromise arose from his weak political situation in Rome. He had forced the Colonna family, his predecessor's relatives, to return large chunks of papal properties that Martin V had given to them, and so the Colonna plotted against him in Rome. In May of 1434, Eugenius had to flee Rome in disguise, and he lived mostly in Florence for the next nine years.)

At this point, two divergent developments occurred. First, the fathers at Basel now thought themselves superior to the pope and believed that he had to go along with whatever they did, and what they did was to reorganize church government. The council cancelled a sizeable number of payments previously sent to the pope and the curia (the pope's court), and instead insisted that payments be made directly to the council, effectively bankrupting papal government. The council also involved itself in the day-to-day business of the church, negotiating with princes and recommending or approving appointments to ecclesiastical offices. Quite literally, a second, rival church government arose at Basel.

Naturally, government by the hundreds was not easy to achieve, and disputes broke out right from the beginning. Furthermore, the monarchs and nobles fearfully saw at Basel a budding democracy when the council began to extend voting rights to those other than bishops, such as theologians; political support for Basel became tepid. The meetings at the council became increasingly chaotic.

Eugenius would probably have benefited by waiting for the council to offend the monarchs and forfeit their support, but a second development, unrelated to the first, turned the tide firmly to him.

By the fifteenth century, what had been the Byzantine Empire now consisted of Constantinople and a small territory around it. The Ottoman Turks, the new Muslim power in the Near East, occupied most of what had been the empire, and the Turkish sultans determined to take Constantinople, reduced now to a population of fifty thousand, a far cry from the half million people who lived there in its glory days. In 1402, 1411, and 1422, Turkish forces besieged the city, but, fortunately for the Byzantines, each time the Turks had to raise the siege in order to deal with political unrest or threats elsewhere. The empire depended heavily upon foreign, Western mercenaries, and the Italian seafaring city-states, especially Venice, dominated its commerce. The emperors realized that the city could not survive much longer on its own, and they also realized that their only hope for help lay in the West.

Inevitably, religion intervened into politics. The Byzantine emperors realized that they could not expect serious Western assistance as long as the schism between Catholicism and Orthodoxy existed. A union of the two churches was essential, but the emperors realized that Rome would exact a high price. Negotiations had to proceed very carefully, since the Byzantine population rightly considered the conquest of the city by the Fourth Crusade and the establishment of a Latin kingdom in imperial territory as the ultimate causes of the empire's fatally weakened position. The emperors had to ask for salvation from the descendants, so to speak, of the very people who had created Byzantium's perilous situation. Loathing of the West in general and of the papacy in particular would keep the population opposed to plans for reunion, but the emperors literally had no choice. But, like most Byzantines, Emperor John VIII (1425–48) had great faith in councils, and he hoped for one that could meet in Constantinople to effect reunion.

The popes also wanted reunion, albeit on their terms, and after the Great Western Schism had ended, Martin V began negotiations with the Byzantines, but to no avail. In 1431, when Eugenius IV became pope and the Council of Basel opened, the Byzantines again raised the question. Naturally they knew about the council if not much about conciliarism, but they learned quickly as embassies from both Basel and the pope came to Constantinople. Much diplomatic maneuvering occurred, but eventually the emperor decided to work with the pope. He knew the papacy; he was a monarch himself; and he did not wish to travel to Switzerland, the middle of nowhere to the Byzantine.

Eugenius showed himself to be very diplomatic with the Byzantines, even agreeing to a proposal to have the reunion council meet in Constantinople, but a number of problems, especially financial ones, caused the Byzantines to accept a council in Italy, which the pope guaranteed to underwrite. A council in Italy would require transferring the existing council from Basel to the city agreed upon by the pope and the Byzantines.

The pope sincerely wanted reunion, but it also gave him a powerful weapon to use against the council. Would the fathers at Basel stand in the way of ecclesiastical reunion? The answer turned out to be yes.

On September 18, 1437, the pope officially transferred the council from Basel to Ferrara, the city agreed upon with the Byzantines. A minority of the participants, including the council president, Cardinal Cesarini, obeyed the command to move. The majority stayed in Basel. Significantly, Europe's monarchs, having no particular political benefits to gain from the reunion of Rome and Constantinople, remained mostly neutral, while some continued to support the council. A new schism had begun, this time with one pope and two councils.

The council at Basel became increasingly radical, even proclaiming the superiority of the council to the pope to be an article of faith, that is, disagreement with conciliarism meant heresy. Naturally Eugenius rejected the decree, thus committing heresy, and since no heretic could be pope, the council deposed him on June 25, 1439. But the church needed a pope, so on November 5, 1439, the council elected as pope a pious Italian layman, Duke Amadeus of Savoy, who took the name Felix V (1439–49). The schism now had two popes and two councils.

The election of Felix V began to scare off the council's political supporters who envisioned decades of two competing popes. Felix himself turned on the increasingly beleaguered council when he learned that even as its pope, he could not get the council to follow his wishes. He soon retired to his estates at Savoy, while the council, constantly diminishing in size, continued to meet.

Negotiations between the Greeks and Latins dragged on for months, but finally all was done, and the Greeks arrived in Italy. The emperor John VIII and the patriarch of Constantinople headed the delegation, which, with attendants and servants, numbered seven hundred, all of whom had to be housed and fed as well as to have their travel costs paid for. To this was added all the diplomatic niceties, that is, which step befitted the emperor's dignity, which one the pope's, who calls on whom first, and the like. But both Eugenius and the city of Ferrara rose to the task, and the council opened on April 9, 1438. But the cost of maintaining the council in Ferrara became prohibitive, and Eugenius, anxious for papal finances, gratefully accepted a generous offer from the city of Florence and moved the council there. It opened on January 16, 1439.

The council opened with a great disappointment for the emperor John VIII. He had hoped that Western princes, that is, those who could help him militarily, would be there, but not one put in an appearance, although some sent representatives. John clearly realized that no help would be forthcoming until reunion had been achieved. To his great credit, the emperor, who considered himself a divinely appointed monarch and, as such, head of the church, did not order his bishops to reunite with the West no matter what. Instead, he let the theologians and bishops debate the points separating Rome and Constantinople, most especially the *Filioque* or procession of the Holy Spirit through the Father and the Son, and, of course, papal authority.

The debates went on for months, and for three reasons. First, both churches had centuries of tradition behind them and were reluctant to compromise long-held beliefs and positions. Second, the problem of language— the bane of the early councils—arose again, complicated by the fact that few of the Greeks spoke Latin and few of the Latins spoke Greek, so that most participants could not directly follow what was being said and instead had to depend upon translators. Third, both sides did theology in different ways. The Greeks supported their views by providing quotations from the Fathers of the Church, especially the Greek Fathers. They believed that an amassing of sources would be sufficient to prove a point. The Latins, on the other hand, relied upon the techniques of scholastic theology, which was open to the thought of the ancient, pagan Greek philosopher Aristotle and which had developed a sophisticated method of study and debate in universities. When a Greek theologian quoted a Father, a Latin theologian often took the Father's statement, broke it down into parts, and began logically to examine each of the parts, their relationships to one another, and what might be deduced from them. The Greeks had literally never experienced theology being done that way. They felt both uncomfortable and puzzled. They could not deny the efficacy of the scholastic method, but neither could they accept it. (To use a modern analogy, many conservative Christians prove a point by citing biblical texts. Mainstream biblical scholars instinctively want to know who wrote the text, when, where, what literary devices the biblical author used, and in what historical situation the text was composed.)

Progress emerged with the discussion of the *Filioque* as the Byzantines realized that the Westerners could use that term in such a way that it did not contradict the Christology of the Greek Fathers. Papal supremacy raised a different set of difficulties, but the Byzantines reluctantly recognized that some form of acceptance of it was needed to get Western support for the beleaguered empire. Finally the theologians managed to come to agreement on all the major points, and a decree of union was signed on July 5, 1439, although a few Greek bishops declined to sign it. It appeared now that the Greeks would leave, but that was not the case. Some went sightseeing, others wanted to discuss nonecclesiastical matters, and the emperor wanted to arrange for Western help for Constantinople. On this latter point, he experienced only disappointment. Some Western leaders made vague promises that went unfulfilled. The pope alone stood by the emperor, and he worked hard to get at least the Italian city-states to support Byzantium.

The emperor left for home on October 19, 1439, and did not arrive in his imperial city till February 1, 1440. There he learned of the death of his wife during his absence.

Back in Florence the Latins were negotiating with Armenian Christians for reunion with Rome. This was achieved with considerable speed, a decree of union being issued on November 22, 1439. In 1442 the papacy effected a decree of union with the Monophysites in Egypt.

The stay in Florence had grown very long, and in February of 1443 Eugenius transferred the council to Rome, where as late as August of 1445 the Latins were negotiating with other Eastern groups (Chaldeans, Maronites) for union. Scholars do not know exactly when the council ended.

Although normally called the Council of Basel, the seventeenth ecumenical council's true name is the Council of Basel-Ferrara-Florence-Rome.

After the Council, West and East

Through a combination of hard work, careful planning, much patience, considerable endurance, and some diplomacy, Eugenius IV had achieved what no previous pope had been able to do: reunion with the Byzantines. This was wonderful for the church and a great personal triumph for Eugenius, whose status in Catholic Europe rose accordingly, although the Council of Basel continued to sit and, with enough political and financial support, to survive. Yet the pope's triumph at Florence impressed the monarchs, and the progressively radical and democratic character of Basel discouraged them. By 1446, when the German empire declared allegiance to Eugenius, almost all of Europe had deserted Basel, and its leaders moved it to the Swiss town of Lausanne, partly for lower costs and partly because Basel's citizens were sick of the whole affair. Yet this rogue council outlived the beleaguered pope, who died in February of 1447, his last words supposedly expressing regret that he had ever left his monastery.

The cardinals chose a new pope, Nicholas V (1447–55), who worked with the king of France to convince Basel's pope, Felix V, to resign. By then Felix had become embarrassed by the council and fearful of what could happen to his noble family if he stood out against all of Catholic Europe. In April 7, 1449, Felix V, last of the antipopes, resigned, and the Council of Basel came to an end. Nicholas generously created Felix a cardinal and made him papal legate to Savoy, where he was duke. For the first time since 1378, the Western church was at peace.

When the Byzantine emperor and his bishops were journeying home, they put in occasionally at some Greek islands, where they found the local populace complaining about the union. The real trouble, however, lay in Constantinople, where antiunionist parties organized against the "sellout" to the hated Latins. One of the emperor's own brothers used the unrest to attempt a coup d'état, which failed. Depressed by his wife's death, John VIII did not have the energy to combat the antiunionist forces strongly enough, while unlearned, virtually illiterate monks stirred up hatred against the Latins among the populace. But the emperor never backed down from the union, and most bishops supported him.

The Turkish threat, which had prompted John's desire for reunion, did not diminish. The papacy tried to help. Cardinal Julian Cesarini, who, on behalf of the pope, had opened the Council of Basel, went to the Hungarian court and convinced the king to attack the Turks. In 1444, near the city of Varna in Bulgaria, the Turks routed the Hungarians, and Cardinal Cesarini was among the slain Westerners. This defeat guaranteed that no Western military aid to Constantinople would move overland. If the emperor John VIII could not count on Western armies, at least he did not have to see the fall of his capital. He died on October 31, 1448, and was succeeded by his brother Constantine XI (1448–53).

While the new emperor did not have his brother's investment in the union, he did recognize that he needed Western help. But the opposition to the union never diminished; some opponents even used the phrase "Better the turban than the tiara," that is, better to be ruled by the Muslim Turks than by the papacy.

An external threat soon changed everything. In 1451 Mehmed II became sultan and made it clear that he would do what his predecessors, including his father, had failed to do: he would take Constantinople. Turkish forces began to build a new fortress close to the city, and Constantine could do nothing. He appealed to the West for help, but to no avail. As the situation worsened, only the pope stood by him, negotiating with the Venetians to outfit a fleet, but time was fast running out. The populace of Constantinople, recognizing the danger, dropped their opposition to the union, and on December 12, 1452, in the great church of Santa Sophia, the Byzantines officially accepted and proclaimed the decree of union agreed to at Florence fourteen years earlier. The religious obstacle to Western help had finally been removed.

But the empire's time had run out. On April 2, 1453, the Turkish army laid siege to the city that had been founded 1100 years before by Constantine the Great and that had been the leader and pillar of Orthodoxy through so many trials. On May 29 the Turks captured Constantinople; the emperor Constantine XI died defending his city. The Turks turned Santa Sophia into a mosque, and, in future, the sultans would appoint the city's patriarchs. The union of Constantinople and Rome was now a dead letter.

Toward Lateran V

The popes had defeated the councils, but they had not defeated conciliarism. Many in Catholic Europe, both clerical and lay, believed that the papacy would never reform itself and that only a council could truly reform the church. For the next eighty-seven years (1447–1534), the papacy went a long way to proving that belief.

This is the period of the so-called "Bad Popes," a silly and inaccurate name since several of these popes led pious lives and believed in reform. A better name would be that given by Monsignor Philip Hughes: "A Papacy of Princes." With a few exceptions, the popes came from noble Italian families, and their political concerns, especially their mastery of the Papal States, often outweighed ecclesiastical ones. Most practiced almost ruthless nepotism, giving church offices and even church lands to relatives, including their own illegitimate children. They often resorted to violence to achieve their ends.

They also lived in Italy during the Renaissance, and, starting with Nicholas V, the popes supported the arts, especially in Rome, where magnificent churches, public buildings, and, unfortunately, palaces for the cardinals arose almost everywhere. Wonderful as this support was, it demanded enormous amounts of money, and complaints about this extravagance flowed into Rome, especially from northern Europe. The belief in the curative powers of a reforming council never died out until the Reformation.

But conciliarism served another purpose. Europe's monarchs, as usual, wanted concessions from the popes on numerous issues, and they routinely brought up the threat of a council to force an issue on the pope. This too would continue until the Reformation.

When the Council of Basel officially closed, Nicholas V turned the rest of his pontificate to his real interest: collecting books. Thanks to him, scholars have the Vatican Library, one of the world's great treasure houses, and he invited artists and humanists to work in Rome. But the papacy lost ground politically. In 1438 the French king Charles VII (1422–61) had issued the Pragmatic Sanction of Bourges, which limited the right of the pope to appoint prelates in France, a privilege now reserved to the king, as if the Investiture Controversy had never occurred. Charles backed this up with threats to withhold funds due to Rome and by asserting the superiority of the council to the pope, a weapon he threatened to use, and Nicholas could do nothing to change this.

In 1452 the German emperor Frederick III (1452–93) journeyed to Rome for his imperial coronation but after him no other emperor believed a papal coronation was necessary. German emperors would still request a formal coronation in Rome, as Charles V did in 1530, but papal approval for the office of emperor had become a thing of the past.

Pius II (1458–64), a personally good man and former supporter of the Council of Basel, published a bull in 1460 that forbade appealing above the pope's head to a council or future council, which settled the matter as far as the papacy was concerned, but Europe's monarchs ignored it, just as they ignored Pius's pleas and plans for another crusade.

For the rest of the fifteenth century this Papacy of Princes lived in style, supported the arts, enriched their families, connived in Italian politics, spent enormous amounts of money, and negotiated their ways in and out of political crises. People still spoke hopefully of a council, but no meaningful steps were taken. All of that changed, however, with the election of Julius II (1503–13).

Best known as the pope who forced Michelangelo to paint the Sistine Chapel ceiling, Julius was "a forceful ruler, ruthless and violent . . . [determined] to restore and extend the Papal State . . . and to establish a strong, independent papacy in an Italy free of foreign domination" (Kelly, *Popes*, 255). The great Florentine Renaissance historian Francesco Guicciardini (1483–1549) said of this pope: "There was nothing of the priest about him except his clothing and his title." True, but Julius was indeed a remarkable man. He raised an army, attacked all of his Italian enemies, enjoyed stunning success over the papacy's old foe Venice, and often led the papal armies in person, wearing a full set of armor! The Italians nicknamed him "O Boots."

When Julius had defeated his Italian enemies, he then turned to depriving France of its dominance in northern Italy. Louis XII of France

(1498–1515) tried to fend off the pope with an ecclesiastical weapon. After renewing the Pragmatic Sanction of Bourges, he listened to advice from some cardinals opposed to Julius and opened a council at Pisa in 1511. Louis did not threaten to depose Julius but rather to have a council that would have more authority than the pope. The Holy Roman Emperor Maximilian I (1508–19) did not actively support the council but neither did he oppose it. Conciliarist traditions ran strong in northern Europe.

Despite the French king's protestations of religious concern, the council's crudely political motives fooled no one. But Julius still feared the Council of Pisa and with good reason. For more than a half century the popes had avoided calling a council and had also avoided reforming the church. Might not other monarchs and secular leaders support the French venture? Louis seemed to be riding high, but it was not by accident that Julius had survived the snake pit of Renaissance papal politics to rise to the top. He negated the Pisan council in one bold, brilliant stroke—he called a council of his own to meet in Rome on April 19 of 1512 (it actually opened on May 1).

The Fifth Lateran Council

All of Catholic Europe agreed that only the pope had the right to call a council; the complaints had dealt with the unwillingness of popes to do so. Now Julius had done so; he had given the church what people wanted: a council. What justification could Louis XII claim for his council, which had such meager attendance that it was soon nicknamed the *conciliabulum* or "mini-council."

The popes include Lateran V among the ecumenical councils, which thus makes it one, but all Catholic church historians, accepting the Vatican's decision as an ecclesiological one, still have difficulty accepting the ecumenicity of Lateran V as a historical fact. "There was an average attendance at the council of about ninety to a hundred bishops, and almost all of them were from sees in one or other of the Italian states. . . . There were no more than twelve public meetings of the council in all: four in 1512, four in 1513, and one in each of the years 1514, 1515, 1516, and 1517. The legislation of the council appeared in the form of papal bulls, published in the several sessions" (Hughes, *Crisis*, 256). One cannot help but note that the immensely successful and permanently influential Fourth Lateran Council (1215) met for three sessions in three weeks, while Lateran V averaged fewer than three sessions *per year*.

Historians also consider Lateran V more a papal than a truly ecumenical council since Julius and his successor Leo X (1513–21) made no attempt to get any serious representation from outside of Italy, largely because the Italian bishops as a group strongly opposed conciliarism. Even though this council welcomed the first bishop from the Americas, he too was an Italian, representing a Spanish colony.

The sessions meeting during Julius's reign had one purpose and one purpose only—to counter the *conciliabulum* of Pisa. This turned out to be easier than expected. After considerable military and political success in northern Italy, Louis XII's position there deteriorated quickly. The French withdrew from Italy, fulfilling a major goal of Julius's pontificate, and the *conciliabulum* of Pisa soon followed, moving first to the Italian city of Asti and then to Lyons in France, site of two previous ecumenical councils. In December of 1512 the German emperor Maximilian repudiated the Council of Pisa and announced his adherence to Lateran V. Julius had won a major victory over the French but also over the threat of conciliarism, thwarting a monarch's attempt to use it as a weapon against the papacy.

French politics dominated the pope's other main concern at the council, the revocation of the Pragmatic Sanction of Bourges. He founded a commission to study how that might be done, but before any decision could be made, Julius II died in February of 1513.

A month later the cardinals elected the thirty-seven-year-old cardinal Giovanni de Medici to be Leo X (1513–21). A son of the great Florentine Renaissance prince Lorenzo the Magnificent, Leo had been a cardinal for twenty-four years, having been raised to that rank at the age of thirteen. He had never taken holy orders, so after his election, he had to be ordained a priest. "A polished Renaissance prince, Leo was also a devious and double-tongued politician and an inveterate nepotist. His aim was to keep Italy and his own Florence free from foreign domination and to advance his family [the Medici] outside Florence" (Kelly, *Popes*, 257). Leo was a man of great cultivation who contributed much to Rome's artistic and cultural life, but spirituality claimed precious little of his time.

In 1513 Leo made sure that Lateran V continued, and he received the acknowledgment of the French king Louis XII that Lateran V and not the king's own Council of Pisa was the true council. But Leo generally ignored his council. He called just one formal session per year in 1514, 1515, 1516, and 1517. He preferred personal negotiation for dealing with the church's problems. In 1515, the new French king, Francis I (1515–47), invaded Italy to reclaim territory that the French had lost, in the process defeating a league of enemies that included the papal army. Leo promptly made peace with Francis and convinced him to abrogate the Pragmatic Sanction of Bourges, which, in French law, gave the king virtual control over the church in France.

In return, Leo concluded a concordat with Francis that gave the king the right to nominate (= appoint) all bishops and all abbots in France, along with a number of personal privileges. Denounced as a concession in both Paris and Rome, the concordat was actually a work of political brilliance. The French king kept all his power but received that power from the pope, so both saved face and avoided future disputes. But what about the conciliar commission that Julius II had established to look into the Pragmatic Sanction? Leo simply ignored the council on a matter that Julius had ordered it to take up.

Many bishops at the council were good, sincere men, anxious to reform the church, and they drew up a number of reform decrees. But the papal victory over the conciliar movement meant that the bishops in council could do nothing without papal support, and Leo had little concern for reform. He approved the council's statements on reform as well as a dogmatic decree affirming the individuality of the human soul, but he did so in papal bulls, prepared by his secretaries. By 1517 he had tired of the council; he also had other matters on his mind. He had discovered a plot by some dissident Italian cardinals to poison him. He had the ringleader, the cardinal of Siena, executed, and he imprisoned several others. Fearful of plots and harangued by Italian city-states opposed to his aggrandizement on behalf of Florence and his family, Leo had no time or interest for the council that he closed on March 11, 1517. Ignoring its worthy decrees on reform, the pope returned to politics and hunting.

Leo X may have prevented Lateran V from reforming the church, but six months after the council closed, a German Augustinian priest named Martin Luther (1483–1546) would initiate a reform, but one that no one had envisaged. We are on the cusp of the Protestant Reformation.

CHAPTER SEVEN

The Council of Trent

The Protestant Reformation

Martin Luther (1483–1546) was a German Augustinian friar and theologian who taught at the University of Wittenberg, which had been founded in 1502 by the elector of Saxony, Frederick the Wise (1463–1525). Luther was and remains a controversial figure, but the rise of ecumenism in the latter part of the twentieth century has enabled scholars to take a broader and more objective view of him. It has also clarified our understanding of his protest against the Roman Catholic Church.

The Protestant Reformation centered on doctrinal matters and on which ecclesiastical authorities had the competency to judge in such matters. The Reformation was not about the abuses rampant in the Catholic Church (and against which many Catholic reformers also railed). Yet it was one of these abuses that forced Luther, who was a pastor as well as a university theologian, to reconsider his fidelity to Catholic teaching.

The Catholic Church teaches the existence of purgatory, a postmortem place of purging where the deceased make satisfaction for the transgressions committed during their earthly lives and for which God has forgiven them. After this purging, they will enter heaven. To use an everyday example, suppose I borrowed a wrench from a friend and then lost it. I would apologize to my friend, who would accept my apology and "forgive" me, but we would both understand that I had the obligation to make "satisfaction" for what I had done, that is, I would buy him a new wrench.

Purgatory is a place of punishment, and naturally Catholics wished their deceased relatives and friends to spend the shortest amount of time there. In the Middle Ages the church had established a system of indulgences, whereby people could do pious works and have the spiritual value of those works offered to God for the alleviation of the suffering of those in purgatory. Many medieval theologians testified to the value of this practice, but it contained potential for serious abuse. Suppose a Catholic were too ill or otherwise unable to perform pious works? She or he could make a financial donation to the church in lieu of the pious works. By the late Middle Ages, it had become far more common for people to obtain indulgences by making donations than by earning them, and to meet this need there arose the office of indulgence seller. Catholic reformers repeatedly warned against the harm of this practice, which they believed demeaned the image of purgatory and increasingly made helping the suffering souls there a matter of money.

In the early sixteenth century, the dominant family in Germany was the House of Habsburg, but an ambitious new family, the Hohenzollerns, hoped to replace them. At the time the Holy Roman Emperor, ruler of Germany and some lands beyond German borders, was chosen by seven electors, four secular (one of them Luther's lord Frederick the Wise) and three ecclesiastical. The Hohenzollerns held a secular electorship, that of Brandenburg. In 1513 a second electorship, the archbishopric of Mainz, became vacant, and the Hohenzollerns wanted it to give them two of the seven electoral votes. Their candidate was Albrecht, younger brother of the elector of Brandenburg. Although not a priest, Albrecht was bishop of Magdeburg, so he would need a papal dispensation to transfer to the see of Mainz (traditionally a bishop spent their episcopates in one see, in keeping with the image used at Nicea I, that a bishop was married to his see); Albrecht would also need a second dispensation because he was not of legal age to become an archbishop. Fortunately for the Hohenzollerns, the pope at the time, Leo X, had no difficulties with reasonable dispensations. The only issue would be the price, which Pope Leo set very high since he needed funds for the building of Saint Peter's Basilica.

The Hohenzollerns could not meet Leo's price on their own, so they turned to bankers for a loan. Albrecht got to be bishop of Mainz and elector of the Holy Roman Empire, and the money to cover all this would be raised by indulgence preaching in Germany. The bankers mistrusted the Hohenzollerns, and so they arranged that when the indulgence preachers collected funds, a representative of the banking house would be seated alongside the preacher, with one coin going into the preacher's money box and the next one going into the bankers' money box. The reader can imagine the impression this made on pious and reforming Catholics.

Luther's lord Frederick the Wise did not permit the indulgence sellers to enter his lands, because he himself had a large relic collection that produced revenues of their own. Luther soon discovered that his parishioners went to towns where the indulgences could be purchased. Luther the pastor gave sermons against this abusive practice, but Luther the theologian had for some time been thinking intensely about the larger issue of how salvation might be gained. The Protestant Reformation began in his ruminations.

Like his theological mentor Augustine of Hippo, Luther had a strong sense of his own sinfulness. He fretted constantly over what he could do to justify himself before God for his sins. He reached a monumental conclusion: he could do nothing to justify himself before God. Instead, God would have to justify him. "Luther came to realize that we are not to think of the righteousness of God in the active sense (that we must become righteous like God) but rather in the passive sense (that God gives us his righteousness). The good news, Luther discovered, is that justification is not what the sinner achieves but what the sinner receives. . . . The Christian before God is therefore at one and the same time both sinner and righteous," because God would impute righteousness to sinners, that is, a created righteousness, not God's own righteousness (Lindberg, *Reformations*, 69–70, 72).

Luther's theology deserves far more space than this survey can provide, but clearly he had moved away from traditional Catholic teaching, which offered sinners several ways to become justified. Had Luther become a heretic? Not really, and his *Ninety-Five Theses* proved it.

This "revolutionary document" was anything but. The traditional image shows Luther nailing the theses to the church door in Wittenberg while the population stands about aghast, thinking *So beginnt die Reformation!* ("So begins the Reformation!") In Lindberg's words, "The 'Ninety-Five Theses' were a typical academic proposition for a university debate. They were written in Latin, and most Wittenbergers could not even read German" (ibid., 76). Rather than break from the church, Luther wished to debate his theses about salvation and various religious issues with other theologians.

He sent a copy of the "Theses" to Albrecht, the new Hohenzollern archbishop of Mainz, who forwarded it to Rome, where the pope passed it on for review to Dominican theologians who had little sympathy for Luther's attack on the scholastic theology that underlay the church's teaching on indulgences and many other issues. Learning of this, Luther was frightened and for good reason. If the Roman theologians concluded that he was a heretic, he would have to recant or ultimately face execution. But politics intervened and, indeed, saved Luther.

By 1517 Catholic Europe realized that the Holy Roman Emperor Maximilian I would not live much longer and that the emperor wanted his grandson Charles Habsburg, king of Spain since 1516 and heir to Maximilian's lands, to succeed him as emperor. This terrified Leo X since the Spanish ruled much of southern Italy, and if Charles became emperor, the Habsburgs would rule Spain, southern Italy, and Germany, which intervened constantly in Italian affairs; to all this would be added Spain's enormous and growing empire in the Americas. Charles Habsburg could threaten the pope's independence.

Understandably, Leo had more concern about the imminent imperial election than about the theological meanderings of a German Augustinian. He allowed the Roman theologians to continue their investigations into Luther, but Luther's lord Frederick the Wise, one of the seven precious imperial electors, liked Luther and resented what he deemed Roman persecution of his university's best theologian. When the Roman theologians concluded that Luther was a heretic, Frederick saw to it that nothing happened to him.

The emperor Maximilian died in 1519, and Europe awaited the result of the election. Blatantly drawing upon Spain's wealth, Charles Habsburg bribed enough electors to secure the imperial title for himself, a title he would hold until 1556. Leo had failed in his campaign to limit Habsburg domination, but he still needed to pacify Frederick the Wise because the pope hoped the German *Diet* (parliament) would vote to finance a crusade against the Turks in Eastern Europe. The proceedings against Luther would continue, and politics would still impact them.

But an important moment had passed for the papacy. In the time since the publication of the *Ninety-Five Theses*, Luther had become a celebrity and then a hero in Germany, where resentment against perceived Roman abuse of the German church was widespread. Furthermore, Luther had had the time to refine his thinking and, to his surprise, found other theologians in Germany agreeing with him. In 1519 he went to the Diet of Augsburg to meet the great Roman theologian Thomas de Vio, Cardinal Cajetan, who had been instructed by the pope to debate Luther. But the Roman peremptorily told Luther there would be no debate; he must simply abjure his teachings. Morally unable to comply, Luther quickly made his escape from Augsburg, and Cajetan complained bitterly to Frederick the Wise about his continued support of Luther.

Luther realized that his theological views needed support. By what authority was he proposing his own views about salvation and rejecting those of Rome? Luther argued that all doctrine must rely upon Scripture and upon Scripture alone. He rejected the authority of ecumenical councils and of the popes, who, he believed, had usurped the authority of Scripture in order to augment their own power in church and society. In 1520 Leo X excommunicated Luther, but the papal emissaries entrusted with disseminating the bull in Germany found themselves resented and occasionally threatened. One wrote to Leo that of every ten people in Germany, nine shouted "Long live Luther" while the tenth shouted "Death to the pope." Luther also found himself picking up political support.

But Germany's most important politician loathed him. Charles V, now emperor, wanted to settle the matter, but he had left Spain (which he loved) and come to Germany (which he disliked but where he spent most of his adult life) and now had to move carefully. Rome wanted a condemnation of Luther, but Charles granted Luther a hearing at the Diet of Worms in 1521. There Luther made his views clear: "Unless I am convinced by the testimony of the Scriptures or by clear reason . . . I cannot and will not retract anything, since it is neither safe nor right to go against my conscience. I cannot do otherwise. Here I stand. May God help me. Amen." He impressed the German princes in attendance, but the emperor considered Luther a blatant heretic and ordered him to recant or face punishment. Luther did not recant and so became an outlaw in the empire, a burden he carried for the rest of his life. But, once again, Frederick the Wise protected him from arrest.

In the 1520s Luther's movement grew rapidly, helped by the reformer's many writings, including his magnificent translation of the Bible into German, a foundation block of the modern German language. Since the Catholics relied upon development of doctrine for much of the elements of their faith, Luther's Bible showed German readers that many Catholic teachings and practices, such as the seven sacraments, had no explicit biblical foundation. When Catholics began buying Luther's Bible to see what the Bible actually said, the German bishops commissioned Catholic translations. No longer a troublesome theologian, Luther had become a major figure in German life. His support grew constantly, especially in German cities, where middle-class merchants, resentful of the dominance of church and nobility, found his teachings attractive.

Imperial opposition continued, but Charles V soon found German affairs beyond his ability to control, especially with the French and the Turks attacking either end of his German lands. At the Diet of Speyer in 1529, Charles, hoping to settle matters in Germany, proposed some anti-Lutheran measures, but several German states sympathetic to Luther issued a formal *protestation*, leading to their being labeled *protestantes*, that is, "those who protest" in Latin, and thus the name Protestant.

Luther's ideas spread beyond Germany into Switzerland, where the Protestants (the term we shall use from here on) found that without a central authority, there was no way to prevent groups from going their own ways. But Protestantism did not have to be a united movement to spread. From Germany it moved north into Scandinavia, and in 1533 it attracted an important convert, a Frenchman named Jean Cauvin, better known as John Calvin (1509–64), who would prove to be the greatest of Reformation theologians. The unity of the church was becoming a memory.

Leo X focused on politics until his death on December 1, 1521, but to the end he maintained an interest in the Luther affair. In January of 1522 the cardinals chose Cardinal Hadrian of Utrecht, a commoner, a Dutchman, and the last non-Italian pope until John Paul II (1978–2005). A formidable scholar, Hadrian VI (he kept his own name) had been tutor to the Holy Roman Emperor Charles V, so the cardinals may have hoped that diplomatic relations between papacy and empire would improve. While in Spain, Hadrian had twice served as an inquisitor and was no friend of theological innovation or speculation. He came to Rome hoping to halt the Reformation and to organize a crusade against the Turks. He quickly learned that the Romans resented this northern "barbarian" who had little interest in the arts. The cardinals quickly learned that he considered them in need of reform but not in need of the financial handouts they had expected. They promptly turned against him.

As a Spanish inquisitor, Hadrian had condemned Luther's teachings, and he expected Charles V to move against Luther, only to find that his former pupil expected his former teacher to join him in attacking not Luther but the French! Hadrian stayed neutral, only to find that the French were plotting against him. Reluctantly he became involved in the complex of European politics, but his health deteriorated, and he died on August 3, 1523, having done little to halt the Reformation.

Having learned their lessons with the northerner Hadrian, the cardinals chose an Italian nobleman, Clement VII (1523–34), an illegitimate son of Lorenzo di Medici of Florence. Clement brought to the papal office experience and diligence, but he focused mainly on political issues, often to his detriment. He was a poor choice to deal with the Reformation because he simply did not realize it was a spiritual revolution that challenged the foundations of Roman Catholicism and that it required a strong spiritual response.

Like Leo X, Clement feared that the emperor Charles V and the House of Habsburg would dominate the papacy, and so he looked to France as a bulwark against Charles. But the emperor was genuinely trying to combat Protestantism, while the French king, delighted at the havoc the Reformation was reaping upon his German enemy, encouraged and quietly helped the Protestant cause. Furious with Clement's reluctance to abandon France and favor Germany, Charles stood by while on May 6, 1527, imperial troops, with German Lutheran mercenaries augmenting the Spanish regiments, sacked the city of Rome, raping and pillaging as they went. Clement went into hiding in the Castel Sant'Angelo, but Charles's troops discovered him there (some of the Lutherans threatened to roast and eat him). The emperor effectively kept the pope a prisoner for six months, allowing imperial troops to remain in Rome, although the pope was still safe in the Castel. After he resumed his office, Clement supported Charles and, as it happened, Charles's aunt Catherine.

Henry VIII of England (1509–47) worried about his dynasty. His Spanish wife, Catherine of Aragon, had produced a daughter, Mary, but no son, and by 1529 Henry concluded that she could never give him the son he believed the dynasty needed. He wished to divorce her, but a divorce was not possible according to Catholic matrimonial teaching. Clement denied Henry's request, and eventually the king led England out of the Roman communion. Until 1570, however, when Pope Pius V excommunicated Queen Elizabeth I and declared her deposed from the throne, the popes entertained hopes of England's return to the church, but it was not to be.

By the time Clement died in 1534 the Reformation had spread widely in northern Europe, and Protestant groups, usually meeting in secret, began to appear in France and Italy. Only true, extensive, long-lasting reform could preserve the church, but that required a pope committed to this enormous task. In 1534 the cardinals chose the right man, a truly great pope who took the name Paul III (1534–49) and whose reform program would include calling the Council of Trent (1545–63).

Great does not mean perfect, and Paul III had faults aplenty, those typical of Renaissance princes. Although not ordained a priest until the age of fifty-one in 1519, he held a number of bishoprics, few of which he ever visited but from all of which he drew sizeable revenues. He had a Roman noblewoman for a mistress, and she bore him three sons and a daughter. Throughout his life, especially as pope, he practiced nepotism on a wide scale, naming two of his grandsons cardinals at the ages of fourteen and sixteen. His nepotism provoked his enemies to murder one of his overly ambitious sons. Yet in 1509 he proved to be a responsible bishop of the city of Parma, and by 1519 he had recognized the Protestant threat. When he became pope, he left much of his previous life behind and made reform his priority.

Reform took many shapes. In 1542 Paul III established the Roman Inquisition (later the Holy Office) to combat heresy and to impose censorship on books. He approved the establishment of several new religious orders, the most important of which was the Society of Jesus or Jesuits, founded by the Spaniard Ignatius Loyola (1491–1556). The Jesuits would prove to be the most effective agents in carrying out reform. But the central piece of Paul's reform was calling an ecumenical council.

The Council of Trent, Period I

Like all Renaissance popes, Paul feared a revival of conciliarism, but many Catholics, especially the emperor Charles V, believed that only a council could convince both Catholics and Protestants of the pope's commitment to reform. Naturally politics entered in. Charles hoped that a council would aid his struggle against the German Protestants, whose leaders had banded together in a league. Francis I opposed a council precisely because it would benefit Charles; the French king preferred to see Germany in a state of anarchy. When Luther heard of plans for a council, including one that would invite Protestant attendees, he said that he could only accept "a free council held in German lands," that is, a council that would be independent of the pope, something to which Paul could never agree. Even the nature of the council provoked problems. Charles V wanted a focus on reform, hoping to placate the German Protestants, but Paul first wanted to settle the doctrinal issues and to refute Protestant theological challenges. (Paul may also have concluded by then that the Protestants could not be placated.)

The royal-imperial-papal negotiations began. Paul called a council for the Italian city of Mantua in 1537, but the Mantuans were hesitant about the costs of hosting it, and the pope had to abandon that idea. He next announced a council in Vicenza in 1538, but both the French king and Holy Roman Emperor had objections. He tried again in 1542, but two weeks after Paul proclaimed a council for the Italian city of Trent, hostilities broke out between France and the empire. The war ended in late 1544, and Paul called a council for 1545, again with Trent as the place. The city was in imperial territory, and thus technically in "German lands" as Luther had requested, but 90 percent of the population was Italian, and Trent lay on the Italian side of the Alps.

Paul III had no intention of attending the council, but to represent papal interests, he appointed three legates: Giovanni del Monte, Marcello Cervini, and an Englishman, Reginald Pole, who would all play great roles in Catholic reform.

The council opened on December 13, 1545, to what can safely be called an inauspicious beginning with only thirty-one bishops in attendance. The French king boycotted the council and forbade his bishops to attend. The turmoil in Germany prevented attendance from there. Except for some Spaniards, the bishops were almost all Italian, although several of them lived in imperial territory, and so, like the Spaniards, owed their offices to the emperor.

The emperor wanted the council to deal with reform, but the legates, following the pope's wishes to discuss doctrine, saw to it that the council simultaneously discussed issues in both their doctrinal and reform aspects. This was a wise decision. No matter how obvious was the need for reform, the Protestants had challenged several Catholic doctrines, and so the fathers at Trent chose to clarify those. In long, often stormy, debates, the bishops set to work.

On April 8, 1546, they passed a decree on divine revelation, which they said was contained in the written Scriptures and in unwritten traditions, which they sensibly declined to enumerate, thus responding to Protestant questions as to where the Catholic Church got its authority and to the basic Protestant assertion of "Scripture alone." The reformers equated revelation with Scripture, while the bishops asserted a wider understanding, and one that allowed for revelation to continue in the church. In this same decree, they then listed the books of the Bible, affirming the Catholic canon, which most Protestants repudiated, disagreeing with Catholics on the number of books in the Old Testament. (Catholics accepted more than the Protestants did.) The bishops then set out conditions and restrictions for the publication of Bibles. They confirmed, with no prejudice to the Greek and Hebrew originals, that the Latin Vulgate text of the Bible was sufficient for doctrinal matters, and they called for a new edition of the Vulgate. Because Luther's translation of the Bible had had such a stunning effect on the Germans, many bishops wanted to condemn vernacular translations, while others thought the church should support and encourage them. But neither side could muster a majority, and so the matter was dropped.

In preparing the decree on original sin of June 17, 1546, the bishops naturally accepted the historicity of Adam and Eve, and so they accepted that all humans inherit the consequences of the first parents' sin. These consequences include the loss of grace, mortality, and concupiscence, that is, the inclination to sin. The grace bestowed upon humans by the sacrament of baptism removes the guilt of original sin, but concupiscence remains. Differing, however, from Luther, the bishops did not teach that concupiscence is sinful.

They then moved on to justification, a major issue for both Protestants and Catholics. The decree on that topic took almost six months to prepare, receiving conciliar approval on January 13, 1547. The bishops accepted that only God can justify humans, but they insisted that humans can prepare for justification: ". . . when, understanding themselves to be sinners, they, by turning themselves from the fear of divine justice, by which they are salutarily aroused, to consider the mercy of God, are raised to hope, trusting that God will be propitious to them for Christ's sake" (Schroeder, *Canons and Decrees of the Council of Trent*, 32). After humans have received this divine grace, they can go on to do good, that is, not the ordinary goods that all humans do, but the goods necessary for eternal salvation. But note that the council spoke of humans "understanding themselves to be sinners." This realization also results from divine grace, so God initiates the process of salvation, although humans can then play a role. This addressed one of the most disconcerting elements of Luther's teaching for Catholics—that humans played no role in their own salvation. The council also taught that humans were indeed sanctified through grace, whereas Luther taught that God reckoned them as righteous.

The preceding paragraph sums up more than twenty pages of conciliar text, but the last few pages of the decree dealt with the central problem of reform: the residence of bishops in their dioceses. It was quite common for a bishop to hold title to one or more dioceses but not reside there, even though he collected funds due to his office as bishop. This was pluralism, so widespread as to include the reigning pope during his earlier career. The bishops at Trent insisted that governing a diocese was "a burden formidable even to the shoulders of angels" that should be held by those of "unblemished character" in order "to restore a very much collapsed ecclesiastical discipline and to reform the depraved morals of the clergy and people." (Also problematic, but not as serious because it affected fewer people, was the absence of abbots from monasteries, who often left their abbeys on business.) Obviously, a bishop holding more than one diocese received revenues from all the sources, so many bishops at Trent literally voted to reduce their own incomes, no small step and one that proved the sincerity of their commitment to reform.

Not all bishops were pluralists, and the church had strong examples of what a good bishop could do. Abolishing pluralism appeared to be a reform no one could oppose, but a problem did arise: several bishops believed that the obligation of residence for a bishop was a matter of divine law (*ius divinum* in Latin), although no biblical text said anything like that. This caused concern in Rome, where the specter of conciliarism always haunted the pope and his advisors. The pope routinely appointed bishops to act as emissaries or to serve in Rome on committees and commissions. If divine law insisted that a bishop must reside in his parish, would this not infringe on papal authority? The final form of the decree, produced in Trent's third period (1562–63), came out strongly in favor of residence but still preserved the pope's right to call bishops from their dioceses for special needs. This sounds like a loophole through which a truck could be driven, but the popes of Trent and later never acted like that, instead insisting on residence. This one decree removed much of the pastoral neglect that had plagued the episcopacy, although *ius divinum* would return. Paul III showed his goodwill by forbidding the cardinals to hold more than one bishopric, thus initiating an important reform without going through the council.

The Protestants had attacked the notion of seven sacraments, insisting that the Bible speaks only of two: baptism and Eucharist (in fact, the New Testament never uses the word "sacrament"). On March 3, 1547, the bishops passed a decree specifying that all seven Catholic sacraments were instituted by Christ, that they have efficacy via their actual administration (*ex opere operato*) and independent of the disposition of the recipient, and that a sinful but lawfully ordained priest could validly administer sacraments. The bishops gave a special boost to confirmation, which the Protestants had severely attacked. But they took up questions relating to specific sacraments, such as the Eucharist and penance, during the council's second period.

The council had been doing good work, and its achievement won it not only approval but more participants. By the time the bishops voted on the sacramental decree, their number had doubled to sixty-four. But trouble was brewing. The pope and his advisors feared imperial influence on the proceedings. When several bishops became ill, fear of the ever-recurring bubonic plague seized the council. In March of 1547 the papal legates used this opportunity to transfer the council to the Italian city of Bologna, outside of imperial territory and influence. This infuriated the emperor, who withdrew his bishops, and in February of 1548 Paul III suspended the activities of the council. No one knew if it would meet again. Charles V angrily responded by making an interim arrangement with the German Protestants that "allowed the provisional continuation in Protestant lands of married clergy, communion in both kinds, and a form of the doctrine of justification" (Lindberg, *Reformations*, 244).

The first session of Trent also demonstrated that the biblical-humanist approach to theology had run its short course. Although the bishops never established an official theological method, they did make it clear that scholasticism would be the preferred theology, even voting down a proposal to have the education of priests include the biblical and humanist methods.

Paul III died in 1549. No clear candidate emerged, and one of the papal legates to Trent, Reginald Pole, came within one vote of election (he would have been only the second English pope). Eventually cardinals chose another of the papal legates at Trent, Giovanni del Monte, who took the name Julius III (1550–55). Hopes quickly rose for the reopening of the council, and Julius did not disappoint.

The Council of Trent, Period 2

After negotiations with the emperor, Julius reopened the council on May 1, 1551. The council had been suspended after issuing a decree on the sacraments in general and on baptism and confirmation in particular. Now the bishops turned to other sacraments, specifically the Eucharist, issuing a decree on it on October 11, 1551. They defended the real presence (denied by some Protestants) and gave conciliar approval to the scholastic term "transubstantiation" to explain how the Eucharist bread can become the body of Christ. Several Protestants believed in the real presence, but the fathers wanted to explain the Catholic position clearly. Transubstantiation meant that at the consecration during Mass, the substance of the bread and wine was changed into the substance of the body and blood of Christ. Yet the "accidents," that is, the nonsubstantial parts of the bread and wine remained. Thus the eucharistic bread and wine looked and tasted like bread and wine. In scholastic terminology, substance and accidents form an indissoluble unity in a person or thing, and such unity was maintained in the Eucharist, but now the substance was not that of bread or of wine but of the body and blood of Christ, the same body and blood that came forth from the womb of the Virgin Mary. The fathers at Trent considered transubstantiation to be not just miraculous but unique (*singularis* in Latin). Protestant theologians, generally critical of scholasticism, challenged this teaching, but the bishops focused on clarifying the teaching for Catholics. They explained how Jesus could be present in heaven (by nature) and present in the Eucharist (sacramentally); they also affirmed the excellence of the Eucharist over the other sacraments. In addition, they wisely acknowledged the eucharistic presence of Christ to be a mystery of the faith, lest anyone accuse them of using transubstantiation to "explain" a mystery.

Working at a good pace, the bishops issued the decree on penance and extreme unction on November 25. As with the Eucharist, the bishops did not anticipate winning over Protestant theologians but rather wanted to clarify Catholic teaching on penance. They began with the logical problem of what would happen to believers who sinned after receiving baptism and pointed out that in early Christianity some form of penance had existed, and thus modern penitential teaching and practice continue a long tradition.

Again using scholastic terminology, the bishops taught that "the form of the sacrament of penance, in which its efficacy chiefly consists, are those of those words of the minister, 'I absolve you' . . . but the acts of the penitent himself, namely, contrition, confession, and satisfaction, constitute the matter . . ." (Schroeder, *Canons and Decrees of the Council of Trent*, 90). The bishops went on to explain what contrition is and, importantly, to emphasize that imperfect contrition, fostered either by a horror of the sins committed or by a fear of damnation, is yet a gift from God and valid for confession. This frank acknowledgment of the natural frailties of human nature—the inability to achieve perfect contrition, which could only be known by God anyway—gave the teaching a humanity that a rigid approach could not.

The bishops defined confession as auricular, complete, and secret: auricular because the penitents had to tell their sins to a priest; complete because the priest needed to know what the sin was and under what circumstances (some possibly mitigating) the sin was committed; secret because only in that way would penitents speak freely. Satisfaction for the sins usually consisted of prayers or acts of charity, that is, small acts that emphasized that true penance is in the soul, not in acts following confession.

Shortly after this decree the council fathers heard the exciting news that some German Protestants would be attending the council. They arrived early in 1552, traveling to Trent under a safe conduct granted by both the council and the emperor. This demonstrates the continuing Catholic hope that the split in Western Christianity could be healed, but it was too late. While the earliest reformers, such as Luther (1483–1546), had grown up Catholic and understood the church from the inside, so to speak, by the 1550s a new generation had grown up Protestant. To that generation the Catholic Church was an alien and indeed a hostile body.

The bishops at Trent quickly recognized the new situation. Some Protestant representatives refused to meet with papal officials, instead dealing only with imperial envoys who were German. In private negotiations, the Protestants demanded that the bishops abandon their oath of allegiance to the pope and that the pope accept conciliarism, that is, acknowledge the superiority of the council over the pope. Since the first period at Trent (1545–47) had passed decrees on Scripture and on justification, two major Protestant concerns, the Protestant representatives wanted to reopen discussion of those topics, basically nullifying what the first period of Trent had done. Clearly the bishops could not accept such demands, nor would Rome ever have agreed to them. The German Protestant representatives basically asked Trent to give up its Roman Catholic character. When the impasse became obvious to all, the Protestants departed from Trent.

This early exercise in ecumenism soon became irrelevant. In March of 1552 the German Protestant princes revolted against the unwary emperor, who had to flee through the Alps to escape a Protestant army. Charles V never returned to Germany. The bishops at Trent feared for their safety since no power stood between the conciliar city and the victorious Protestants. Furthermore, the papal legate was desperately ill, and Julius III decided it best to suspend the council, effective on April 28, 1552. The official decree diplomatically—and perhaps wryly—blamed the suspension not on the emperor but on the devil: ". . . suddenly such tumults and wars were enkindled by the craftiness of the enemy of the human race, that the council was at much inconvenience compelled to pause as it were and to interrupt its course . . ." (Schroeder, *Canons and Decrees of the Council of Trent*, 119).

Julius made no attempt to reconvene the council, but he did not abandon his interest in reform—for example, he encouraged and supported the work of the Jesuits. In 1553 he received the news that the Catholic Mary Tudor had succeeded her brother Edward VI to the throne of England (she reigned until 1558) and that she intended to reinstate Catholicism as the state religion. Julius contacted his old colleague from Trent, Reginald Pole, who was a cousin of the king through his mother, whom Henry VIII had executed. Pole returned to England in 1555 as papal legate and aided Mary in her attempt to restore Catholicism.

Although supportive of the council, Julius still safeguarded papal authority. When Spain and Portugal began to implement some of the decrees of Trent, the pope pointedly informed them that conciliar decrees had no validity without papal approval and that Trent's decrees had not yet received such approval.

Julius III finished his reign quietly, paying attention to personal concerns. Upon his death, the cardinals showed their deep desire for reform by choosing the third papal legate to Trent in its first period, Marcello Cervini. He kept his name and was styled Marcellus II. He moved immediately to give strong personal examples of reform, forbidding his relatives to even come to Rome, much less ask for funds and appointments. He simplified his coronation ceremony and cut down the size of the papal court. This good man wished to make it clear that reform would start at the top. But twenty-two days into his pontificate he died of a stroke.

The cardinals reassembled for the second conclave in two months, and again they chose a reformer. But this time they chose a tiger.

Gian Pietro Carafa was the oldest of the cardinals, seventy-nine at the time of his election, and he had spent his ecclesiastical career fighting for reform principles. He led a life of strict asceticism, had dealt with abuses when he served as a diocesan bishop, and had founded a religious order, the Theatines, which committed itself to restoring the (supposed) simplicity of apostolic life.

But he mixed his desire for reform with severity in achieving it. Paul III appointed him head of the Roman Inquisition in 1542. Even before his appointment, Carafa established an interrogation center in his own residence.

He once remarked that if his own father were convicted of heresy, he himself would carry the burning torch to set the stake aflame.

His fondness for the Inquisition was matched only by his hatred for Spain. A Neapolitan nobleman, he had served as archbishop of Naples when Spain ruled southern Italy, and he could see no good in anything or anyone Spanish, even if that Spaniard were one of the greatest, if not the greatest, Catholic of the day. Upon hearing of Carafa's election, Ignatius Loyola acknowledged that his bones rattled from head to foot, so terrified was he of what this Spanish-hating pope might do.

Carafa took the name Paul IV (1555–59). Convinced that the Holy Spirit was responsible for his election (like later historians, he could find no human explanation for it), he decided that he would reform the church on his own, and he did not need an ecumenical council to help him, although he did establish a large advisory committee of bishops and scholars to study the council's decrees. But he let this group disband without following its advice. Simply put, he had no use for Trent.

Paul actively practiced reform. He chose good men for vacant bishoprics, and he told several diocesan bishops resident in Rome to return to their dioceses. In 1558 he began work on an Index of Forbidden Books, publishing his index in 1559. To no one's surprise, the list of books not to be read included the major Protestant authors, but it went on to include the works of people such as the Dutch scholar Erasmus, a lifelong Catholic. Italian literary classics such as the *Decameron* of Boccaccio made the list as did everything published by no fewer than sixty printers whom the pope disliked, fourteen in the city of Basel alone. Peter Canisius (1521–97), the great Jesuit preacher in Germany, observed that even the most pious Catholics lamented such unnecessary severity.

But no one would cross Paul because his other great instrument of reform was the Inquisition. Regardless of the great demands of his office, he always took time out to attend the sessions of the Inquisition. Originally founded to root out heresy, the Roman Inquisition now prosecuted people for moral lapses, and the number of death sentences increased significantly.

Paul IV made it clear that he would never compromise, but only a person who controls every situation can afford such an attitude. He quickly learned that in his dealings with England. Thirty-seven at the time of her accession, Queen Mary had married a foreign prince, Philip II of Spain, who usually remained in his own country and was widely resented in England. Mary often found herself virtually alone when she needed help. She had no children and no prospect of having any, which raised again the specter of a problematic succession and thus weakened her authority. In 1556 Queen Mary arranged for Reginald Pole to become archbishop of Canterbury and thus primate of England. Mary trusted Pole, but Paul IV had long believed him to be a heretic and had suggested so at the conclave of 1551 to prevent Pole from being elected pope. Had Paul IV supported Pole and had Mary not persecuted Protestants, the restitution of Catholicism might have had a chance. But Paul removed Pole as papal legate and ordered him to return to Rome and an almost certain visit to the Inquisition. The queen prevented Pole from leaving. On November 17, 1558, this unhappy woman died, followed to the grave twelve hours later by Reginald Pole. The succession to the throne of Elizabeth I (1558–1603) guaranteed that England would not be a Catholic country.

Paul suffered another diplomatic disappointment in Germany. Charles V finally understood that he could not reunite Germany religiously by force. In 1555 he agreed to the Peace of Augsburg with the Protestant princes. This agreement recognized the legal existence of Catholicism and Lutheranism (Calvinism was excluded) and accepted that in each land the people would follow the religion of their ruling prince (in Latin, *cuius regio, eius religio*, that is, "whose region, his religion"). Charles also decided that, after thirty-six grueling years of dealing with religious conflict, he would abdicate in 1556. Rulership of the Holy Roman Empire, that is, the Central and Eastern European lands, would go to his brother Ferdinand I (1556–64), while Spain, the Netherlands, and his endless territories in the New World would go to his son Philip II (1556–98). Paul IV opposed this and actually forbade Charles to abdicate. He also denied that Ferdinand could be emperor because he had not gotten the pope's approval. But Paul IV was not Innocent III, and the Habsburg brothers ignored him. Paul actually considered deposing the Habsburg brothers but decided against an astonishingly provocative and surely useless step.

Without doubt, Paul's worst diplomatic error was to follow the advice of his nephew, Cardinal Carlo Carafa, and join France in a war against Spain. The miserable papal army stood no chance against Spanish veterans. After routing the papal forces, the Spaniards occupied the Papal States and forced the pope to sign a treaty. Soon after this, Paul learned that Cardinal Carlo and another of his nephews had been using their ecclesiastical offices to create great fortunes for themselves. Uncle Paul initially wanted to send them to the galleys but settled instead on imprisonment and exile from Rome. But his numerous enemies gleefully pointed out that the great reformer had never extended his inquisitorial energies to his own rapacious nephews.

Paul IV died on August 18, 1559. Upon learning of his death, the Roman mob invaded the offices of the Inquisition, set free all the prisoners, and destroyed the building and most of its records.

The Council of Trent, Period 3

The cardinals met in conclave for almost four months before choosing a Milanese cardinal who took the name Pius IV (1559–65). As was common with the reforming popes of the period, Pius had not been a lifelong reformer. He had three illegitimate children, and he rose in the papal bureaucracy because one of his brothers had married into the family of Paul III. Like most popes of the era, he advanced his own relatives. But, like Paul III, Pius rose to the challenge of reform.

The fanaticism of Paul IV had frightened him, even to the point where he left Rome in 1558 for his own safety. Once in office, he began reversing Paul's policies, restricting the power of the Roman Inquisition, revising the Index of Forbidden Books, and opening up friendly relations with Spain. In a dramatic exercise of power, he ordered Paul IV's two imprisoned nephews, one of them a cardinal, to be executed for prompting their uncle to war against Spain.

Not surprisingly, Pius also changed papal policy toward the Council of Trent. He wanted it reopened, and he appointed no fewer than four presidents to preside, although the leaders were two cardinals, Ercole Gonzaga, from a princely Italian family, and Gerolamo Seripando, who had represented his order, the Augustinians, at the earlier phases of the council. The council reopened at Trent in January of 1562.

Fierce disputes marked the opening. The new French king Charles IX (1560–74) had decided to support the council, so the French bishops demanded that the council be considered a new one and not a continuation of the two phases in which they did not participate. The Holy Roman Emperor Ferdinand I also wanted a new council because he had worked out a peace with the German Protestants and feared that they would reject and resent the earlier two phases. On the other hand, the Spanish king Philip II wanted a continuation, believing that the council had done good work. The pope joined Spain on this issue, wisely realizing if he denied the validity of the first two periods, some future monarch could urge the same be done to the third one. Although annoyed, the French and German monarchs accepted this.

The council had opened seventeen years before, and so sympathy was strong for an active council that would work quickly and finish its task. For example, the council had debated revising the Index, but a Spanish bishop pointed out that a committee, no less a council, would take years to agree on the contents, and therefore the council should ask the pope to take up the task. The fathers at Trent agreed.

A long-simmering issue again came to the fore: the residence of bishops in their dioceses. Many bishops wanted this to be defined as divine law (*ius divinum*), that is, that God wanted bishops in their dioceses. But the Roman Curia included many bishops who had left their dioceses for papal service. Many papalists feared that declaring residency to be divine law would challenge papal power, and so they fought the issue. A vote on April 20 showed that a plurality of bishops supported *ius divinum*, while the other bishops either opposed it or wanted the matter left to the pope. The presidents of the council tried to negotiate a way out of this by saying that since the vote was inconclusive, they would bring the matter up again when the council discussed holy orders. Pius, who strongly opposed *ius divinum*, was furious at the papal legates for even allowing the vote to occur, and he debated recalling them. He stopped short of that but never fully trusted them again.

Shortly after the vote, King Philip II, fearful that this debate might derail the council, told the Spanish bishops to drop the matter, which they did.

The council quickly moved on to the sacraments, defining the sacrificial character of the Mass, which Luther had attacked. Since the Protestants practiced communion under both species and since many Catholics in Germany and Eastern Europe liked the practice, the emperor Ferdinand wanted the council to approve communion in both species. The council fathers, recognizing this as a political issue, deftly avoided it and instead pronounced that Christ was fully present in communion under both species, so that the reception of bread alone still meant that Christ was fully received in his body and blood, soul and divinity. After the council had closed, however, Pius IV allowed communion under both species in parts of Germany and Eastern Europe as a concession to the emperor.

But communion under both species was not the only reform issue related to the Mass. The bishops outlawed priests from bargaining for Mass stipends and urged that superstitious practices be curbed. And no discussion of the Mass can ignore a popular legend about Trent—that the bishops had planned to ban the use of polyphonic music in churches but relented when they heard the *Missa Papae Marcelli*, the "Mass for Pope Marcellus," by the great Italian composer Giovanni de Palestrina, who wrote the work specifically to counter the proposed ban. (The pope of the title is Marcellus II (1555), the former legate at Trent.) But Palestrina had composed the Mass before the council even met! In any event, the ban never materialized.

While real progress was being made at the council, an undercurrent of discontent continued. The bishops at the council, mostly diocesan bishops, wanted a real reform of the Roman Curia, whose bishops, they believed, knew little of diocesan life. (To use a modern analogy, many governors of

U.S. states believe that Washington bureaucrats do not know the difference between Idaho and Tennessee, and yet they make decisions that those states must obey.) But the curial bishops served the pope directly, and he saw the council's resentment of the curia as a criticism of his government. When the council took up the issue of holy orders, the legates kept their promise and allowed the matter of *ius divinum* to be brought up again. Many eyes in Rome were focused directly on Trent, while national considerations had begun to play a role in the debate as the rulers made their views known.

Then, suddenly, the council changed. On March 2, 1563, one of the legates, Cardinal Gonzaga, died, and on March 17, the other legate, Cardinal Seripando, also died. Pius IV had lost confidence in both of them some months before, and now he had a chance to appoint as legate a man who could represent papal views and who could move the council. His choice was Cardinal Giovanni Morone.

Morone (1509–80) had spent his career working on reform and had tried to improve dialogue between Catholics and Protestants. In 1543 Paul III wanted him to be legate to Trent, but plans for a council at that early date fell through. The ferocious Paul IV naturally loathed someone as open-minded as Morone, charged him with heresy, and in 1557 had him put in prison, where he remained until he was released by Pius IV. To this distinguished churchman would go the honor of bringing Trent to a successful conclusion.

Realizing *ius divinum*'s political overtones, Morone went first to confer with the emperor; then he went to Trent, where he sidelined the papal hard-liners and offered the French a compromise. Working with Morone, the pope wrote to the king of Spain to give him a personal assurance of his commitment to reform. Soon Morone had his decree.

On July 15, 1563, the council declared holy orders to be a sacrament, and it specified the qualities desired in a priest. Then it went on to say that it is a divine commandment that bishops should know their people, thus raising the dignity of the episcopate above that of a mere papal appointee. The council furthermore said that no bishop is free of the obligation of residence, but, if the pope needs someone for special service, he can temporarily absolve the bishop from his residency requirement, although suitable steps must be taken to ensure that someone qualified will fill in for the bishop. The decree tactfully avoided mentioning a "divine law" that bishops be resident in their dioceses. Shortly after the decree was passed but before he had officially confirmed it, Pius IV began telling diocesan bishops resident in Rome to return home.

This same decree also established the seminary system. This still surprises modern Catholics—that a system for educating priests did not exist until the sixteenth century. Till then the local diocese had the responsibility for educating priests. In large dioceses like Milan and Paris, the education, often in conjunction with a local college, could be very good, but in poor dioceses the situation was reversed. Historical examples actually survive of priests who could barely read Latin, but who memorized the words of the Mass. Now the larger church would see to it that all priests received a basic education, no matter what their diocese. The impact of this upon Catholic life cannot be gauged.

With the *ius divinum* controversy now behind him, Morone pushed the council to finish its business. Next came a decree affirming the sacramental nature of marriage (an issue contested by the Protestants) along with canons for reform that insisted that a marriage could not be valid unless performed by a priest in front of two witnesses and that documentary evidence be kept, which led to the establishment of marriage registries in parishes.

The council had dealt with the major issues, but many of the bishops, aware of what was happening in their dioceses, wanted a statement about indulgences, relics, images, and veneration of the saints. These issues may not have had the weight of justification or Scripture and tradition, but the bishops knew how important these were to the people, most of whom were illiterate and for whom venerating a saint had much more meaning than advanced sacramental theology. Morone wisely agreed to take up the matter, and so council committees began work on the decree.

But then a thunderbolt struck Trent. News arrived from Rome that the pope had had a stroke and was in mortal danger. The specter of conciliarism quickly rose from the ashes. The curia feared that if Pius IV died while the council still sat, the bishops at Trent would claim the right to elect the new pope. Morone rushed to finish this last decree and close the council. News soon came that the pope had survived and was recovering, but Rome still wanted the council to finish, a view by this time shared by most of the bishops.

The council met for the last time on December 3–4, 1563, passing a decree that defended and clarified Catholic teaching on images, purgatory, relics, and veneration of the saints. Teaching on these points had been established for centuries, but the bishops felt they could not deal with abuses without clarifying the teaching. For example, they made it clear that images were material objects pointing to the spiritual reality beyond them, that is, an image of Jesus reminds believers of the Savior. The bishops taught that Catholics venerated the saints because of the excellence of their lives; further, that veneration of God's saints pays honor to God. The saints are great, often heroic, figures of the church who can still intercede for those in the communion of saints still on earth. Since relics, especially physical remains of the saints, remind believers that the saints' bodies were temples of the Holy Spirit, Catholics can appropriately venerate relics. Finally, while not conceding any points to Luther, the council quietly urged reform in the promulgation of indulgences.

The council then held a closing ceremony, expressing thanks to the popes, the legates, and the monarchs who had supported the council. By December 13, 1563, the legates and bishops had left Trent.

By the time of this last decree, the bishops, cardinals, and patriarchs present at the council had numbered almost two hundred, a far cry from the thirty-one at its opening in 1545. Trent had proven a success. It had clarified Catholic teaching, responded to the Protestants, and established a program of reform and organization that would carry long into the future.

The council had ended, but, with conciliarism now in the past, the council decrees and canons had no intrinsic binding force; they had to be confirmed by the pope. Pius IV proclaimed his official confirmation of the decrees and canons on January 26, 1564. The Latin word for "Trent" is *Tridentinum*, so the phrase "Tridentine decrees" came to stand for the documents from Trent. But the tone of the canons and decrees was juridical and scholastic, assuming a static church in a static world, and thus a "minimal awareness of the historical conditioning of norms, axioms, principles, and authoritative statements" (O'Malley, essay in *From Trent*, 305), an attitude that would survive until Vatican II.

Several issues remained undone by the council; for example, Luther had written two successful catechisms, which briefly and accurately summed up his teachings, and the council saw the need for a Catholic catechism. But such tasks would fall to the popes.

After Trent

Pius IV's commitment to Trent never waivered, but he quickly established his role as the council's interpreter. He instituted a Congregation of the Council, consisting of cardinals who would evaluate the decrees and recommend to him how they could be authentically understood and enforced. No matter what happened at Trent, Rome would decide what Trent would mean. Yet Pius truly followed the lines of the council. He got bishops out of Rome and back to their dioceses. He revised the Index of Forbidden Books. He allowed the use of the chalice in the Eucharist in parts of the Holy Roman Empire. Pius also continued his reform of the Roman court. But any reconciliation with Protestants had become a thing of the past. This very active, reforming pope died on December 9, 1565.

To succeed him, the cardinals chose Paul V (1566–72), a protégé of Paul IV, who shared that iron pontiff's fixation with the Inquisition, even rising to the office of inquisitor general. But unlike his namesake, Paul V appreciated the work of Trent and tried to implement its decrees. To aid priestly formation and spirituality, he revised the Roman Breviary (1568), which contained the readings from which priests would daily say the Divine Office. To improve and standardize worship, Paul published the Roman Missal (1570), which Clement VIII (1592–1605) emended in 1604, producing the edition from which other emendations were made. The Clementine edition remained the standard text until the nineteenth century.

Doctrinal issues had played a great role at Trent, especially in response to multitudinous Protestant criticisms. The need of a popular authoritative manual arose from a lack of systematic knowledge among pre-Reformation clergy and the concomitant neglect of religious instruction among the faithful. Paul V saw to the publication of the Roman Catechism (1566), which provided a summary of Catholic teaching and would, by virtue of papal support, remain a standard text until the late twentieth century. It differed from previous catechisms by being intended for priests rather than a literate laity. Many other catechisms, often ones suited for believers in particular countries, appeared in the centuries after Trent, but none had the authority of the Roman Catechism.

Several subsequent popes saw to the implementation of the Tridentine decrees, including getting the Catholic rulers to accept them or even to allow them to be published in their countries, which the French did not do for decades. But Tridentine reform went steadily ahead. After Paul V, Sixtus V (1585–90) played the greatest role in implementing the decrees, albeit in his own way. In 1588 he set up the system of twelve congregations to handle most of the church's affairs, congregations whose members he appointed, thus centralizing papal power and weakening that of the college of cardinals who had been appointed by various popes. Sixtus continued the Congregation of the Council but created congregations for the Inquisition, for Rites and Ceremonies, for bishops, for religious orders, for the Index of Forbidden Books, and several for the administration of the Papal States, such as the Congregation for the Navy (ten ships). Ironically, Trent had emphasized the responsibility of bishops in their dioceses, but the congregations now gave Rome the authority to intervene, when deemed necessary, in diocesan affairs. But this reorganization of the papacy fit into the growing movement in Europe toward royal absolutism; Sixtus was a man of his age.

He also tried to effect a revision of the Latin Vulgate edition of the Bible, but he undertook it himself rather than use experts. The resulting, disastrous edition was quickly withdrawn after his death, and Clement VIII saw to the revision of the Vulgate.

The popes of the late sixteenth and early seventeenth centuries had much else to worry about besides implementing the Tridentine decrees. Slowly but with increasing tempo the number of Catholics in the Americas was increasing. Elizabeth I succeeded in making England into a state that could challenge Catholic powers such as Spain, France, and the Holy Roman Empire. The wars of religion in France tore that country apart until almost the end of the century and hampered the progress of reform. Philip II of Spain supported reform but in his own way, and he always dominated the Spanish church. Yet the popes still found ways to make the reforms of Trent felt in almost every aspect of Catholic life, a phenomenon matched only by Lateran IV (1215) and Vatican II (1962–65).

CHAPTER EIGHT

The First Vatican Council

From Trent to Vatican I: Enlightenment and Revolution

More than three centuries separated the end of the Council of Trent (1563) from the opening of the First Vatican Council (1869). Obviously a great deal of history occurred over those centuries, and we can only cover those issues that impacted Vatican I. For the long term, most important was the church's spread to many corners of the world, especially to the Americas and then Africa. Missions also went to Asia, although they never made the conversions that occurred on the other continents. However, Vatican I responded not to global concerns but to European ones, and the perennial issues, such as the status of the Papal States and the relation of the church to the European states, returned again and again. Thus the background to the twentieth ecumenical council will cover mostly European events.

The splits caused by the Reformation did not heal, and the Catholic Church existed in a divided Europe. While the Protestant states were often hostile to Rome, it was, as usual, the "Catholic" monarchs who caused the popes the most difficulty. Louis XIV of France (1642–1715) virtually took over the church in his country, and in 1682 summoned the French clergy to a national council, at which they agreed to the Declaration of the Clergy of France, which gave the king, among other rights, the right to approve papal pronouncements for them to be valid in France, a significant diminishment of papal power. The popes may have defeated conciliarism, but European royal absolutism continued to challenge their authority in the church. By the mid-eighteenth century the Catholic powers had gained so much ascendancy over the popes that in 1773 they could force Clement XIV (1769–74) to suppress the Jesuits, whom several monarchs loathed for their strict loyalty to the pope. (The suppression continued until 1814.) The

149

popes continued to rule the Papal States, but their political influence outside Italy was declining.

Yet in spite of their constant attempts to control the church, the monarchs remained Catholic and valued the church. But the nineteenth-century church, that of Vatican I, reacted against an immensely powerful movement not from the right but from the left—the French Revolution.

Although portrayed in literature and films solely as an upsurge of an angry urban proletariat, the Revolution was actually led by educated men influenced by the Enlightenment, an eighteenth-century intellectual movement that enshrined the primacy of reason over all else, faith included.

The Enlightenment itself grew out of the Scientific Revolution of the sixteenth and seventeenth centuries.

Catholics had always accepted the authority of scriptural revelation as interpreted by the church. Furthermore, they accepted the authority of ecclesiastical traditions, and of decrees and doctrines promulgated by ecumenical councils and by the popes. The church had produced many great scholars over the centuries, and all of them saw reason as subordinate to faith. These scholars wanted a reasonable faith, that is, a belief in a deity whom intelligent people could accept rather than the silly pagan gods of field and stream; and these scholars, especially the university-trained scholastic theologians of the High Middle Ages, applied reason to faith so rigorously that conservative Catholics objected that they gave too much to rationalizing and not enough to simple belief.

But ultimately faith had priority. The scholastics denied the notion of double truth, that is, that something could be true in faith and its opposite be true in reason. God is the source of all truth, and thus all truth must be one. The scholastics considered philosophy to be the *ancilla theologiae*, the handmaiden of theology, helping theology but never overcoming it. For example, the philosopher most used by the scholastics, Aristotle (384–322 BC), had taught that the universe is eternal and claimed he had proved that rationally. But the biblical book of Genesis said that God created the heavens and the earth, which previously had not existed. For believers, which the scholastics were, Aristotle's reasoning had to give way to biblical faith. The universe had a beginning, and the doctrine of the Last Judgment made it clear that the universe would also have an end.

Christians, both Catholic and Protestant, had other, very serious reservations about reason. Augustine of Hippo had taught that original sin not only tainted human souls with the guilt for Adam and Eve's disobedience to God but also weakened our natural faculties, both rational and physical: we make mistakes, we forget things, we become ill, we die. Since original sin had weakened reason, which could easily mislead us, we should not trust it too much and instead must rely on divine revelation, tradition, and church authority. With characteristic vigor Luther once called reason "a whore."

But the Scientific Revolution changed this attitude. Scripture, tradition, and church authority could tell scientists nothing about topics like the circulation of the blood, which the scientist William Harvey announced to the world in 1628. In that same century Galileo discovered the craters on the moon, and Isaac Newton created a new physics. Clearly reason, unaided by faith, could produce some remarkable achievements. It became increasingly difficult for educated people to speak of the primacy of faith over reason when scientists obligingly pointed out that one could *see* the results of their work while one had to *accept* what the churches taught.

Science grew rapidly in this era, especially with the foundation of scientific societies and the introduction of science courses into universities. It also impacted society. As people began to look for natural explanations for physical events, it became increasingly difficult to believe in witches flying through the sky but also more difficult to believe in saintly apparitions. While European and American churches did not directly oppose science (many scientists were also clergymen or devout believers), prescient churchmen could see what the rise of science could or would do to traditional ecclesiastical authority.

In the eighteenth century, European intellectuals, especially in France, began to turn reason against traditional Christianity, first attacking superstitions and those who promoted them but then quickly moving on to larger targets like miracles, common in the Bible and still widely accepted in the eighteenth century. For them miracles were fantasies intended to bewilder illiterate peasants. The Scottish philosopher David Hume (1711–76) snidely claimed that the only thing miraculous about miracles was that people believed in them. Soon the Enlightenment intellectuals turned on doctrines, such as the sacraments, which they called tricks to keep people obedient to ecclesiastical authority.

Original sin was the primary target. Is it reasonable, the intellectuals asked, to believe that a loving God would condemn the entire human race to eternal damnation because two prehistoric people took a bite out of a piece of fruit? Would people really think that they were born evil if the church had not bludgeoned them into believing that so they would accept that they needed the church for salvation? No heretic had ever attacked the faith with such persistence and, among educated classes, with such success.

The seventeenth century had seen many monarchs claim that they reigned by divine right. But, intellectuals asked, were we actually expected to believe that a king who is gluttonous, adulterous, violent, alcoholic, and moronic was chosen to rule by God? Such a belief made no sense. Rulers, the intellectuals concluded, were just men in favored positions, not more-than-ordinary beings chosen by God. The Enlightenment intellectuals thus encouraged and praised democracy.

They took a great interest in the fledgling United States, where a Europeanized intellectual, Thomas Jefferson, became a moving force in establishing a democracy based upon rationalist principles. But democracy meant that the views of all counted, not just those of aristocrats, and that in turn meant that all should have the right to voice their views. The eighteenth-century intellectuals pushed for freedom of speech and freedom of the press. Since churchmen as well as monarchs took it for granted that they could censor both books and speech, the intellectuals added freedom of religion to the list.

Soon these new ideas entered the wider political realm. The French Revolution, which overthrew the Catholic ruling dynasty, took steps against religion far beyond anything a monarch would do. Claiming to offer people "Liberty, Equality, and Fraternity," its leaders had strong anticlerical feelings and worked not just to weaken the power of the Catholic Church but even to eliminate its very existence in France, claiming that the hierarchy was allied with the monarchy (which was true) and the clergy had no sympathy for the people (which was totally false—most parish priests lived as poorly as their parishioners). The revolutionaries proclaimed freedom of speech, of the press, and of religion, goods in themselves and already practiced in the United States; but in association with the Revolution, these freedoms caused many European monarchs and aristocrats, including the popes and bishops, to be suspicious of them and even to try to repress them.

Pius VI (1775–99) was the first pope to deal with the Revolution. An aristocrat who had appeased the Catholic monarchs, he hesitated when the Directory, France's revolutionary governing body, in 1790 made the Catholic clergy employees of the state. Pius condemned this step in 1792, but the Revolution was established by then. In 1796 an ambitious French general named Napoleon Bonaparte invaded Italy and annexed part of the Papal States. The French began to secularize the States, introducing practices such as civil marriage and legal divorce. When Pius protested, the Directory had him arrested and eventually brought to France, where he died in 1799, if not a martyr then certainly someone who had suffered for his church.

In that same year Bonaparte staged a coup d'état, initially ruling as First Consul and then in 1804 proclaiming himself emperor. His astonishing military successes up to 1812 spread revolutionary ideas wherever the French army went, ideas that would plague the papacy. But, knowing how many French citizens still practiced their traditional religion, Napoleon wanted to get along with the church, so he chose to negotiate with Pius VII (1799–1823).

Pius VII had proved himself open to new ideas and in 1797 had preached a sermon on the compatibility of Roman Catholicism with democracy, but by 1801 democracy was fading in France. In that year the pope and the First Consul signed a concordat that recognized that Catholicism was the religion of most Frenchmen. This eased tensions, although the following year Bonaparte, on his own, revised part of the concordat, showing what he really thought of it. When he decided to become an emperor, he invited the pope to come to Paris to crown him. Pius was wary, but this offered a chance for him to influence the most important person in Europe as well as to reaffirm the church-state link reminiscent of the Middle Ages when popes had crowned emperors. But Napoleon had different plans. When the pope arrived in Paris, he learned that the emperor would crown himself. Pius now knew that Napoleon simply planned to use him, and the pope did his best to thwart the emperor's plans. When Pius refused to bow to his increasing demands, Napoleon had him arrested in 1811 and eventually brought to France in 1812. After Napoleon's final defeat, Pius returned to Rome for good in 1815.

The allied leaders who had overcome Napoleon met in 1815 at the Congress of Vienna, where the papal secretary of state had to labor for the restoration of the Papal States, most of which were returned. But the European leaders, including the Catholic ones, made it clear that they were returning the States to the pope; he did not automatically get them back.

It was unfortunate for the church that the antireligious Enlightenment, the anti-Catholic French Revolution, and the ambitious Napoleon came to define so many modern values for the nineteenth-century popes. As absolute monarchs, the popes could not be expected to be sympathetic to democracy, but they saw democracy largely in the form of a secularist government that wished to abolish religion. They also saw freedom of religion as indifferentism, the idea that there are no distinctions among religions and that one is as good as any other. Unlike people living in democracies, the popes did not understand freedom of religion to mean that people can believe one religion to be necessary for salvation but still accept that all persons have the right to practice their own religion freely. Had democracy, freedom of religion, freedom of speech, as well as freedom of the press come to the papacy in different forms, some of the papacy's problems with the nineteenth century might have been avoided. One Catholic who tried to present those freedoms in a favorable light was the first American bishop, John Carroll of Baltimore (1735–1815). Scion of an aristocratic Maryland family and a Jesuit, Carroll had traveled in Europe and seen the harm done by clerics interfering in politics and by nobles interfering in the church. He strongly supported democracy, freedom of religion, and freedom of the press but found few European Catholics interested in his justification for his views.

But another revolution was changing much of the world, including the church, in the nineteenth century. The Industrial Revolution transformed society forever. For all previous generations, wealth had resided in land, and thus the landed monarchy and aristocracy, traditional supporters of religion, enjoyed both prestige and power. Thanks to the Industrial Revolution, entrepreneurs and capitalists gained unheard-of wealth and the influence that went with it. The traditional peasantry with generations of land-bound loyalty to dukes and counts was steadily becoming an urban proletariat that wanted political rights.

Many monarchists and aristocrats resented and tried to halt this new world, but in Great Britain, the Industrial Revolution was welcomed. British industry made the country wealthy, powerful, and ruler of an empire on which the sun never set. Jealous and prescient Europeans could not help but notice that Great Britain was both democratic and Protestant, while the previous dominant power, autocratic and Catholic Spain, could not even hold on to its multitudinous American colonies. This new, industrialized world would quickly impact the Papal States and thus the popes' outlook on the modern world.

In post-Napoleon Europe, the restored monarchs and nobles tried to bring back the world before 1789, but they failed. Most held on to their power but only by making concessions. Pope Gregory XVI (1831–46) would make no concessions.

Gregory XVI

France had occupied the Papal States for some years, and the citizens of the States wanted some liberties. Their initial demands were modest, for example, that towns should have laymen as mayors rather than clerics. They also wanted the industrialization that they saw going on in other parts of Italy and Europe. Gregory would have none of that. Linking industrialization to democracy and even revolution, he refused to allow railroads in the Papal States, a move that guaranteed that the States could not industrialize and would be less prosperous than other parts of Italy and Europe.

A revolt quickly broke out in the States, and the pope turned to the Austrians, who, at the Council of Vienna in 1815, had gotten sovereignty over much of northern Italy, and their territory bordered the Papal States.

Austrian troops entered the States to repress the revolt. The image could not have been worse: an Italian pope calling in foreign troops to battle the Italians of his own States. The Austrians succeeded, but the inevitable atrocities and innocent suffering made Gregory look like a despot using outsiders to oppress his own people. Significantly, the rebels proclaimed that they did not wish to weaken the papacy's spiritual authority but rather to achieve a lay, secular government for the States. Future rebels would maintain this claim.

The Austrians needed the Papal States to survive in order to preserve their own power in northern Italy. Should a revolution succeed and Italy become united, they would be forced to leave. In 1832, the French, realizing what the Austrians were up to, sent an army of their own to a part of the States the Austrians had not occupied, ostensibly to prevent revolts. Now two foreign armies were stationed on papal soil.

The European powers, Catholic and Protestant, urged Gregory to ease restrictions. He made some minor changes but would not allow elections or a council of state with lay members. On the contrary, repression increased: the Jews had to live in ghettoes, Roman taverns could not serve alcohol, women could not wear tight dresses, anonymous denunciations were accepted by the police.

The fear of revolution reached regrettable limits. When the severely oppressed Catholic Poles revolted against an anti-Catholic czarist oppression, Gregory condemned the Poles, even when "Russia began a brutal campaign of reprisal without parallel anywhere in Europe" (Duffy, *Saints*, 230). Polish Catholic patriots felt betrayed.

Convinced that the problems arose not from his treatment of the people but from modern ideas, the pope decided to fight those ideas. In 1832 he wrote an encyclical, *Mirari Vos*, which traced all the church's ills back to indifferentism, the notion that people of different religions could be saved. The encyclical went on to condemn the "delirium" of freedom of conscience along with those of speech and of the press. Gregory denounced the separation of church and state because "the princes . . . received their authority not only for the government of the world but especially for the defense of the Church" (Mioni, *Popes Against*, 12). "Indifferentist" democracies would not defend the church.

Gregory could accept some modern realities, such as recognizing, over Spanish protests, the independence of Spain's former colonies; he also condemned slavery and racism. But he could not accept any idea that would question his absolutist worldview.

In 1838 the French and Austrian armies withdrew from the States, leaving "public order to the Pope's Swiss mercenaries and the nasty volunteers enlisted by the (papal) Secretary of State (into a small army)." But revolution continued to simmer, and by 1843 "lone terrorists grew into guerilla bands" (Chadwick, *Popes*, 53, 59). In 1845, in spite of some successes by papal forces, the revolutionary movement got to the point where the Austrians had their forces on the alert.

Pius IX

When Gregory died on June 1, 1846, the cardinals, recognizing the need for a change in direction, chose an affable moderate to be Pius IX (1846–78). The new pope had advocated changes in the Papal States and proclaimed his Italian nationalism by his resentment of Austrian occupation of parts of northern Italy. After becoming pope, he proclaimed an amnesty for prisoners and introduced a partially representative form of government. Many in Europe thought the church had a liberal pope; some conservatives, especially in Austria, feared what Pius might do. In Italy itself, people's hopes rose quickly, only to be dashed almost as quickly.

Pius was a thoughtful, industrious, and patriotic man, but he accepted completely the millennium-old belief that the pope could not be an effective spiritual leader unless he ruled an independent state and was thus beholden to no government. He simply could not acquiesce in the uniting of the Italian peninsula into a single, secular state because he believed such a development would irreparably harm the papacy and thus the church. When his attitude became known, a rebellion broke out in the States. In 1848, the pope's prime minister was murdered, and Pius ignominiously had to flee from Rome in disguise. The Romans proclaimed a republic in 1849. Having gone to the town of Gaeta in the kingdom of Naples, Pius appealed to the Catholic powers to restore him. The French obliged, and once again an Italian pope called in foreign troops to battle the Italians of his own States. In 1850, under French protection, Pius returned to Rome.

Any inclination toward openness or democracy now disappeared. Pius IX would rule as did Gregory XVI. But developments had moved past him. The French would keep him in power in Rome, but their ruler was now the self-proclaimed emperor Napoleon III, a cynical despot who did not take religion seriously. He did, however, take Austria seriously, and so he chose to preserve the Papal States in order to check Austrian power in Italy. Looking over their shoulders at the rising might of Protestant Prussia, the Austrians did not want trouble in Italy, and so in 1855 they signed a concordat with Pius, which ended the emperor's traditional control over the Austrian church. But this link with Austria further convinced the Italians that the pope was a tyrannical tool of foreigners. Trouble in the States continued, and slowly but surely most of the States became "no-go" areas for papal officials.

The nature of the attacks on the States became far more dangerous. In the southern part of Italy, including the despotically-ruled kingdom of Naples, the rebels now found a charismatic leader, Giuseppe Garibaldi (1807–82), whose very adventurous life included exile from Italy, revolutionary activities in South America, a return to Italy, and eventually a great and heroic role in the *Risorgimento*, Italian for "Resurgence," the term given to the reunification of Italy.

Formidable as Garibaldi was, Pius's "most dangerous enemy" (Chadwick, *Popes*, 131) was not a soldier but a diplomat, Camillo Cavour (1810–61). He considered himself a Catholic, but he wanted a state free of ecclesiastical domination. Premier of the northern Italian kingdom of Piedmont, he worked to expand the kingdom's borders by allying with the French to get the Austrians out of Italy. Slowly but surely he and his king, Victor Emmanuel II (1849–61 king of Piedmont, Sardinia, and Savoy; 1861–78 king of Italy), forced the Austrians from northern Italy. The Piedmontese then stationed an army on the borders of the Papal States. This army soon replaced a group of guerillas as the invaders of the States. By 1860 the pope ruled only Rome and its environs, protected by French troops stationed in the Holy City. For Pius, "Italy was witnessing an apocalyptic struggle between the forces of good, led by himself, and the forces of evil, led by [Piedmont]" (Duffy, *Saints*, 224). He remained convinced that, by divine providence, the States would somehow survive in the modern era. Like Gregory XVI, he did not see the problem in the nature of papal rule but rather in the false ideals of the modern world. Also like Gregory, Pius would challenge those ideals.

The Immaculate Conception

Pius believed that one effective method to challenge modern errors would be to strengthen the pope's teaching office. Here he was helped by a long-standing and, in the nineteenth century, growing belief that the Catholic Church spoke infallibly on matters of faith and morals, and the companion belief that the pope could speak for the church and thus he too could speak infallibly. Pius considered this a benefit in a confusing world, and he wanted to demonstrate it, but on what issue? Ecumenical councils had determined the canon of Scripture, the real presence in the Eucharist, and a host of other issues. But a new one had arisen in the nineteenth century: had the Virgin Mary been conceived without original sin? Such a belief is called the Immaculate Conception (to be distinguished from the biblical virginal conception of Jesus).

This belief dated back to at least the fifth century with the Syrian Christian belief that Mary had not died. Death is a consequence of original sin, and thus Mary's freedom from death implied freedom from that sin. But if Jesus died to redeem all of humanity, would that not include Mary? Many theologians, including the master of Catholic theology Thomas Aquinas (1225–74), believed that only Jesus had been conceived free of original sin because these theologians could not reconcile Jesus' universal salvific activity with the notion of an immaculate conception of Mary.

Thomas's younger contemporary John Duns Scotus (1265–1308) had defended the notion by arguing that Mary would normally have been conceived in original sin, but her heavenly Son preserved her from this. He could not have been the perfect mediator between God and humanity had he been unable to preserve his own mother from sin. Duns Scotus further argued that God's perfect love for Mary resulted in a special privilege for her. (The arguments of Thomas and Duns Scotus are far more nuanced than could be presented here.)

But theological discussions had little impact on the growing popular belief in the Immaculate Conception, a belief that was furthered by claims from Catholics in France, the home of the Revolution, that the Virgin Mary had appeared to them. In 1845 the American bishops had named Mary Immaculate patroness of their country. Gregory XVI had believed in infallibility and in the Immaculate Conception but hesitated to define the doctrine. By 1854 Pius IX prepared to take that step.

Commonly seen as the most autocratic of popes, Pius IX genuinely cared for the views of his bishops. He asked the papal ambassadors to various countries to sound out the bishops on two points: the doctrine itself and the pope's right to proclaim it. Overwhelming episcopal support for both convinced Pius to go ahead. On December 8, 1854, he solemnly proclaimed the Immaculate Conception of the Virgin Mary to be a doctrine of the Catholic Church, saying that "the most Blessed Virgin Mary in the first instant of her conception, by a unique grace and privilege of the omnipotent God and in consideration of the merits of Christ Jesus the Savior of the human race, was preserved from all stain of original sin." This doctrine demands obligatory acceptance for all believers, and Pius made that demand on the authority "of Jesus, of the Apostles Peter and Paul" and "on our own authority," that is, he as pope defined the doctrine. He had, in effect, made an infallible statement.

Pius knew the consequences of his act, and so did the bishops. One of the pope's advisors acknowledged that the method of defining the doctrine was more important than the doctrine itself. Four years after the definition, in the southern French town of Lourdes, a teenage girl named Bernadette Soubirous claimed to have received a vision of the Virgin Mary, who told Bernadette: "I am the Immaculate Conception." Pius accepted the reality of the apparition as celestial approbation for what he had done. Certainly there was popular approval by the world's Catholics among whom devotion to Mary was very strong.

The Syllabus of Errors

In 1864 Pius IX published an encyclical, *Quanta Cura*, to which was attached a list of eighty errors of the modern world. The list quickly became known as the *Syllabus of Errors*. Much of what was in it had come from earlier papal writings and a list drawn up by a French bishop, but the *Syllabus*, by listing so many errors seriatim, had great force. Combined, the encyclical and the *Syllabus* condemned freedom of conscience, freedom of religion, freedom of the press, public schools, civil marriage, separation of church and state, the intellectual independence of philosophy, and democracy in general. It ended on an overarching, defiant note: it is an error to say that the pope should come to terms with modern civilization.

One can imagine the impact this had on the increasing number of Catholics living in democracies. The year the *Syllabus* appeared, American Catholics were dying in a Civil War to defend a country that had enshrined the very values the pope was condemning. In the U.S., "modern civilization" had increased literacy, made long-distance train travel feasible, begun to extend life spans, and even made it possible for people of every means to afford kitchen utensils, previously owned only by the wealthy. Most American Catholics liked the modern world.

Many of them also believed that the United States provided a good example of how a modern, democratic state could benefit the church. Starting with John Carroll, American bishops had supported the separation of church and state, and they believed that the faith would flourish as a free church in a free state. By 1864 Catholicism had become the largest church in the U.S., living proof that the bishops were correct. Furthermore, the American government gave the popes what they had wanted for centuries from European rulers: absolute neutrality in the appointment of bishops, no governmental approval before papal letters could be published, freedom from taxation for church revenues, even in time of war. But, working from a European perspective, Pius could see none of this, and, of course, American bishops had to go along with the pope.

The *Syllabus* disheartened many Catholics who favored democracy, freedom of speech, freedom of religion (denied to Catholics in places like Ireland and Poland), freedom of the press (also denied to Catholics in some countries), and the modern world in general. To many northern Europeans, the *Syllabus* meant that Pius was simply out of touch with the new world around him. More and more French Catholics wondered why their troops should risk their lives in Italy to save an absolute monarch who still required visitors to kiss his foot. Pius would get French protection for Rome and its environs, but serious intervention to restore the Papal States to him became increasingly remote.

Yet, just as his political power was diminishing, Pius found his spiritual and ecclesiastical stature soaring among Catholics worldwide. First, his struggles against the revolutionaries had won him much sympathy, even among people who may have disagreed with his views on society. Clearly this pious, sincere man had suffered mightily for what he believed to be best for the church.

Second, many of the states whose constitutions Pius disliked actually strengthened his authority. Unlike the European monarchies, democratic governments that separated church and state had no interest in interfering within the church and thus had no interest in the appointment of bishops, which they left completely up to the pope. Furthermore, the new states in the Americas carved out of former Spanish colonies also accepted the bishops whom the pope selected; previously bishops for those countries had been chosen by the king of Spain. Pius IX found himself with more control over the church hierarchy than any pope in history.

Third, many people shared his uncertainty with the new world. Agricultural workers and peasants belonged to families that had lived on the same land for generations, and if the land belonged to an aristocrat, their ancestors had known his ancestors, and thus a personal relationship, even a bond, existed. In an industrial age, workers had no ties to the land and no commitment to their place of work, except for a salary. Instead of working by the sun, they worked by a clock. Instead of having a relaxed winter when crops could not grow, they had to work throughout the year. They did not know their employer personally, whether he even lived in the same city, or even if the employer were an individual or an anonymous board of directors. Many industrial workers made so little money that for the first time in history, large numbers of women worked outside the home, sometimes in untoward circumstances. Even children had to work outside the home, often in factories where safety standards were minimal and rarely enforced; some boys actually worked in mines.

Aristocrats who were losing both wealth and influence to capitalists also resented this new world. Venerable titles carried no weight in the business world and progressively less in the political one.

Fourth, many religious people genuinely feared knowledge produced outside the control of the church. Scientists like the geologist Charles Lyell and the biologist Charles Darwin proved the Genesis creation account could not be taken literally, thus weakening the traditional biblical base for the doctrine of original sin. In abolishing the Garden of Eden, they were joined by nineteenth-century biblical exegetes who demonstrated the mythic nature of the Genesis account, making these religious scholars traitors in the eyes of their coreligionists. Many believers also interpreted Darwin's phrase "natural selection" as the banishing of divine activity from the physical world. Yet no religious scholar had the scientific credentials to respond to Darwin.

When traditional values are overturned, many people long for certainty. In the 1860s, Pius IX would provide it, at least for Catholics. He may have represented a disappearing past, but he was not alone in resenting its modern replacement.

Vatican I

In the mid-1860s, after his challenge to the modern world, Pius concluded that he could better make his case to all Catholics if his understanding of his office received the acknowledgment of an ecumenical council. He had been nursing the idea of a council since 1849, but curial officials had opposed this. After the definition of the Immaculate Conception, Pius began sounding out groups of bishops about a council; most agreed with the idea. In 1867 he announced that a council would meet in the Vatican in 1869.

The announcement met with enthusiastic approval from conservative Catholics whom scholars call "Ultramontanes." The word in Latin means "those on this side of the mountains," in this case, on the Italian or papal side of the Alps. At the council, the term referred to those who "backed papal authority, sometimes almost rabidly, over the entire world" (Bellitto, *General Councils*, 117–18). This sizeable and very influential group loathed democracy, opposed freedom of speech even though many of them were writers and publishers, and firmly believed that a council that would proclaim the pope's infallibility would answer all the ills of the modern age. For the Ultramontanes, there was no such thing as too much papal authority. The sword of infallibility would slay the monsters of Darwinism, Marxism, socialism, democracy, and liberalism. This, of course, would not happen, but the belief that it would energized the Ultramontanes to dominate the council. Making their task easier was a very powerful ally: Pius IX.

Pius believed in papal infallibility, and he wanted the council to define it, yet he truly wished the bishops to express their own views and freely make their own decisions, although he was confident that most bishops supported him. He worked with the Ultramontanes to assure that those sympathetic to him would run the council.

(This may disturb the modern reader, but every pope has the right to bring his own views to a council and to appoint whom he wishes to run the council. Paul III, Julius III, and Pius IV appointed all the presidents at Trent. Many popes went to councils with predetermined agendas; in 1245 Innocent IV called Lyons I with the express intent of condemning Emperor Frederick II of Sicily, which the council did.)

As noted earlier, most bishops believed the church to be infallible when making pronouncements on matters of faith and morals. They believed that there were passages in Scripture, definitions of ecumenical councils, and doctrines taught for centuries by the church that could be considered infallible, even if that term had never been used, for example, that Scripture is divine revelation. By assenting to the definition of the Immaculate Conception, the bishops had effectively extended this infallibility to the pope. Why then would any bishop oppose a conciliar definition of infallibility?

Some bishops simply disagreed with it; they did not consider the pope able to speak infallibly on his own and without the concurrence of the church. Others worried about how the document proclamation of infallibility would be worded: would the pope be personally infallible? In that case, could anyone ever disagree with him on anything? Would everything he taught be infallible, even on matters outside the faith, such as politics? Would all his teachings about the faith be infallible? If so, what would happen if facts arose to prove him wrong (evolution versus the historicity of the Garden of Eden)?

Many other opponents were "Inopportunists," an awkward neologism coined by historians to mean bishops who believed in papal infallibility but who feared that its definition at that time would be inopportune. Some European bishops, especially from France and Austria, knew it would offend their governments. American and British bishops feared it would promote anti-Catholicism at a time when Catholics were making real progress in heavily Protestant countries.

These groups of bishops would form the minority on the question of infallibility.

What If?

Pius had a limited worldview, seeing almost everything, especially anything political, through European eyes. When the American Civil War was raging, he expressed sympathy for the South, seeing the Southerners as rural aristocrats being besieged by the proletarian hordes from the industrialized North. Many French, Italian, and Spanish bishops shared his outlook. This Eurocentric myopia prevented the bishops assembled for Vatican I from recognizing and exploring new paths for the church.

For example, for the first time in church history a council welcomed bishops from the countries of North and South America—not European missionary bishops but bishops born in those countries or naturalized citizens of them. Missionary bishops, almost all European, represented the Catholics of Asia and the Pacific, and they could have offered unique perspectives on how the church functioned in cultures so diverse among themselves and, of course, so different from Europe.

Also present for the first time were bishops from largely Protestant countries, such as Great Britain and Prussia. These bishops had learned to function in a Protestant society and could give sage advice on getting along in a multireligious world, but most of the bishops at the council were not interested because they came from almost completely Catholic societies. Furthermore, Italian tradition promoted the idea that every Catholic community should have a bishop, and many Italian bishops represented small rural or mountain towns. The bishops of the larger Italian cities sometimes referred to them as *episcopetti* (mini-bishops), but they were true bishops, they had votes, and, like Pius, they loathed and feared the Italian revolution. They had no concern about getting along with non-Catholics because most had literally never met someone who was not Catholic. When, at the council, a Croatian bishop, Cardinal Joseph Strossmayer, observed that many Protestants were pious people, he was greeted with shouts of "heresy" and "the new Luther." Ecumenism would have to await Vatican II.

Another "first" at Vatican I was the presence of bishops from countries that enshrined the very freedoms that the *Syllabus of Errors* had condemned. As a group, the American bishops supported Pius and infallibility, but they accepted their country's values right from its founding when John Carroll had supported American democracy and its attendant freedoms. Millions of European immigrants had gone to America precisely to enjoy these freedoms, such as that of religion, which was especially enjoyed by Polish and Irish Catholics who had lived under Orthodox and Protestant governments that restricted the rights of Catholics and occasionally resorted to oppression. The American bishops used freedom of the press to found diocesan newspapers that the American government, unlike the "Catholic" European states, did not censor. American Catholics worked alongside Protestants and Jews, some of whom became friends and even relatives. By the time the council opened, Catholics had served in the Congress and in presidential administrations; the Catholic jurist Roger Taney had been attorney general and then chief justice of the Supreme Court; General Philip Sheridan was one of the great Union commanders of the Civil War. Many Catholics had given their lives in wars to preserve America's freedoms.

European bishops from absolutist states could have learned from the Americans how a free church can flourish in a free state, but they had no interest in doing so. In fact, their attitude was just the reverse. One of the more colorful events of the council occurred when the Spanish-born bishop of Pittsburgh, Michael Domenec, having heard one criticism too many of the U.S., announced on the council floor that one day there would be more Catholics in America than in Italy (this actually happened in the twentieth century) and that the church's future did not lie exclusively in Europe. The bishop then asserted that American Catholics were "real" Catholics who went to Mass, not like the Romans who were just nominal Catholics. This provoked a great outcry and an admonition to Domenec from the president of the council. (In fairness to Bishop Domenec, every American Catholic who goes to European Catholic countries is surprised at the empty churches. It is a matter of culture, albeit one that many American Catholics cannot understand.)

Sometimes modern, democratic attitudes did appear at the council. More than one bishop of a large diocese expressed, privately, his chagrin about his vote being worth no more than that of a bishop representing a hill town of five thousand people. "According to some calculations, the bishops of the minority [those opposed to the definition of infallibility] represented, in terms of the populations of their (in many cases, large) dioceses, over half the worldwide Catholic population" (Tanner, *Councils*, 95).

Ecclesiastically, all bishops were equal at the council, but numerous bishops objected to what they saw as the preponderance at the council of French and Italian supporters of infallibility. Indeed, not just the numbers of the Ultramontanes but also their deplorable educations disturbed many minority bishops. Hughes quotes an Irish bishop: "When I read the school of theology in which they were trained, I am not surprised that they treat every doubter as a heretic" (*Crisis*, 310). Other minority bishops lamented that some Ultramontanes came from such a limited social and political background that they could not begin to understand the modern world. But such concerns would sway neither the council nor the pope.

But if the council would not be moved by bishops bringing an unfamiliar outlook, the council did reach out, sort of, to Protestant and Orthodox Christians: "a letter was directed to all Orthodox bishops in September 1868, in which they were asked to return to Catholic unity in order to be able to participate in the council; a few days later a global letter was sent to Protestants and Anglicans. But this clumsy double procedure was generally badly received and to us, today, from an ecumenical point of view, appears as one of the saddest cases of missed opportunities" (Roger Aubert, *Hist Ch* viii, 316).

The Council

Although infallibility would be forever the symbol of Vatican I, technically that was not the reason the council met. "What Pope Pius IX had in mind in summoning the council was set forth in his bull convoking it (*Aeterni Patris*, 29 June 1868): to restate the faith in certain matters where it had been attacked or misunderstood, to review the whole matter of clerical life and its needs, to provide new safeguards for Christian marriage and the Christian education of youth, and to take up in this new age problems of the relation of Church and State and provide appropriate guidance, so as to promote peace and prosperity in national life everywhere" (Hughes, *Crisis*, 298–99). Pius did not mention infallibility nor did the preparatory committees, although almost everyone planning to attend the council knew that the matter would come up. When that happened, it would probably be in the context of a definition of the church. The Council of Trent had defined many topics and reformed many abuses, but it never dealt with the question: what is the church? Given the difficult circumstances under which Trent met, this may be understandable, but it was also unfortunate, and so Vatican I hoped to rectify it.

The preliminary work began late in 1868. The consultants selected to prepare the conciliar decrees were "sixty Romans and thirty-six foreigners, almost all of them known for their unequivocally ultramontane and antiliberal views" (Aubert, *Hist Ch* viii, 316). Few non-Europeans played any significant role; on the other hand, the minority (non-Ultramontane) bishops were also mostly Europeans, but they would have little voice in the preparation.

The council opened on December 8, the feast of the Immaculate Conception, 1869. About seven hundred bishops attended. "Among them were 60 prelates of Eastern Rites who were affiliated with Rome, for the most part from the Near East, and almost 200 fathers from outside of Europe: 121 from America, 49 of these from the United States, 41 from India and the Far East,

18 from Oceania, and 9 from the missions in Africa" (Aubert, *Hist Ch* viii, 318). But, diverse as this sounds, 52 percent of the bishops came from just two countries, France (17 percent) and Italy (35 percent). Furthermore, all five of the council presidents appointed by the pope were Italian.

At Trent, the popes had allowed the council fathers to determine the agenda, but here Pius controlled it:

> It was evident that the most important of the [conciliar] commission or committees would be the commission on doctrine, called the Deputation on the Faith, for it would take the comments of the fathers about the draft [of a proposal] into consideration and present a final version to the Pope. The Ultramontanes, headed now by the English Archbishop Henry Edward Manning of Westminster [who once spoke of "the beauty of inflexibility"], made sure that not a single member of the minority was put into this commission of twenty-four members. . . . the most important of the commissions was made unrepresentative of the Council as a whole. (Chadwick, *Popes*, 203)

In January of 1870 the bishops received a draft entitled *On the Church of Christ*. It sounded much like the *Syllabus of Errors*, and many bishops objected to it. "It was redrawn for redrafting and never came back" (ibid., 205). Part of the pressure against the document came from a modern phenomenon, the newspaper, which guaranteed that what happened in Rome quickly reached audiences in much of the world, especially Europe. The bishops soon learned the stark difference between what happened at the council and what the world at large was told happened at the council. Furthermore, the newspapers reached people immediately, so complicated theological positions went through a journalistic filter that simplified them so that the average, nontheologically trained reader could "understand" them.

No previous council had worked in such an environment, and newspapers alarmed many bishops who could not control what the reporters might write. The pope and the curia expected the bishops to maintain silence, but that was an unrealistic expectation of almost seven hundred bishops and the multitude of assistants and attendants who accompanied them. Documents were leaked as were accounts of procedures and meetings. Reporters soon recognized which council participants were reliable sources. This initially appeared threatening to the Ultramontanes who loathed freedom of the press, but since the newspapers would not disappear and since the Ultramontanes dominated the conciliar committees and often had access to the pope, their information was always more reliable and up-to-date than that of the minority. Newspaper reporters soon looked to them to get copy.

Since modern thought, especially philosophy and science, posed a challenge to traditional teaching, the Deputation on the Faith issued a document entitled On the Catholic Faith, later renamed *Dei Filius*, "Son of God" in Latin. To the surprise of many, the document did not take a harsh tone. The bishops strongly approved it in a preliminary vote. When it was submitted to them as a dogmatic constitution, 667 fathers voted unanimously to approve it on April 24, 1870.

The document's first chapter defined Catholic teaching on the nature of God; the second chapter explicated revelation and Scripture, largely following Trent; the third chapter explained the nature and necessity of faith; the fourth and last chapter established, following scholastic theology, the bounds and goals of faith and reason. The document was clear and conservative but attacked no modern thinker by name, although it did excoriate such "-isms" as atheism, pantheism, naturalism, and rationalism, the last two being understood to claim that there is no supernatural being or world and that reason takes precedence over faith. But the document in no way criticizes the power of reason; on the contrary, it acknowledges that God "has endowed the human mind with the light of reason." Following all Christian thinkers and not just Catholics, the bishops asserted that faith, also given to us by God, takes precedence over reason because faith allows people to know truths that reason could not reach. For example, the bishops believed that one could reason to the existence of God, but reason could not fathom that the one God sent his only-begotten Son to become incarnate to redeem us from our sins. Only faith could do that. The council's teaching could not be accepted by radical rationalists, but the bishops wished to clarify Catholic teaching about faith and reason, not to win over atheists.

Appended to the document are eighteen canons, in the form of "If anyone should" deny or question church teaching or say something contrary to it, "let him be anathema." In opposition to Enlightenment cynicism about miracles, one canon insists on the possibility of miracles and specifically mentions scriptural ones, but it does not enumerate any, which thus allows modern Catholic exegetes to understand some miracles as literary devices employed by the biblical authors. Another canon condemns the reception of scientific assertions that are "opposed to revealed doctrine," although once again not providing any specific example, thus avoiding an awkward question such as, does a literalist interpretation of the Bible constitute "revealed doctrine" that must be defended against scientific conclusions? The bishops were, however, careful not to condemn scientific investigations or research.

The last canon condemns the notion "that with the progress of knowledge it is sometimes possible that dogmas proposed by the Church can be given a meaning different from the one that the Church has understood and still understands." But the council said nothing about development of doctrine, which would be a major but unstated issue at Vatican II.

After the passage of *Dei Filius*, attention turned to infallibility. In January of 1870, Archbishop Manning and other Ultramontanes circulated a petition that requested the pope to put infallibility on the council's agenda. The petition garnered more than 450 signatures. The pope said that he would go along with the request of the bishops. No matter how Pius wanted the council to approve of infallibility, it was indeed desired by a sizeable majority of the bishops.

Yet the Ultramontanes wisely decided that there would be no decree specifically on infallibility but rather that the topic would be part of a constitution on the church, with the discussion focused on the role of the pope in the church. Carrying on such a discussion would be very complicated, and Hughes gives a good picture of the procedure:

> The debate was in three "acts," so to speak: (I) the discussion of the draft as a whole, 13 May to 3 June, fifteen meetings of four hours each in these three weeks, with sixty-five speakers in all, thirty-nine *pro* and twenty-six of the Minority; (II) the detailed discussion of the text dealing with the primacy of the pope, 6–13 June, five meetings, thirty-two speakers; (III) the detailed discussion of the text of the infallibility proposal, 15 June– 4 July, eleven meetings, fifty-seven speakers, thirty-five *pro*, twenty-two of the Minority. The bishops were fortified for the work before them by a folio of one hundred four pages (in Latin) that contained the amendments proposed by various of them to the original draft of the primacy section of the Constitution, and a second folio of two hundred and forty-two pages with the like amendments to the section on infallibility. With the amendments were printed the comments of the theological experts. (*Crisis*, 313)

It is not difficult to imagine what a trial this was for hundreds of middle-aged and elderly men who had to read texts and listen for hours to debates in a language that many had difficulty understanding, to say nothing of trying to keep track of the points made by more than one hundred speakers. Bishops who knew their church history no doubt longed for the simple days of Lateran I (1123), which finished its work in ten days!

The minority bishops had no specific leader, but they looked to Strassmayer of Croatia and Félix Dupanloup of Orléans in France, who had rendered valuable service to bishops in democracies and states hostile to Pius by explaining and nuancing the *Syllabus of Errors* in such a way that it seemed far less threatening to the modern world. (Even Pius IX commended him for this work.) The minority did not have the votes to stop infallibility, but they hoped to convince the pope and maybe some other bishops that it would be embarrassing if the issue were approved against so much opposition. They also repeatedly tried to convince the pope that although infallibility might be ecclesiastically acceptable, it would have political repercussions in several states, not the least of which were largely Protestant Britain, the world's leading power; newly powerful Prussia, soon to emerge as the dominant continental power; and the rising United States, which, by the 1880s, would have a larger economy than Britain. In the end, all the minority's efforts failed, and, as it happened, their fears proved unjustified.

Often overshadowed by infallibility and overlooked by historians is the section of the constitution that deals with papal primacy, which, on a practical level, has had more impact than the teaching on infallibility. The primacy had been taken for granted for centuries, and no one questioned it, but Vatican I moved it to a new level. Chapter three of *Pastor Aeternus* ("Eternal Father"), the council's Constitution on the Church, reads: "the Roman Church possesses the pre-eminence of ordinary power above all other Churches; and this power of jurisdiction of the Roman Pontiff . . . is truly immediate. . . . This is the teaching of Catholic truth. No one can deviate from it without danger to faith and salvation" (Broderick, *Documents*, 57–58).

What this wording states is that the pope has the right to intervene in any diocese at any time on any issue. For example, theoretically, a pope could transfer a priest from one parish to another, if a pope were ever to get involved in so minor a matter. But would this not reduce a bishop to being just a papal representative? Did episcopal consecration not give the bishop a unique status in his own diocese? The decree insisted that "This power of the Supreme Pontiff is far from obstructing the ordinary and immediate power of episcopal jurisdiction by which individual bishops . . . feed and rule as true shepherds the individual flocks assigned to them. Rather, the power of the bishops is protected, strengthened, and upheld by the universal shepherd" (ibid., 58). But these words could not remove the concern that the bishops' stature was being diminished, if not actually obscured, and ninety years later, at Vatican II (1962–65), episcopal collegiality with the pope would be a major concern.

Now the bishops turned to infallibility. The Ultramontanes were riding high; some extremists even hoped that the council would just acclaim an infallible pope. But many Infallibilist bishops, cautious when dealing with church teaching, wanted to move along established lines. Also, unlike some of the extreme Ultramontanes, most bishops supportive of infallibility had a pastoral concern. It bothered them that so many of their brother bishops had reservations about how the doctrine would be defined, and they tried to find a verbal formula acceptable to as many bishops as possible.

Some Ultramontanes wanted to say that the pope was personally infallible, leading to the possibility that he could claim, or people would think, that virtually everything he said was infallible. But the bishops knew that a pope might, as a theologian, hold a view that did not correspond completely to traditional teaching, as was the case with Pope Honorius I (625–38) and Monothelitism. Personal statements could not be equated with infallible official statements. Others knew about Sixtus V (1585–90), who, with no editorial expertise, had revised the Latin Vulgate and was ready to declare his botched version to be the revision demanded by the Council of Trent, a crisis averted by his death and the withdrawal of his version by Clement VIII. Furthermore, the popes were often elderly men (Pius IX was seventy-eight in 1870), whose memories might fail; would an erroneous utterance caused by weak memory be infallible? No bishop really thought that this was what Pius had intended, so they worked to find a widely acceptable formula.

On June 18, 1870, two cardinals gave major addresses. Cardinal Filippo Guidi, bishop of Bologna and a good theologian, wanted to clarify the wording and thus the meaning of the statement on infallibility. He opposed the phrase "the pope's infallibility," which could give rise to an endless number of meanings and interpretations. Instead, Guidi argued, the pope is not infallible but his dogmatic pronouncements, if properly nuanced, could be. Some poorly educated bishops did not understand Guidi's sophisticated theological approach. Several of them tried to shout him down, but he would not leave the speaker's platform. The presidents of the council supported his right to continue, a move that won the approval of many bishops who, supportive of infallibility but wary of loose wording, agreed with Guidi. After his speech, some bishops of the majority spoke with bishops of the minority "to see whether Guidi's speech did not afford the basis of an accord in which all could agree" (Butler, *Vatican Council*, 356). But one bishop genuinely loathed the speech: the Bishop of Rome.

That evening the pope summoned Guidi to his presence and accused him of desertion. The cardinal defended himself by insisting that he and the many bishops who agreed with him were following ecclesiastical tradition. In the council's most famous scene, Pius, summing up his view of the institutional church, replied, "*I* am tradition."

But despite the papal rebuke, Cardinal Guidi had correctly recognized a problem in the decree's proposed wording, and he had the satisfaction of seeing his interpretation of infallibility prevail at the council.

Cardinal Paul Cullen, archbishop of Dublin, also spoke on June 18, following Guidi and suggesting a rewording of the decree, "the form which, with a few modifications, was the one finally adopted" (ibid., 355). Cullen, however, did not speak just for himself but on behalf of some members of the Deputation on the Faith, who shared his reservations about the initial wording of the decree. It would embarrass those who had prepared the decree if the bishops rejected it that day, so it was diplomatically returned to the deputation for modification.

On July 11, a German bishop, Vincent Gasser of Brixen, gave a four-hour speech explaining what the Deputation on the Faith had prepared regarding infallibility, which would make up the fourth chapter of the Constitution on the Church. The deputation had considered an astonishing 144 proposed amendments. On July 13 the revised document was submitted to the bishops. The preliminary vote showed that 451 approved, eighty-eight disapproved, and sixty-two gave a conditional approval. Since fully one-fourth of the bishops did not give full approval, the Deputation made some minor changes for a final presentation to the bishops on July 16 and a vote on July 18.

The evening before the vote, a group of minority bishops, including such important prelates as Georges Darboy of Paris and Wilhelm Ketteler of Mainz, met with Pius to ask him to change some of the decree's wording in order to make it universally acceptable. As he had on other occasions, the pope followed the wishes of the majority of the bishops and declined to change the wording. After this disappointment and following the advice of Bishop Dupanloup of Orléans, the minority bishops decided to boycott the vote and left Rome the next morning.

On July 18, in the presence of Pius IX, the bishops voted 553 to 2 to approve *Pastor Aeternus*, the Dogmatic Constitution on the Church. The two naysayers were an Italian bishop and an American, Edward Fitzgerald of Little Rock, Arkansas. After the vote, both informed the pope of their full acceptance of the constitution.

And the exact wording of the constitution?

> We teach and define as a divinely revealed dogma that when the Roman Pontiff speaks *ex cathedra*, that is, when in the discharge of his office as shepherd and teacher of all Christians, and by virtue of his supreme apostolic authority, he defines that a doctrine concerning faith or morals must be held by the whole Church, he possesses through the divine assistance promised to him in blessed Peter that infallibility with which the divine Redeemer willed His church to be endowed in defining a doctrine concerning faith or morals; and that such definitions of the Roman Pontiff

are irreformable of themselves, not from the consent of the Church. (Broderick, *Documents*, 63)

Some bishops had concerns about the phrase "not from the consent of the Church," but most believed that since the document referred to the pope's teaching authority that he could not exercise apart from the rest of the bishops, they had not, in effect, handed over to the popes the right to create doctrine out of thin air. Furthermore, infallibility was said to be endowed by Christ upon the church, not upon the person of the pope. In fulfilling his office and under prescribed circumstances, that is, dealing with faith and morals rather than something like the political order, the pope could make an infallible pronouncement, something no other bishop could do.

Theological niceties do not make good copy, and newspapers and popular speakers began to interpret infallibility in any number of ways. Some Catholics hoped that the pope would now make a series of infallible pronouncements; others feared that he would now pronounce infallibly on areas such as science or politics. Both groups' expectations were completely wrong. Since *Pastor Aeternus*, only one pope, Pius XII in 1950, has made an infallible pronouncement.

The day after the vote on *Pastor Aeternus*, the Franco-Prussian war broke out. French and German bishops left Rome immediately; other bishops soon followed. But also leaving Rome was the French garrison that had kept Rome in papal hands. Even with fewer and fewer bishops, the council continued to meet, but on September 20, 1870, after dispersing the pitiful papal forces sent to oppose them, Italian troops entered Rome, effectively putting an end to the council. One month later, Pius officially adjourned it. Vatican I was over.

After the Council

The victorious Italian revolutionaries had a real problem: what to do with Pius IX? The Prussians had already defeated the Austrians, and when they handily defeated the French, the pope and his advisors knew that no Catholic power could intervene and that no non-Catholic power would intervene to get Rome back for the church. But Pius refused to deal with the fledgling Italian government because to do so would recognize its right to rule in Rome. He announced that he was the prisoner of King Victor Emmanuel II, and he then made himself the "Prisoner of the Vatican," the only territory in Rome that the new government would leave to the pope. The Italian government quickly passed the Law of Guarantees (1871), which provided protection for the pope's person and even his honor, exempted much papal property in Rome from taxation, and allowed Pius to keep the Swiss guards as a mini private army. Pius denounced the Law of Guarantees because, in his view, the Italian state had no right to make laws binding on him. He also forbade Catholics to vote in elections staged by the new government. Many Catholics obeyed him, and in some districts voting was very low. But this guaranteed that those who did vote were antipapal, and the initial Italian national legislature included many lawmakers strongly hostile to the papacy.

In the eight years left to him, Pius never left the grounds of the Vatican. Many Catholics worldwide sympathized with him, but all governments, including those of heavily Catholic countries, established diplomatic relations with the new Italian state. Initially lionized as a liberal and an Italian nationalist, by his death in 1878 Pius was excoriated by the people as a pope who had invited foreigners to Italian soil to keep his people oppressed. Pius had requested to be buried in a church on the edge of Rome, a good distance from the Vatican. Fearful that a funeral procession might be attacked, the cardinals tried to move his body secretly at night. But word of this slipped out, and police and even army troops of the state that Pius had so loathed had all they could do to keep a mob from throwing his coffin into the Tiber. This marked a sad end to a troubled, controversial, but in many ways impressive, pontificate that established the papacy as modern Catholics know it.

The Papal States, which had played such an immense role in papal, Catholic, and conciliar history, were now gone, never to return. Popes would no longer have the political rule that their predecessors had deemed so essential to the preservation of papal spiritual authority. Yet, now free of political entanglements, of the burdens of governing a secular state, of balancing the needs and demands of monarchs, and of suspicion that their ecclesiastical and even spiritual acts and pronouncements had a hidden political agenda, for the first time in a millennium the popes could be unfettered religious leaders. Pius IX's successors would now govern the church with an authority undreamed of just a century before and with a spiritual prestige few of their predecessors had ever enjoyed. The loss of the Papal States had not weakened the papacy but rather had given it a new, albeit different, life. Freed from involvement in Italian and European politics, the popes more and more became international figures, impacting not just Catholic Europe but much of the world. Vatican I concluded the twelve Western European councils that started with Lateran I in 1123. Ninety-two years later, a pope with an internationalist outlook would open the most ecumenical council in history, with prelates from all over the world, with the Americas heavily represented, and with native bishops from Africa and Asia.

CHAPTER NINE

The Second Vatican Council

From Vatican I to Vatican II: The Popes

Like his predecessor, Pope Leo XIII (1878–1903), a nobleman, had strong conservative leanings. He hoped to convince some European powers, such as Austria, France, and Germany, to restore, if not the Papal States, then at least Rome to the papacy, and this hope dominated his foreign policy. But no European power wished to invade Italy, and every year the Italian government grew stronger and more acceptable to the people. Leo wanted Vatican representatives at the First Hague International Peace Conference in 1899, but the Italian government, welcomed in Europe and resentful of papal opposition, prevented the Vatican from being invited. Like Pius, Leo refused to leave the Vatican.

But he also knew that the church could not completely ignore the modern world. Recognizing that the Catholic Church was indeed becoming a catholic church, he established bishoprics in many non-European countries, such as India and Japan, along with twenty new dioceses in the United States. But, in spite of the international ecclesiastical prestige these efforts won for him, he still had to accept a diminished diplomatic role.

A well-educated man, Leo believed that modern intellectual systems were flawed. One year into his reign (1879) he published the encyclical *Aeterni Patris* (Of the Eternal Father), urging Western thinkers to study the thought of Thomas Aquinas. Although few non-Catholic intellectuals turned to Aquinas, Neo-Thomism revivified Catholic theology, and sometimes in ways Leo had not anticipated; for example, scholars demonstrated that Aquinas was a very complex thinker whose thought was open to new developments. The Thomistic approach dominated Catholic theology into the 1960s, when the biblical revival began to challenge it. It still remains an important force. To protect Catholic thought, in 1893 Leo insisted that exegetes follow traditional methods of interpretation; in 1902, he founded the Pontifical Biblical Commission to watch for deviations.

Leo also worried about social conditions and the alienation of the laboring classes from the church. In 1891 he published the important encyclical *Rerum Novarum* (On New Things). Its very title had significance. Leo dealt with the status of the working class, insisting on workers' rights, a just wage, and even trade unions. Modern Catholic social thought looks to this great encyclical as its starting point. But, an aristocrat until his death, Leo distrusted democracy, although he increasingly accepted it and tried to work with democratic European states.

Perhaps the cardinals thought Leo had taken too big a step toward the modern world because in 1903 they chose for his successor Pius X (1903–14), who, like his namesake Pius IX, loathed the modern world. Rejecting Leo's attempts to work with the modern nations, Pius X insisted on the church's presumed rights everywhere and in an uncompromising fashion. This led to the cancellation of diplomatic relations with France in 1904 and to poor relations with Portugal. In Italy, however, the pope allowed the bishops, if they wished, to relax the church's ban on participation in elections.

Unlike Leo XIII, Pius X would condemn modern ideas, especially those questioning the historicity of many biblical passages (now a standard element of modern biblical exegesis). He lumped these ideas into a general category called Modernism, "the synthesis of all heresies," that he condemned in two 1907 encyclicals. Professors who expressed new ideas were dismissed; bishops censored publications that might have modernist ideas, and "each diocese was immediately to establish a 'Vigilance Council' whose function was to inform the bishops of anything or anybody possibly tainted with heresy" (O'Malley, *What Happened*, 70). Priests had to take an oath disavowing Modernism. All this set back Catholic biblical scholarship for decades; the oath was not lifted until 1967 by Pope Paul VI. Pius X soon established a secret society to check for orthodoxy; among those denounced was an obscure church historian named Angelo Giuseppe Roncalli, the future John XXIII. Benedict XV, Pius's successor, found among the papal papers a secret denunciation of himself. One of Modernism's chief sins was a "most pernicious doctrine that would make the laity a factor of progress in the church." Pius X's own view was that "the one duty of the multitude is to allow themselves to be led and, like a docile flock, to follow the pastors" (O'Malley, *What Happened*, 56, 69).

Yet, for all his fear of new thinking, Pius accomplished much in the church. He restored Gregorian chant to its former beauty, he encouraged frequent and even daily communion, and he inaugurated a reform of the Code of Canon Law, which put much stress on papal power and viewed the bishops as just papal appointees.

At the time of Pius's death, all Europe anticipated a major war to be fought with weapons never used before: machine guns, aeroplanes, tanks, and submarines. Benedict XV (1914–22), a cardinal for only three months before his election, had had a long diplomatic career. He quickly learned that the Italian state would prevent his gaining any real diplomatic influence in Europe. He made a peace proposal, which the combatants ignored, and the victorious powers barred him from the peace conference at Versailles in 1919. But Benedict never gave up. He offered his support to the League of Nations, and he effected an increase in the number of countries (fourteen to twenty-seven) that had diplomatic relations with the Vatican. The pope also saw to it that extremely competent men got experience as Vatican diplomats. Thanks to this good man, his two immediate successors gained the experience they would need to deal, as best as one could, with the Western dictators and Russian communists. Influenza carried Benedict off at the age of sixty-seven.

Benedict's pontificate witnessed the passing of monarchical, Catholic Europe as a result of World War I. Monarchies disappeared or became constitutional monarchies. No longer would Catholic rulers try to interfere in church affairs, but no longer could popes call on monarchs who were believing Catholics and thought the state should support the church. Now the popes would have to deal with governments of various kinds. Benedict lived long enough to glimpse the immediate future: the Bolshevik Revolution, which destroyed an Orthodox monarchy and dynasty.

A former diplomat, Pius XI (1922–39) saw the "modern" world at its worst: Benito Mussolini, Adolf Hitler, Josef Stalin, and other totalitarians. Pius attributed many of Europe's problems to rising secularism, and he hoped to make the church a stronger voice. He held frequent eucharistic congresses and wrote encyclicals supporting Catholic education and workers' rights, hoping to curb Communist influence in European trade unions. He also encouraged lay activity in the church, an approach that would bear fruit at Vatican II. To protect the rights of the church, he concluded concordats with twenty states, these concordats spelling out the rights of the church in society. Some concordats worked well; not surprisingly, the one with Nazi Germany was violated by Hitler whenever he wished. Accepting that the Italian state would not go away, Pius negotiated with Mussolini the Lateran Treaty of 1929; this created Vatican City as an independent state within Italy, which Pius now recognized. The "Prisoner of the Vatican" was technically no more, although Pius himself stayed within the Vatican confines.

Several right-wing dictators were Catholic (at least by upbringing), and Pius initially thought he could work with Mussolini, Hitler, Francisco Franco in Spain, and António de Salazar in Portugal. Pius hoped that they would help restrain the militantly atheist Soviet Communists whose subjugation of the Russian Orthodox Church made it clear what would happen wherever they might gain power. But Pius steadily found himself disagreeing with the Nazis as they spread their control over every aspect of German life, including, when possible, the churches. Furthermore, as the Nazi racial policies became better known, Pius concluded that Nazism was the equivalent of a pagan religion. In 1937, he condemned Nazism in an encyclical, copies of which were smuggled into Germany and read from Catholic pulpits.

Outside of diplomacy and politics, Pius XI had both conservative and liberal sides. He eased the restrictions on supposed Modernists but without canceling the oath. He allowed negotiations between Catholics and Anglicans but strongly opposed the growing, largely Protestant, ecumenical movement. He forbade Catholics "to be present or take part in any non-Catholic religious service," which meant that Catholics could not attend an Orthodox baptism, a Protestant funeral, or a Jewish wedding.

Although Pius also tried to strengthen the church's missions, especially in East and South Asia, the European situation overwhelmed all else. As his death approached in 1939, Pius feared that war was inevitable, no matter what he did to avert it. His successor would have to deal with it.

Pius XII (1939–58) had served as his predecessor's secretary of state. Committed to diplomacy, he too tried but failed to avert the looming war. After the German invasion of Poland, he tried to keep Italy out of the war, but Mussolini joined the Nazis in June of 1940. The pope found himself in an impossible situation, especially after the Americans entered the war and decisively turned the tide for the Allies, who began pressuring Pius to condemn their enemies. But how could he denounce Germany and Italy when there were Catholics fighting on both sides? Furthermore, the Nazis ruled many Catholics in both Eastern and Western Europe, while the U.S. and Great Britain had allied themselves with Stalin's Soviet Union, and Pius well knew what a Soviet victory would mean for the Catholics of Eastern Europe. After the war some critics accused him of not condemning the Nazi treatment of the Jews and thus doing nothing to stop the Holocaust. His defenders pointed out that he did condemn Nazi racial policies, even if he did not use the word "Jews," and he sheltered the Roman Jews in the Vatican during the German occupation of the city. Ever the diplomat, Pius opposed the Allies' demand for unconditional surrender, correctly realizing it would prolong the war.

However annoyed the Allies might have been with him during the war, when it was over and Soviet Union became the enemy, they applauded the pope's strong anti-Communist stance.

His experience with the European dictators, before and after the war, caused Pius to be the first pope to commend democracy, acknowledging that it aligned best with the dignity and liberty of citizens, a far cry from previous papal denunciations of democracy.

In purely ecclesiastical affairs, Pius encouraged biblical scholars to use modern historical methods, although scholars had more leeway to use modern techniques on the Old Testament than on the New. He wrote an encyclical that clarified Catholic teaching on the church as the Mystical Body of Christ. Pius encouraged a liturgical revival, internationalized the college of cardinals, and established bishoprics in Asia. Thanks to television and movie newsreels, Pius XII became the first pope to be physically recognizable to Catholics worldwide.

Pius also became the first, and so far the only, pope since Vatican I to make an infallible definition. In 1950 he affirmed of the Virgin Mary that "when the course of her earthly life had ended," she had been assumed body and soul into heaven. Although some Catholic theologians had reservations about this and Protestants pointed out its lack of a biblical foundation, Pius XII infallibly defined the Assumption and made it a part of Catholic doctrine.

But Pius too fell victim to anti-Modernist fears. His 1950 encyclical *Humani Generis* spoke of original sin, "which proceeds from a sin actually committed by an individual Adam and which through generations is passed on to all and is in everyone as his own" (Mioni, *Popes Against*, 362). He warned about theologians who were "desirous of novelties" and too ecumenical. During his pontificate several prominent theologians, such as the Frenchmen Yves Congar, Pierre Teilhard de Chardin, and Henri de Lubac, along with the German Karl Rahner and the American John Courtney Murray, found their works questioned and themselves forbidden to teach and/or publish. Pius XII emphasized papal authority and frowned on those who did not support it wholeheartedly.

Pius XII became very ill late in life and turned to questionable remedies that occasionally had untoward side effects. By 1957 he was making almost a speech a day, reading and writing at a frenetic pace. He spoke of visions, and when he telephoned someone in the Vatican, he expected the person receiving the call to kneel down. This was a sad end for a sincere, hardworking man who had led his church through the difficulties of World War II and the Communist advances of the 1950s.

Prelude to Vatican II:
The Changing World and the Changing Church

Every ecumenical council occurs at a unique point in history, but Vatican II took place in a world unlike that of any of its predecessors. Most notably, "divinely appointed" emperors and kings had faded into history. Somewhat ironically, the ruler of a minuscule city-state, completely surrounded by the city of Rome, was the last absolute monarch in Europe.

The Western European nations (Great Britain, France, Spain, Italy, and Germany) had lost much of their ability for self-determination. By the time the council opened most of their colonies, especially in Africa and the Near East, had become independent states. The Soviet megalith in Eastern Europe threatened them, and they could not stop it on their own, relying instead upon a young nation on the Western side of the Atlantic Ocean. The only industrial nation to survive World War II with its cities, factories, and roads intact, the United States, the largely Protestant democracy mocked by European bishops at Vatican I, now dominated the world. America exported its goods but also its ideas. Convinced that democracy offered the best defense against Communism, they promoted it endlessly and often with success, as in West Germany and Japan. The values loathed by the Ultramontanes— freedom of speech, assembly, the press, and religion—spread throughout Catholic Europe and, to a lesser extent, in Catholic Latin America. Increasingly Catholics came to accept and appreciate these values and, inevitably, to wonder why, officially at least, their church opposed them.

The question of values became acute in 1960 when the largely Protestant U.S. elected a Catholic president. During the campaign, some Protestants raised the question of how John F. Kennedy could govern a country committed to those values when his church opposed them. Kennedy said that he would not allow his religion to determine his duty as president, a statement that no other presidential candidate ever had to make. In an increasingly democratic world, the old, condemnatory attitudes seemed out-of-touch and even oppressive.

Not just more democratic, the modern world abounded in scientific and technological advances. People ate better, and these better diets, along with medical advances, allowed them to live longer and healthier lives. Earthlings were entering outer space, and images of Earth from outer space showed that we really do inhabit together a small planet in a vast space. Air travel shrunk the world, and if people could not travel to exotic places, they could see them on television. People became increasingly aware of their common humanity; Catholics, Protestants, and Jews increasingly intermixed and even intermarried; attitudes that separated people, such as requiring Catholics to get a bishop's permission to attend a Jewish wedding, seemed outdated and shortsighted. Universal education in democracies was wiping out illiteracy and allowing people to get better jobs, live better materially, and explore new facets to their lives. Modernity increasingly seemed like something good to more and more people.

Many social changes occurred, but few would impact the church more than the combination of democracy and education. Catholics in democracies enjoyed increasingly higher standards of education. When Vatican II opened in 1962, for the first time in history the pope and bishops had to deal with educated laity, both men and women. More and more of them truly wanted to contribute to the church they loved, but not just as members of parish social groups but as educated people whose voices deserved attention. Inevitably, educated laity questioned procedures taken for granted by ecclesiastical leadership: Why do priests say Mass in a language no one can understand? Why do authorities silence theologians instead of letting them air their ideas, to which the authorities can respond? Why do celibate clergy not listen to laity on matters like sex and marriage? Educated, democratic Catholics were not the "docile flock" so desired by Pius X.

Not only were Catholics better educated but the methods and content of education had changed. Science and business courses focused on the material world, challenging not only the traditional arts education common to Catholic institutions but also the way in which Catholics had traditionally done theology, relying upon a medieval, static worldview. Anthropologists demonstrated that primitive cultures have different understandings of right and wrong and that Western ethical ideas are hardly intrinsic to humanity. Sociologists demonstrated the impact that group membership has on individual behavior, including moral behavior. Psychology showed that many human traits are caused by upbringing, that humans are moved by unconscious forces they cannot always recognize, and that the desire for money, sex, and power is normal rather than a consequence of the concupiscence caused by original sin. Moral theologians could not ignore these new disciplines and quickly demonstrated that they could be adapted to Catholic teaching but only with great difficulty to traditional scholastic norms.

These new disciplines had another effect: they raised the question of where values and teachings came from, that is, who formulated and articulated them. Women scholars quickly pointed out that "universal values" and "eternal verities" were in fact all produced by dead, white, European men. It did not take long for Catholic women to note that all Catholic teaching had been largely formulated by celibate, medieval, white, European men. Obviously there is no reason why a medieval celibate man could not articulate ideas and doctrines that have value to modern women, but in the 1960s, when Vatican II met, popes and bishops found themselves and their teachings being challenged in democracies in new and very difficult ways.

But the most important change resulting from the twentieth century was the attitude toward change. People accepted it as a normal and inevitable part of life; indeed, change was a sign of life. Naturally, they liked some of the changes and disliked others, but they could not accept that the church never changes or that denunciations could stop change. If the church wished to impact the modern world, that required living in it, understanding it, and working with it. The church remained a tremendous force for good but now had to work with democracies that enshrined the freedoms condemned in the *Syllabus*. This required an attitudinal sea change, and John XXIII recognized that.

Serious changes had also occurred in how Catholic theologians and scholars viewed the church and the world. Neo-Thomism may have revived medieval scholasticism, but great Neo-Thomists like Étienne Gilson insisted that scholasticism was not closed or rigid and that Catholic scholars had to take advantage of new research methods. Jacques Maritain insisted that Catholicism could keep its identity and still adapt to the world and that "it was silly to try to remake the world in a medieval pattern . . ." (O'Malley, *What Happened*, 79). The German theologian Karl Rahner brought modern philosophical ideas into his understanding of Thomism. The French theologian Henri de Lubac had emphasized the church as a mystery rather than a juridical institution.

Other Catholic scholars also returned to the past, but they jumped over the scholastics and went to the Fathers of the Church, who often linked their theology to spiritual life and values in contrast to the heavily academic scholastics. These patristic scholars also pointed out that many things the church had "always" taught were unknown to the Fathers or often unknown in the form enshrined by later theology. It was not by chance that several prominent French patristic scholars found themselves under investigation and even silenced. But the study of the Fathers continued.

Modern biblical scholarship threatened traditional views even more. Modern New Testament scholarship demonstrated that the gospels were not lives of Jesus but rather theological accounts of his person, teachings, and public career. Some miracles were understood not as physical events but as literary devices created by the gospel writers. More and more, biblical exegetes understood Jesus in a Jewish and historical context. New Testament texts traditionally thought to support church teaching, such as Jesus instituting all seven sacraments himself, were quietly discarded in favor of the idea of the historical development of doctrines. Exegetes rejected the traditional "proof-text" method, by which a text was taken from its biblical context to support a doctrine, for example, the "I Am Who Am" passage in Exodus 3:14 as a philosophical explanation of the divine nature (still taught in U.S. Catholic universities in the 1960s, as this author can attest).

In sum, much of the worldview of twenty previous ecumenical councils had disappeared by the time of Vatican II. The church's teaching remained, but its understanding and formulation had to be changed, as John XXIII would often say. For example, original sin may not have been caused by two prehistoric people eating a piece of fruit, but the doctrine could still teach that by their own actions, humans estrange themselves from God and stand in need of divine grace for salvation. No longer did Catholic scholars have to defend the historicity of the Garden of Eden.

John XXIII recognized that the church was living in a very new world, and he feared that Catholicism would lose its beneficial influence in that world if the church did not change. But he soon found out that many Catholics did not want the church to change because they believed that the church could not change, in spite of the now wide acceptance of the principle of development of doctrine. The American Jesuit theologian John Courtney Murray (1904–67) would point out that at Vatican II "development of doctrine [was] *the* issue under all issues" (O'Malley, *What Happened*, 39). Murray also acknowledged that the most difficult task was convincing the bishops that the church does change and that there is nothing wrong with that.

John XXIII and the Calling of Vatican II

Unlike many of his predecessors, Angelo Giuseppi Roncalli (1881–1963) came from a peasant family. A good student, he entered the seminary at Bergamo but soon went on to Rome, where he earned a doctorate in theology at the age of twenty-three. He taught church history at the Bergamo seminary, where he found himself suspect of heresy by the secret society Pius X had established to check on orthodoxy. After Pius X's death, he was given appointments by Benedict XV and Pius XI, who in 1934 made him apostolic delegate to Turkey and Greece. This post brought him into friendly relations with Muslims and Orthodox Christians. When the German armies occupied Greece (1941–44), Roncalli worked hard to prevent the deportation of Greek Jews to concentration camps. His experiences in this diplomatic post led him to see Jews, Muslims, and Orthodox Christians not as infidels and schismatics but as good, often pious, people, loved by God and hopeful of salvation—and this at a time when many Catholics believed and taught that, except by a special divine dispensation, only Catholics could be saved.

After World War II, Roncalli was the papal observer at UNESCO, where he again came in contact with diverse people and diverse beliefs. This good man could see the good in others, including people of Asia and Africa who stood outside Abrahamic religions. In 1953, when Roncalli was seventy-two, Pius XII gave him a cardinal's hat and appointment as patriarch of Venice so he could spend his last days in his northern Italian homeland. The new patriarch engaged in historical writing, and his understanding of history and the historical process would greatly influence him in his papacy and in his calling of Vatican II.

When Pius XII died in 1958, the cardinals found themselves divided on his successor. As the balloting continued, the cardinals began moving toward a compromise candidate, an elderly pope who would be a caretaker and not take many initiatives. On the twelfth ballot, they chose Roncalli, who took the name John XXIII. He knew why he had been chosen and actually commented in public that popes of his age rarely had long reigns, causing some understandable squirming on the part of the cardinals.

To a generation of Catholics grown up with Pius XII, John did not appear to be "papal." Pius was tall and thin; John short and pudgy. Pius was an ascetic; John smoked cigarettes and enjoyed a martini. Pius seemed remote; John loved and was loved by everyone. He visited Rome's penitentiaries, and hardened criminals knelt and wept as they asked for his blessing. When Jacqueline Kennedy visited Rome, John fretted over how he should address her ("Mrs. Kennedy," "Madame President"), only to spontaneously greet her as "Jacqueline" and give her an embrace.

But the new pope had no intention of being an affable caretaker. He truly feared for the situation of the church in the ever-changing modern world and felt an obligation to do something about it. Eschewing the "Rome knows all" view, he truly wanted and needed to know what the world's bishops thought. He also wanted to know what the world at large thought. Both the communist and democratic powers responded positively to this pope who wanted to understand and not condemn the modern world.

Accepting that he would indeed not have a long pontificate, in January of 1959, only three months after his election, John announced that he would call an ecumenical council. This alarmed some conservative Vatican prelates; one cardinal actually told John that it could take up to ten years just to plan the council. The elderly pope just smiled and went ahead with his plans.

Shortly after the announcement of the council, John had established a group to plan for it. On May 17, 1959, he formally announced what came to be called the Pre-Preparatory Commission of ten members, almost all officials who worked in Rome; all of the Roman congregations were represented. By July the pope had decided the council would be Vatican II, definitely not a continuation of the abruptly ended Vatican I.

John consulted all the bishops about the council and received two thousand written proposals and suggestions for actions the church could take. "The majority of these writings demonstrated surprise and disorientation. Rome was not issuing orders but asking for collaboration!" (Alberigo, *Brief History*, 12). The Pre-Preparatory Commission sorted the material.

On June 5, 1960, John established a Central Planning Commission and ten commissions to deal with thematic areas, all but one headed by curial cardinals. The exception was the Secretariat for Christian Unity, headed by Cardinal Augustin Bea, a German Jesuit biblical scholar who knew of ecumenism via biblical conferences; he was also an old Vatican hand, which likewise recommended him. While these commissions dealt with theological problems, other Vatican officials had to deal with very practical ones, such as arranging for two thousand bishops—all of whom brought at least a secretary and a theological advisor—to travel to Rome and to be housed there. The cost stretched the Vatican treasury, but several North American dioceses provided help.

John XXIII made it clear that this would be a truly ecumenical council by inviting observers from other traditions without even the hint that they must return to the fold in order to be admitted. He also wanted it to be pastoral, focusing on renewing the life of the church and of the faithful rather than just making pronouncements on faith and morals along with canons and anathemas. Indeed, Vatican II would be the first council to issue no anathemas, relying instead upon the positive messages of its documents. John also wanted the assembled bishops to be active participants, "leaving behind the attitude of passivity that had characterized the Catholic episcopate, especially after the definitions of the primacy and infallibility of the pope" (Alberigo, *Brief History*, 14).

John set the opening date of the council for October 11, 1962. Before the council opened, the bishops received copies of documents prepared by the theological commissions. Taking seriously John's injunction to be active, many bishops expressed dissatisfaction with the documents along with their fear that conservative Roman clerics would frustrate the pope's goals. Two important cardinals, the Belgian Léon-Joseph Suenens and the Canadian Paul-Émile Léger, met with John to express their concerns about this. John listened to them.

"The work [of the council] was to be directed by a Council of Presidents (ten, later twelve, cardinals), assisted by a general secretary. Each commission was to be headed by a cardinal designated by the pope, who would also appoint eight bishops, one-third of the twenty-four members, while the other two-thirds—or sixteen bishops—would be elected by the council" (Alberigo, *Brief History*, 16). The pope wanted the bishops to have a major voice in who would be on the commissions that would draw up the documents.

Vatican II would also see the presence of experts, *periti* in Latin, who would provide theological advice to the bishops. Eventually more than eight hundred *periti* participated. John saw to it that several prominent European theologians who had been silenced or warned about their writings were invited, including Rahner, whose works were still under scrutiny when the council opened. Most theologians came as advisors to bishops; for example, Rahner advised Cardinal Franz König of Vienna. In a surprise move, the very conservative Cardinal Francis Spellman of New York invited John Courtney Murray to come. Despite the cloud hanging over Murray's writings, Spellman wanted to bring the best American theologian, just as the Europeans were bringing their best. The *periti* often held informative meetings about modern theology for the bishops, most of whom were glad to learn about the new trends and methods.

Not included in formal Vatican planning, but expected nonetheless, were more than one thousand journalists, now representing radio and television networks as well as print news organizations. Reporting on the council was constant, and with two thousand bishops along with secretaries, advisors, *periti*, and lesser functionaries, "leaks" became inevitable. One writer, an American priest named Frank Murphy, wrote "under the pseudonym Xavier Rynne and published in *The New Yorker* (magazine) . . . a gossipy but engrossing account of what was going on . . ." (O'Malley, *What Happened*, 34–35). Murphy originally got his information secondhand, but in 1963 Pope Paul VI appointed him as a *peritus*, and his information became more reliable. "The fact that . . . Murphy, a priest in good standing, felt constrained to adopt a pseudonym speaks volumes about the intimidation the Holy Office could bring to bear" (ibid., 152–53). Murphy and others guaranteed that Vatican II would work more openly than past councils, which delighted many of the bishops who objected to the proposed secrecy.

The First Session (1962)

On October 11, 1962, John XXIII solemnly opened Vatican II. Present were 1,041 European bishops, the majority at previous councils but now less than half the attendees. Representing the Americas were 956 bishops; 379 represented Africa; just over 300 represented Asia. John's inaugural address, *Gaudet Mater Ecclesia* (Mother Church Rejoices), laid out the pope's hopes for the council. He wanted the bishops to explore how the church could interact with the world in an open, indeed friendly, way. The church must discern the signs of the times and reject those "prophets of doom" who see "in the modern era nothing but transgression and disaster, and [claim] that our age has become worse than previous ones." He insisted that the church faithfully preserve the deposit of faith, but "even this must be elaborated and presented according to the forms of inquiry and literary expression proper to modern thought. The substance of the ancient doctrine of the *depositum fidei* is one thing, and the manner of presenting it is another." John wanted the council to use a pastoral approach even in teaching doctrine, "showing the validity of doctrine instead of issuing condemnations" (Alberigo, *Brief History*, 22–23). Finally, he insisted that the council be "ecumenical" by being open to all Christians, open to all the faithful of every religion, and open to all people of goodwill. This council would address the world.

John's attitude was routinely summed up by the Italian word *aggiornamento*, which meant "bringing up to date," and did not imply abandoning the goods of the past.

When the council set to work, it was governed by regulations set down by the pope, who established ten (later eleven) commissions to prepare and submit texts to the council; almost all committee heads were those who had headed the preparatory commissions, but the bishops would vote for most of the members. Immediately the influence of the *periti* surfaced. Hubert Jedin, historian of Trent, had advised some European bishops to be vigilant about who served on the council's committees, since they would wield much power. On October 13, the preparatory commissions proposed candidates for the council's commission and wanted an immediate election, believing it would favor the Roman members of the preparatory commissions. But French and German bishops insisted on a delay so that the bishops could get to know each other before voting. When the bishops did vote, many members of the preparatory commission were not elected, and the conciliar commissions better reflected the council's participants.

The bishops first took up the document on the liturgy. The proposed document won much approval, although it insisted on the primacy of Latin in the Mass. Many bishops wanted a vernacular liturgy for several reasons. First, the document itself had spoken of the importance of having everyone present participate actively in the liturgy. How could this be done, bishops asked, when the priest had his back to the people and used a language they did not understand? That forced the people into a passive role. Second, if the council was open to the world, then it should prove it by allowing all languages, including non-European ones, to be used. Third, the local language reflected the local church and thus the importance of the local diocese and bishop.

Many bishops spoke on this issue, but none made more impact than Maximos IV Saigh, a Melkite bishop from Syria, who reminded the bishops that Latin was the language not of the universal church but of the Roman rite. He insisted that all languages are liturgical languages and that "Christ spoke the language of his contemporaries." If Jesus used his own language, why should modern Catholics not follow his lead? The document eventually included this statement: "Let it be left to episcopal conferences in different parts of the world . . . to propose to the Holy See the degree and modes for admitting vernacular languages into the liturgy" (quoted in O'Malley, *What Happened*, 132).

Another proposed change dealt with the Liturgy of the Word, that is, the scriptural readings in the Mass. Before Vatican II, Catholics could "make Mass" by getting to church in time for the offertory. Hearing the scriptural readings was not necessary to fulfill the attendance obligation, something that scandalized Protestants, who rightly considered this a diminishment of the Scripture for worship. Liturgical *periti* urged a change, making it clear that the scriptural readings were an essential part of the liturgy. To some bishops, this smacked of Protestantism. "Many bishops were wary of liturgical changes, and some harbored suspicions about the orthodoxy of the liturgical experts" (O'Malley, *What Happened*, 128). But this change won approval from the majority of bishops.

Many bishops also objected to the document's juridical tone and institutional overtones, insisting that the vitality of the liturgy should be emphasized.

On November 14, the bishops voted on the basic soundness of the proposed document, subject to revisions by the Liturgical Commission. Ninety-seven percent of them approved, and Vatican II had just changed how Catholics would worship worldwide. Unlike theological statements, liturgical change was immediate and visible. The council took its final vote on *Sacrosanctum Concilium*, the Constitution on the Sacred Liturgy, on December 4, 1963, with the approval of Pope Paul VI.

(The vote provided an amusing anecdote. Cardinal James McIntyre of Los Angeles opposed a vernacular liturgy but, due to his poor Latin, misunderstood the nature of the vote. Having voted to approve the decree, he confidently told a colleague, "Well, I guess we fixed those liturgists today" [Sullivan, *101 Questions*, 34].)

Next the bishops received from the Doctrinal Commission a schema on "The Two Sources of Revelation." Its first chapter "presented Scripture and Tradition as essentially two distinct sources. . . . [It also declared] that the task of preserving, defending, and authentically interpreting the two sources fell exclusively to the ecclesiastical Magisterium, by which was meant the pope and the Roman congregations" (O'Malley, *What Happened*, 143). The second chapter spoke of modes of interpreting Scripture. The third chapter understood the Old Testament exclusively as pointing to Christ and with no ecumenical concern about how Jews might understand it. The fourth chapter insisted on the historical accuracy of the gospels, including the words of Jesus, which, in fact, differed in some of the gospels, such as the two versions of the Lord's Prayer in Matthew and Luke. The fifth chapter dealt with the versions of Scripture, exalting the Latin Vulgate and warning about how laypeople might misunderstand the Bible if they read it in the vernacular without recourse to church teaching. "The authority of the Magisterium was an overriding theme of the whole schema" (ibid., 144).

Opposition to the proposed document was immediate, vocal, and deep. Critics pointed out that the Council of Trent had specifically avoided using the phrase "Two Sources" and instead spoke of the Gospel of Christ as the one source to which Scripture and tradition give witness; the notion of two sources was post-Tridentine. The document had a negative tone throughout. It took a cautious approach toward Scripture in the life of the church. An American cardinal, Joseph Ritter of St. Louis, said it cast suspicion on modern Catholic biblical scholars; scriptural and theological *periti* strongly opposed the document and told their bishops so. Maximos IV Saigh lamented the document's lack of ecumenical awareness as did a Belgian bishop, Joseph De Smedt, who spoke on behalf of the Secretariat for Christian Unity.

But the Doctrinal Commission did not back down, and on November 20 the bishops voted 1,368 to drop the text from the immediate agenda, 822 for further discussion, and 19 ballots were ruled invalid on technical grounds. Of those making a decision, 60 percent had voted against the text, a strong rebuke to the Doctrinal Commission. Then the commission members seized a technicality. The regulations guiding the voting insisted that a document needed a two-thirds vote for approval but also for rejection. That meant that a document rejected by 60 percent of the bishops would continue to be the basis for discussion. On November 21, after "hearing appeals from leaders of the majority, John XXIII decided to protect the Council's freedom and . . . decreed that the two-thirds majority needed for approval of a text was not required to reject it" (Alberigo, *Brief History*, 27). Importantly, the pope insisted the document be reworked not by the Doctrinal Commission alone but also by the Secretariat for Christian Unity, guaranteeing an ecumenical approach. As O'Malley puts it, "The importance of the vote of November 20 and of the papal intervention of November 21 can hardly be exaggerated" (*What Happened*, 151).

The last document taken up in Session I was *De Ecclesia* or On the Church. This too came from the Doctrinal Commission. It was wide-ranging, but Bishop De Smedt, who had played a role in the dispute over the scriptural document, denounced *De Ecclesia* for triumphalism, clericalism, and juridicism, which fostered a pyramidal image of the church in which all moves from the top down and implies that the vast majority of Catholics contribute little or nothing to the church. (The document actually referred to the members of the church as "subjects" [*subditi* in Latin].) De Smedt also insisted that a juridical approach did not adhere to the council and the pope's pastoral emphasis. Other bishops soon joined in, and a crisis was approaching.

Another major issue was the nature of the episcopal office within the church. For the juridically minded, the bishops were just papal appointees, an approach many bishops resented. They acknowledged their fidelity and obedience to the pope, but the episcopal office went back to the early church. (The word *epískopos* appears in the New Testament; the word "pope" did not come to mean the Bishop of Rome exclusively until the seventh century.) Many bishops and theologians wanted a statement on collegiality, that is, on the bishops as ordained members of the episcopal college. This did not mean conciliarism because the college of bishops naturally included the Bishop of Rome, but it did mean the episcopal office had an inherent dignity.

With the encouragement of the pope, on December 4 the Belgian cardinal Suenens proposed a new view of the church. Suenens urged the bishops to look at the church in two ways: within itself and in relation to others. Abandoning the juridical approach, which was necessarily exact and detailed, Suenens spoke of the church within itself as a mystery, as the French theologian Henri de Lubac, a favorite of John XXIII, had begun to do in his book *The Splendor of the Church*. The church could be understood only by faith and reflected the salvific life of Christ, who still lives within and guides his church. In relation to others, Suenens asked what the church is saying to "brothers and sisters not now visibly united with it" and what is it saying to the modern world about poverty, oppression, social justice, and war and peace. Many bishops applauded Suenens's presentation. One rather cautious cardinal held back, but only for a day; then Cardinal Giovanni Montini rejected the proposal of the Doctrinal Commission and supported Suenens.

Through Suenens, John XXIII won the day. The document on the church would be reworked and reworked until it emerged, two years later, as the council's signature document. Thanks to the pope and the cardinal, Vatican II would produce a second document on the church in the modern world.

On December 8, John XXIII adjourned the council's first session. He would not live to see the second one.

Knowing that stomach cancer gave him only months to live, John created a Coordinating Commission, which included Suenens and others outside the curia, to make sure that the work of the council would continue during its recess. It overhauled the agenda, mandating revisions of the other drafts according to the pastoral priorities brought to the fore in Session I. From this commission would come the recommendation for a separate document on the church in the modern world. The council also reworked *De Ecclesia*, focusing on the mystery of the church.

In his last months, John produced one of the great documents of Catholic history, his encyclical *Pacem in Terris*, the first papal encyclical written to "all men of good will" and not just to bishops or Catholics. As the title suggests, the document dealt with world peace, naturally condemning war in a nuclear age but also focusing on the sources of conflict, such as widespread poverty and denial of human rights. It won the praise of both Soviet premier Nikita Khrushchev and John F. Kennedy. John XXIII published the encyclical on April 11; he died on June 3, 1963.

Never had so brief a pontificate so changed the church and the world.

A brief conclave elected Cardinal Giovanni Batista Montini to be Pope Paul VI (1963–78) on June 21. Unlike John, he came from a wealthy family. An omnivorous reader, his library contained "his now legendary ninety crates of books" (Kelly, *Popes*, 322). He served as an assistant to Cardinal Eugenio Pacelli, the papal secretary of state, and remained close to him after he became Pius XII. A man who liked to see both sides, Montini was not rigorous enough for Pius's other associates. When he defended a suspect French theologian, "the inevitable happened. The Pope's mind was poisoned against Montini by a whispering campaign, and he was dismissed from his Vatican post and kicked upstairs to be archbishop of Milan. This post invariably carried with it a cardinal's hat, but Pius XII signaled his displeasure by withholding it. In this way, Montini, who was increasingly being seen as the inevitable choice for the next pope, was deliberately excluded from the succession" (Duffy, *Saints*, 268). Less than two months after his election, the man who did become pope appointed Montini a cardinal in December of 1958. He helped John with the preparations for Vatican II, although he did not play a great role in the first session, publicly speaking only twice.

Yet his support for the council helped him to be elected pope because most members of the college of cardinals, internationalized by Pius XII and by John XXIII, supported the council. After his election, Paul VI said in his first message: "The most substantial portion of this pontificate will be occupied by the continuation of the ecumenical council Vatican II." But how would he relate to the council?

With the infallibility of hindsight, historians know Paul to have been a man who wanted, where possible, unanimity, and he micromanaged to achieve it. John XXIII made but two interventions in the council, but Paul intervened constantly. Since the minority at the council turned out to be the conservatives and since Paul wanted unity, he often found himself cautiously trying to slow down the council's pace. He used his authority to modify council documents even after they had been approved by the bishops, but Paul maintained an unwavering support of the council and, after it closed, to the implementation of its decrees.

The Second Session (1963)

The second session opened with two outstanding questions on the bishops' minds. First, how would the new pope interact with the council? Second, what to do about the troublesome decree on the church?

The first question received a quick answer. Many bishops had complained about the slow pace of conciliar discussions, so Paul VI appointed four moderators to guide the council's discussions. Unfortunately, he did not make clear the relationship of the moderators to the presidents to the Coordinating Committee and, of course, to himself. Yet this unclarity did not prevent the council from making progress on the decrees.

The pope opened the council on September 29. The Doctrinal Commission had reworked the decree on the church, and the bishops voted overwhelmingly to use its document as a basis for discussion. By this time most bishops were comfortable with imaging the church not as a juridical, clerical hierarchy but as the entire People of God, and all agreed on the universal call to holiness. Bishops from Latin America and other areas that had a shortage of clergy argued for a restoration of the permanent diaconate (known in the early church), an office open even to married men; some bishops feared this would weaken the notion of clerical celibacy.

But many bishops were unsure how to formulate the wording about collegiality. Throughout October the bishops debated this, with many insisting on the sacramentality of the episcopal office. Alberigo well sums up what this meant:

> Through this sacrament a new bishop becomes part of the body of bishops, the episcopal college, with the purpose and authority not only of administering the sacraments but also of teaching and governing the Church. He exercises this power within his own local Church, but, in communion with the other bishops and the pope, he also exercises it in regard to the universal Church. (*Brief History*, 44)

Yet some conservative bishops saw even this as a weakening of papal authority.

The vivid discussions and the constant reworking of the document produced on October 14 a text with five issues on clerical office, four dealing with the episcopacy and one with the diaconate. The votes proved overwhelming in support of the first four questions, that is, that episcopal consecration is the highest degree of holy orders, that this consecration makes the bishop a member of the episcopal college, that always in union with the pope the episcopal college has full and supreme authority in the church, and that the bishops enjoy this right by divine right. The "closest" vote still garnered two-thirds support for the restoration of the permanent diaconate.

The question arose of a decree on the Virgin Mary. Marian piety appealed to most bishops who wanted a separate statement on Mary. But many bishops and theologians worked strenuously against this, noting that the Scriptures give her just three titles—virgin, mother, and wife—whereas nonscriptural Marian devotions had grown incessantly over the centuries. This group favored putting a statement on Mary within the context of *De Ecclesia*, as the *peritus* de Lubac had done in *The Splendor of the Church*, only to be accused of insufficient devotion to the Virgin. In the closest of all conciliar votes, situating Mary in *De Ecclesia* passed by only forty votes of more than two thousand cast.

The discussion on the People of God proceeded well. The bishops recognized that the gifts given by the Holy Spirit to the church are received by all believers, not just by the clergy, and while the bishops insisted on the leadership of the pastors, they urged pastors to "cooperate" with the laity rather than try to order them about. "Cooperate" became "one of the key words in the vocabulary of Vatican II" (O'Malley, *What Happened*, 186).

On October 30 the bishops approved the revised document.

An embittered minority fought throughout much of November to have the October 30 vote overturned on procedural points, but Paul VI backed the majority. Some more tinkering with the document occurred before the pope formally approved it on November 21, 1964, but the council had settled the main issue. When, however, some bishops wanted to put a practical application to collegiality by creating a kind of permanent synod of noncurial bishops to advise the pope, Paul would not support it. In September 1965, before the opening of the fourth session, he established the Synod of Bishops to advise him, but the synod would meet only every two or three years to advise the pope on issues chosen for discussion by the pope.

In November of 1963 the council turned to the decree on ecumenism, prepared by the Secretariat for Christian Unity and the Commission for the Oriental Churches. With this the council met one of the major objectives of John XXIII in calling the council. The document did not speak of getting the "heretics" (Protestants) and "schismatics" (Orthodox) back to the "true" church but rather approached those "separated brethren" as just that— brethren. This approach appeared in the document's first three chapters and was acceptable to most bishops, but the decree's fourth and fifth chapters took up two issues that brewed controversy: a positive statement about the church's relation to the Jewish people and a validation of religious freedom. "Reasonable though these ideals and principles might seem today, in 1963 they signaled an official turnaround in behavior and a modification of a value system" (O'Malley, *What Happened*, 195).

The decree arrived on the council floor on November 18, barely two weeks before the closing of the session on December 4. While nothing was finally settled, some major issues appeared. Many bishops feared the reaction of the Arab states to a positive statement on the Jews, while others feared such a statement would signal support for the secular state of Israel, which the Vatican did not at that time recognize. Behind these two objections lay what Alberigo calls "traditional Catholic anti-Semitism" (*Brief History*, 55). To the podium went Cardinal Augustine Bea, president of the Secretariat for Christian Unity. He made several points but, as a German, he spoke meaningfully about the anti-Semitism that had caused the Holocaust, and he insisted the church could not persist in actions that could be seen as supporting anti-Semitism. (Only during the pontificate of John XXIII had the denunciation of the Jews as "perfidious" been removed from the Good Friday liturgy.) Bea also insisted that the document dealt with religious issues and not with Zionism or the state of Israel.

Bishop De Smedt spoke about freedom of religion. Most bishops lived in states that guaranteed that, but several Latin American governments had denied Protestants the right to open churches and schools, and the local Catholic bishops had not protested such actions. Bishops from Franco's Spain were also among those most reluctant to accept religious liberty. Thus, since the church had a centuries-old stance of opposing religious liberty, De Smedt spoke about it in a provocative way, under the heading of "development of doctrine."

The council compromised, passing a vote that approved the document's first three chapters but putting off discussion of the fourth (the Jews) and fifth (religious liberty) until the next session.

On December 4 Paul VI closed the second session with a solemn ratification of the decrees on liturgy, *Sacrosanctum Concilium*, and one on the media, *Inter Mirifica*, which encouraged Catholics to use the modern media but which also praises the role of the arts in religion and acknowledges their variety, not insisting on traditional European forms.

But the highlight of the December 4 session was Pope Paul's announcement that he was making a pilgrimage to the Holy Land, where he would meet with local dignitaries and Orthodox leaders, including patriarch Athenagoras of Constantinople. This marvelous ecumenical gesture supported one of the council's main goals. It was also the first trip of a pope outside of Italy (not counting the kidnapping of Pius VI and Pius VII by the French) in more than half a millennium.

The Third Session (1964)

When the third session opened on September 14, 1964, the various conciliar committees worked on the decrees. Pope Paul made some suggestions about the decree on the church, but not ones that fundamentally changed the document. Yet in the summer of 1964, he published an encyclical on the church, *Ecclesiam Suam*, in which he spoke only once of the People of God but used the word "dialogue" seventy-seven times. This word also entered Vatican II's vocabulary.

Paul and many bishops hoped this session would be the last, but the commissions kept on producing documents, and most bishops determined to stay the course, even if it meant another session. The Constitution on the Church loomed large.

The commissions and bishops had rejected a juridical, and therefore exact, characterization of the church, so the document now spoke of the mystery of the church, that is, that the church is essentially a divine reality beyond total human comprehension and thus beyond precise definition. The People of God had also been accepted along with chapters on the laity and on the Virgin Mary. But collegiality remained a problem. On September 21 speakers began the final presentation on the ministry of bishops. The subsequent votes on the different chapters of *Lumen Gentium* overwhelmingly and somewhat surprisingly endorsed the collegial and the sacramental nature of the episcopate. By this point, the bishops had concluded that they should produce a separate document just on the episcopacy, and *Lumen Gentium* would impact that document.

Often overlooked because of collegiality and the People of God is a remarkable statement at the end of chapter one (On the Mystery of the Church): "This is the unique Church which is in the Creed we avow and one, holy, catholic, apostolic. . . . This Church *subsists* (Latin: *subsistit*) in the Catholic Church, which is governed by the successor of Peter and by the bishops in union with that successor, although many elements of sanctification and of truth can be found outside of her visible structure" (*Lumen Gentium* I.8, Abbot, *Documents*, 22–23). Tanner sums up the statement's importance: "It ('subsists') is more comprehensive than 'is,' which would identify the church of Christ exclusively with the Catholic Church—a position advocated by some—yet the Catholic Church retains a privileged position. The statement is clearly a development beyond the earlier teaching, frequently and authoritatively stated, that 'there is no salvation outside the Catholic Church'" (*Councils*, 104). This remarkable statement testifies to the power of bishops working in council and being open to new ideas. One can only wonder how few bishops, in 1962, ever thought they would characterize their church in that way.

Now the council turned to the decrees on religious liberty and the Jews. Religious liberty went against a long-held Catholic view that error has no rights:

> In essence the teaching boiled down to the following. First, if the majority of the citizens were Catholics, the state had the duty to profess the Catholic faith and to do all it reasonably could to promote and defend it. This meant that . . . it was duty-bound to discourage or even suppress other religions. . . . Second, in certain other situations, in order to avoid greater evils, it might be necessary to tolerate other religions and thus allow their free practice. Third, when Catholics are a minority, the state has the duty . . . to guarantee them full citizenship and free practice of their religion because the state must foster the pursuit of truth, which the Catholic Church possesses. (O'Malley, *What Happened*, 212)

By 1964 this attitude sounded outdated and highly offensive since so many bishops either lived in democracies or lived in totalitarian states that denied Catholic religious freedom. The issue was not the nature of religious freedom but whether endorsing it would change church teaching. Murray argued that this was a genuine development; De Smedt insisted that the traditional argument arose in a different era and society; other theologians argued that the very earliest church did not oppose religious freedom, so that religious freedom was "a truth more fundamental than what it wanted to displace" (ibid., 215). Conservatives reminded the bishops that the church had established concordats with several countries, including Italy, Spain, and the Dominican Republic, that accepted the traditional teaching. The leading conservative, Cardinal Alfredo Ottaviani of the Holy Office, went back to Pius IX, equating religious freedom with indifferentism.

But most bishops simply could not envision rejecting freedom of religion in the twentieth century, and they gave their approval to the basic tenets of the document, which was returned to a commission for its final wording.

From religious freedom, the bishops now turned to the Jews. Arguments that today seem appalling were raised with all seriousness: "Were not the Jews of Jesus' time responsible for his death? Was not that responsibility in some sense rightly imputed to the Jews down through the subsequent ages to our own day? . . . Would the document say that the perseverance of the Jews (within their own religion be) without fault?" (ibid., 221).

The Americans strongly supported the document, and one for a very personal reason. Cardinal Richard Cushing of Boston had a Jewish brother-in-law, so this was more than a technical matter for him. He simply could not believe that this good man was guilty of Christ's death, simply for being a Jew. Few bishops could hold to the old ideas less than two decades after the Holocaust. Yet bishops from the Middle East and from Asia raised a good point: why should the council speak only about the church's relationship with the Jews and not with the Muslims and the religions and peoples of Asia? The majority agreed, and the document became *Nostra Aetate*, which speaks of the church's "dialogue and collaboration with the followers of other religions" and that Catholics should "acknowledge, preserve, and promote the spiritual and moral goods found among [them], as well as the values in their society and culture" (*Nostra Aetate 2*, Abbot, *Documents*, 662–63). The Muslims, the infidel targets of the Crusades, "adore one God" and "strive to submit wholeheartedly even to his inscrutable decrees." The decree also notes Islamic veneration for Jesus (as a prophet) and his mother. With the Jews, the decree urges mutual understanding and respect, and the church "deplores the hatred, persecution, and displays of anti-Semitism directed at any time and from any source" (ibid., 696–97). Indeed, not just religious prejudice but "any discrimination against men or harassment of them because of their race, color, condition of life or religion" is foreign to the church. Anti-Semitism did not cease nor did racism, and anti-Muslim feeling has grown in the West, but no longer could anyone claim the support of the Catholic Church for such odious attitudes.

The bishops made good progress on less contentious decrees. The constitution on revelation, now called *Dei Verbum* (Word of God), was presented in a new form, which sees God's revelation in its fullness in the person and saving work of Jesus Christ, whose Gospel then comes to us through Scripture and tradition. Acknowledging anti-Reformation developments that suggested that the church is above God's word, the council affirmed that the "teaching office (*magisterium*) is not above the word of God but serves it," and the church "draws from this one deposit of faith everything which it presents for belief as divinely revealed" (*Dei Verbum* II.10, Abbot, *Documents*, 118), thus scotching the notion held by some that the church can simply create doctrines. To be sure, it may be difficult to find a scriptural basis for some teachings—conservative bishops worried about Marian doctrines—but the document unequivocally states that all teaching must have a basis in revelation.

The decree on the laity met with general satisfaction; the cardinal presenting it to the council summed it up in a sentence: "The laity are not simply in the church, but with us they are the church!" (O'Malley, *What Happened*, 229). Some bishops worried about the document's discussion of the priesthood of all believers as too close to Protestantism, but it is a biblical idea (1 Pet 2:9; Rev 5:10), which biblical exegetes showed could be given a Catholic interpretation. The decree's section on the Eastern Catholic churches also met general satisfaction, although some Eastern bishops again insisted that Catholicism not be equated with the Latin rite. Just two days of discussion won approval for this document, which, in addition to praising the Eastern churches' faith and praying for eventual unity, states that "it is the mind of the Catholic Church that each individual Church (in communion with Rome) or rite retain its traditions whole and entire, while adjusting its way of life to the various needs of time and place" (*Orientalium Ecclesiarum* 2, Abbot, *Documents*, 374). The Catholic Church cannot be equated with the Latin rite.

On October 20 began discussion of the most controversial document, Pastoral Constitution on the Church in the Modern World. To some bishops, the topic alone suggested revolution since the popes and many bishops had been condemning the modern world since the opening of the nineteenth century. But the spirit of John XXIII won out. "[The Church] turned attention from what councils had always before been concerned with, internal church affairs, to the world outside. It addressed concrete, contemporary issues and problems, such as world peace and a just socio-economic order. . . . it projected an image of the church as a helpmate to all persons of good will, whether Catholic or not, whether Christian or not, and as a beacon of hope for a better world" (O'Malley, *What Happened*, 233). This document, named *Gaudium et Spes* ("Joy and Hope"), would be the council's longest, as well as the one most likely to cite nontheological disciplines for its sources.

Speakers would debate most aspects of the document, but, significantly, no one opposed the notion of the church speaking to the modern world, and not as a judge but as a partner, not just as a teacher but also as one who could learn from dialogue. Cardinal Suenens's two-part approach to understanding the church had borne fruit.

An interesting point of conflict arose. Aware of the church's previous unpleasant statements about modernity, the commission working on the decree was emphasizing the positive. Cardinal Joseph Frings of Cologne, whose theological advisor was Joseph Ratzinger, reminded the bishops of the "theology of the cross," which often forces Christians to detach themselves from the world and its goods. Other bishops followed Frings, not so much on the theology of the cross but in insisting that the council look at the ills of the world. African bishops pointed out continuing racism, while several bishops pointed out that discrimination against women was widespread. The document also spoke about the danger of nuclear war, following John XXIII's encyclical *Pacem in Terris*.

The document's discussion of marriage engendered objections from Cardinal Ottaviani and some other very conservative bishops because the document "avoided using the textbook terms 'primary' and 'secondary' ends of marriage, in which the primary end was the procreation of children and the secondary end was a remedy for concupiscence and the mutual help of spouses" (O'Malley, *What Happened*, 236). Concupiscence means sexual desire, so according to this view people got married to have children, satisfy their sexual desires, and help one another. (One can only wonder what the married observers at the council, who presumed that people got married because they were in love, thought when they heard those first two.) The bishops turned a deaf ear to these points, and the document stressed the holiness of marriage and mutual love, proclaiming children as the fruit of love and not the purpose of marriage. This would be a great boon to loving, married Catholics who could not have children and whose marriages were often thought of as somehow incomplete.

The document did not deal with a major marital issue, birth control, because in 1963 John XXIII had established a papal commission to examine the problem. Several bishops, however, did speak in favor of changing the teaching because of the scientific advancements in preventing conception; Suenens went so far as to say that one Galileo case is enough. Privately, an angry Paul VI told Suenens to make a retraction, which he did.

On November 6 the bishops took up a schema on the missions, rejecting the proposed document as too brief and returning it for more work, and this vote occurred only a day after the pope himself had commended the document in its current form to the council. As noted earlier, Paul had hoped that by shortening the documents and reducing their number, he could close the council after the third session, but, rather awkwardly, the bishops still recommended a longer document. The council also dealt with two brief documents, one on religious orders, who were urged to remain faithful to the spirit of their founders but to adapt to modern conditions (*aggiornamento* again). The second was on priests, with an emphasis on the role of the local bishop in priestly formation; this was not at all a rejection of Rome's rights to intervene but just another example of the bishops' focus on the significance of their office in the local churches. Very importantly, the council called Scripture the "soul" of theology, effectively displacing scholasticism as the most important theological element in seminary training. Since most Catholics considered scholasticism to be "the" theology of the church, this displacement had enormous consequences in seminary curricula.

The pope wanted to close the third session on November 21, and the bishops looked forward to a relatively quiet two weeks. But then Paul intervened on three of the schemas. He wanted as much unity as possible among the bishops, and the conservative minority had been besieging him with warnings of the dire consequences for the church if he allowed some of the documents to be confirmed in their present form. Paul tried to find accommodations. He postponed an orientation vote on religious liberty. He sent forty emendations to Cardinal Bea, who accepted nineteen as last-minute changes to the text on ecumenism. Most seriously, he sent an "explanatory note" on collegiality, the subject of chapter three of *Lumen Gentium*. Since the council's schedule called for a vote on the last two decrees by November 21, many bishops were puzzled and annoyed that the pope intervened literally at the last moment.

But the pope's nineteen emendations did not fundamentally change the text of the ecumenism decree, which passed overwhelmingly on November 20. As for the Constitution on the Church, Paul's concern focused on whether collegiality might compromise papal authority, but most bishops believed that collegiality remained secure, even with the adoption of the pope's suggestions. The document received overwhelming approval (only five bishops voted against), and the Catholic Church now had a document that affirmed the traditional structure but likewise affirmed that the church is a mystery, a pilgrim journeying to an eschatological fulfillment, a laity who share in the universal priesthood, ministers who share and care rather than rule and judge, and the People of God—a remarkable document in many respects.

On November 21, at the closing ceremony, Paul VI confirmed both documents, although his speech "repeatedly made reference to the pope's satisfaction with the insistent and continual reaffirmation of papal primacy in the document" (Alberigo, *Brief History*, 87). Paul also announced that he was giving the Virgin Mary a new title, Mother of the Church, a title that the council's doctrinal commission refused to give her, fearing that it would appear that she were above the church and thus differentiate her from other believers, just as biblical exegetes were emphasizing her biblical role as Christ's perfect disciple and a model for believers. Paul had gone beyond the council, and a prominent *peritus* judged this to be "a deliberate assertion by the pope of his primacy. . . . That day Paul's face was grim as he was carried out of the basilica through row upon row of bishops, who applauded perfunctorily or, in some cases, not at all" (O'Malley, *What Happened*, 246). What, they wondered, would the fourth session be like?

But it should not be overlooked that Paul VI, unlike almost every other pope, came into office with an ecumenical council—the largest in history—up and running. He had to learn his office and deal with the council simultaneously, and this challenging combination may explain his awkward handling of some conciliar issues.

The Fourth Session (1965)

Both pope and bishops wanted the fourth session to be the last. During the interval between sessions, commissions and subcommissions worked on the documents awaiting either approval or presentation. On March 7, 1965, the pope offered a Mass in Italian at a Roman parish church, and the world's Catholics saw the earliest and most visible manifestation of the council. On June 24, Paul announced the creation of the Synod of Bishops, which would be called by him when he wished and which would have only an advisory role. The Roman congregation and Vatican bureaucracy would continue their work without formal episcopal input (individual bishops and national synods could, of course, make requests as they wished). The pope also announced that he would go to the United Nations to plead for world peace; he went there on October 4, pleaded for "No more war," and received a warm, appreciative welcome from the assembly, which recognized that Paul spoke from the heart on this issue. His visit also strengthened the image of the UN in the eyes of Catholics who had reservations about giving any authority to a world body dominated by non-Catholics. Paul realized that the UN was the only venue for many Third World countries to have their views heard.

Later that month, on October 28, the council and pope gave approval to the decree on education.

The debate on religious liberty continued but now took a different turn. Bishop Josef Beran of Prague, recently released from a Communist prison, spoke from the point of view of those who had suffered from the denial of religious freedom. He cited the example of Jan Hus, executed by an ecumenical council (Constance), and about the Habsburg monarchy's oppression of Protestants and Jews. Would Vatican II not abolish such infamy? Many bishops, especially from Latin America, announced support for the schema, to the relief of the pope, who feared having to go to the UN with the baggage of a council that, in 1965, could not support religious freedom. The bishops voted to approve the schema; the final vote, with 90 percent of the bishops in favor, occurred on November 21. The doctrine had developed; the Catholic Church now supported religious liberty.

This was the third session in which the bishops discussed the decree on revelation. A minority still wanted the "two sources." Paul VI would not go along with that but did insist on a stronger statement on tradition. The council settled on: "The Church does not draw her certainty for all revealed truths from Scripture alone" (*Dei Verbum* II.9, Abbot, *Documents*, 117). The pope approved of this, and the document went to the printer.

The bishops turned to the Church in the Modern World; many, including Polish bishop Karol Wojtyła, thought the document too positive toward the modern world, which, they claimed, reveled in materialism and consumerism. Many Germans thought it overlooked the human estrangement from God; others considered it more sociological than theological. Yet the majority, conscious of how often the church had looked judgmental and condemnatory to many people, wanted an overall positive statement. As O'Malley put it, "The words that the text uses to express that relationship [the church and the world] are words of mutuality, friendship, partnership, cooperation—and dialogue. That is the great theme of *Gaudium et Spes*" (*What Happened*, 267). These words can only occur when each side has respect for the other and acknowledges that it can learn from the other. The *Syllabus* was history.

On November 18, at a solemn session, the council accepted the decrees on revelation and on the lay apostolate; the pope approved both schemas. On November 30 the bishops approved four documents awaiting final approval; at a solemn session on December 7 the bishops accepted the decrees on religious liberty, missions, priests, and the church in the modern world; the pope formally endorsed them. This last working day ended on a high ecumenical note. Dutch Cardinal Jan Willebrands of the Secretariat for Christian Unity read a declaration from Paul VI that officially removed the 1054 Latin excommunication of the Greeks (Patriarch Athenagoras made a similar declaration for the Greeks but not at the council).

Vatican II closed on December 8, 1965, with more than a quarter of a million people in Saint Peter's Square. Paul VI offered Mass and then offered greetings to all humanity, which he said he could do because the church considers no one a stranger. Next came a series of messages to people in all walks of life. The ceremony finished with a bishop's reading of the pope's letter declaring the council closed. Paul VI then blessed all present and urged them "In the name of Our Lord Jesus Christ, go in peace." The assembled multitude responded, "Thanks be to God." The great council was over.

Every council contains some surprises, but Vatican II exceeded almost all expectations. For a long time, the Catholic Church had viewed the modern world as a threat to the faith. One of the most popular Catholic books of the early twentieth century was James Joseph Walsh's *The Thirteenth, Greatest of Centuries* (1907). The title tells it all. But Vatican II embraced the modern world, not in every aspect, of course, but the bishops affirmed that the church shared the hopes and fears of modern people, and, while insisting that the world can learn from the church, they acknowledged the church could learn from the world.

The laity, the "docile flock" whose task was to pray, pay, and be quiet, were now imaged as sharers and even partners with the bishops in evangelization. Marriage was no longer a baby machine and a remedy for concupiscence but a loving relationship into which people freely entered, with childbearing being one facet of that relationship.

Bishops brought up on traditional theology, which spoke of schismatics, heretics, and infidels, now recognized the goodness of other churches and religious traditions; they also emphasized that all people should be free to worship as they please. And no longer could bigots claim Catholic support for anti-Semitism.

Bishops brought up on scholastic theology now recognized that this theology, for all its brilliance, was but one way to do theology; they furthermore recognized that scholasticism did not take into account the advances in biblical scholarship. Vatican II made Scripture the center of theology and acknowledged the value of modern exegesis.

To be sure, Vatican II's ideals did not always fare well when the council had ended. Anti-Semitism continued; many bishops did not wish to see priests, religious, and laity as partners; conservative theologians resisted the new exegesis. All this was disappointing, but no surprise in an imperfect world. Vatican II had done its best; now the church as a whole had the obligation of putting Vatican II into practice.

After the Council

Previously, this book has recounted the aftermath of a council as preparatory to an account of the next council. But, so far, there is no Vatican III, and since there is no way to determine what would be the forces that would produce its agenda, there will be no sketch of post-conciliar history, although we can at least see how Paul VI's pontificate proceeded.

After the council, he worked for its implementation, setting up commissions to deal with particular issues, such as the liturgy. He also called several episcopal synods to advise him, preserving collegiality but likewise maintaining papal primacy. Paul pursued an active ecumenical agenda, meeting with the archbishop of Canterbury and with the patriarch Athenagoras. He also had Cardinal Bea and the Secretariat for Christian Unity begin dialogues with Anglicans, Lutherans, and other "separated brethren." Paul enlarged the college of cardinals from 80 to 138, considerably internationalizing it, forbade cardinals over 80 to vote in conclaves, and set 75 as the retirement age for bishops. He also worked for world peace. His 1967 encyclical, On the Progress of Peoples, pleaded for social justice. He condemned war and also the arms race. When some American Catholics said that the stockpiled weapons had killed no one, the pope pointedly argued that funds spent on weapons could be spent on helping the poor of the world who die of malnutrition and diseases unknown in Western societies.

But his pontificate changed in 1968. Paul had appointed a commission to look into the question of contraception. The commission had a majority of laypeople, including women. For the first time in church history, people who actually had babies were being consulted, and Paul won much praise for his openness to diverse views. To many Catholics, the commission proved that the "People of God" had become more than a theological phrase. In 1968 news leaked out that more than 90 percent of the commission had voted to change the teaching and permit contraception. But Paul sided with the minority and continued the ban on contraception, which he had every right to do, in his encyclical *Humanae Vitae* (On Human Life).

The international reaction was immediate and mostly negative. Paul VI now saw another side to the modern world. Popes had met opposition from laypeople in the form of kings and emperors, but never had laypeople in general refused to listen to papal teaching. The strongest opposition arose in the Western democracies. Laypeople wished to know why the pope had ignored his own commission; some bishops tried to qualify the encyclical's teaching; theologians rushed to microphones to announce the encyclical was not infallible. Educated people wanted to know why advances in space exploration were acceptable but not advances in reproductive technology;

why contraception was not natural but a heart transplant was; why the Vatican spoke of the People of God and then did not listen to them. Most astonishing was, to use Richard Nixon's phrase, the "silent majority" who did not protest but simply continued to use contraception. By the end of the twentieth century, two previously archetypal Catholic countries, Italy and Spain, had the world's lowest birthrates.

Many scholars have seen the encyclical as initiating the drop in Mass attendance, the virtual disappearance of confession, and even the vocation decline. That view remains unproven, but *Humanae Vitae* definitely hurt the pope's campaign for peace.

The world had one superpower, heavily armed and willing to use military force to achieve its goals. If the pope could not win over the United States, his other efforts could not succeed. But America is a democracy; votes count. Many non-Catholic Americans had been brought up to see Catholics as slavishly obedient to Rome, but the birth control flare-up proved that American Catholics would sometimes disagree with Rome. U.S. politicians learned they could defy the Vatican on some issues and not pay a price at the polls. Against Paul's hopes, the Vietnam War dragged on until 1975, and the arms race continued and got worse. Like Benedict XV and Pius XI, Paul wanted to be a pope of peace but could not get governments to go along. (The situation did not change. In 2003 Pope John Paul II condemned the impending invasion of Iraq and got the American bishops to support him 100 percent. President George Bush went ahead with the invasion, and polls showed a majority of Catholics supported the president—another frustrated papal attempt at peace.)

"Paul never doubted that he had done what had to be done [about contraception], but his confidence was shattered. He never wrote another encyclical, and the last ten years of his pontificate [he died in 1978] were marked by deepening gloom, as he agonized over the divisions within the Church and his own unpopularity, the mass exodus of priests and religious, and the growing violence of the secular world" (Duffy, *Saints*, 281).

A fair man who wanted to win over as many people as possible, Paul VI often appeared indecisive; following the warm and charismatic John XXIII, he often appeared distant and cold—charges that were unfair and were proven so by his passionate commitment to peace and social justice. Endlessly working for peace and for aid to the wretched of the world, he saw Communist and democratic governments patronize his words and go on with their destructive policies. That good man deserved better.

Epilogue

Will there be a Vatican III? If so, when? These are questions we cannot answer. Only a pope can call a council, and not many have done so since the Middle Ages, when seven councils met in less than two hundred years (Lateran I–IV, Lyons I–II, Vienne). Papal authority has increasingly grown, and the popes governed without a council for more than three centuries between Trent and Vatican I. There is no guarantee that any future pope will see the need for a council. But, as the title of Monsignor Hughes's book suggests, when the church is again in crisis, there may be another council.

What might it deal with? One obvious topic will be the church's changing demographics. More than half the world's Catholics live in Africa and Latin America, and many of them are desperately poor, unlike most Catholics of Western Europe and North America. Many are also illiterate or poorly educated, yet they belong to one of the most intellectualized religious bodies in human history. The Catholic Church is a major institution, yet religious sociologists point out that many of these "new" Catholics often have a charismatic approach to their faith. They also live in areas where other traditions compete for believers, such as Pentecostalism in South America and Islam in Africa. Finally, there is the ever-present problem of cultural adaptation. Catholic teaching, formulated largely in Western European terms, must deal with peoples for whom "Western Europe" often means the long-hated and still-not-completely-gone colonialists and imperialists.

Another focus for Vatican III may be dealing with democracies. As Vatican II taught, the Catholic Church is ultimately a mystery, a spiritual reality beyond full human comprehension. But the church also lives in this world and wishes to achieve many goals here, such as halting war and the arms race and helping the impoverished nations of the world. In this regard, the church is a "soft" power, that is, one that cannot carry out its own plans and hopes but instead must rely on "hard" powers, that is, those that can. The church must win the support of powerful governments. In past eras the popes could work with the European monarchs, but now the major powers are very different types.

Several major political and economic powers, such as China, Russia, Japan, India, and the Near Eastern oil-producing states, contain, at best, small Catholic populations. These nations are happy to patronize papal statements that do not challenge their values but can ignore ones that do because they need not worry about a numerous citizenry for whom papal teaching carries weight. But two major powers, the democratic European Union and the United States, have sizeable Catholic populations who can influence their governments, which must listen to the people or run the risk of being voted out.

These two powers can largely determine whether many papal hopes will ever see fruition. Half of the world's defense spending is done by the U.S., which has not been reluctant to use its arms. Many EU countries, members of the North American Treaty Organization (NATO), have also sent troops beyond their borders. Both powers will have a decisive role in the future of the arms race and military actions.

The democratic powers also control much of the world's finances. Their policies routinely determine who will be rich and who will be poor. Many of the world's destitute countries owe the EU and U.S. enormous amounts of money that they will never be able to repay. The popes have argued for the reduction, if not the forgiveness, of debts, but Western governments and banks have done little in that area. Even Western charity can be expensive. American food aid programs use much food grown in the U.S. rather than by local farmers in poor countries; buying locally would significantly aid the local economies.

Today the pope and bishops must win over literally tens of millions of people in order to get a government policy changed. If the voters do not stand with them, the policy will not change. If church leaders cannot "deliver the vote," so to speak, politicians, even Catholic ones, know that they can disagree with church teachings. Strongly pro-choice presidents like Bill Clinton and Barack Obama carried the Catholic vote, as did George Bush in 2004 after John Paul II had condemned the invasion of Iraq.

But there is an answer to these and other challenges: the spirit of John XXIII.

In the course of this book, we have often seen popes worry about what the bishops in council might do and then take steps to control the bishops' activities. At Vatican II, John XXIII intervened on a procedural matter only once, and that was on behalf of the episcopal *majority*. He did not abandon papal authority, but he trusted his bishops. As John O'Malley repeatedly pointed out in his book, Vatican II used a new language—dialogue, *aggiornamento*, collegiality, openness—all as a result of John's approach to dealing with the hierarchy, clergy, laity, other Christians, other believers, and, literally, every person of goodwill.

John XXIII became a great pope in many ways, but especially by understanding the nature of the modern world, appreciating its positive and liberating aspects, and recognizing that modern people would not respond to denunciation or anathemas and certainly not to the idealization of a bygone world of absolute monarchs, second-class status for women, religious oppression, and other medieval ills. John could see possibilities where others saw threats; he could see freedom where others saw anarchy; he could see the goods of the modern world where others could see only evils. This great man cared about, listened to, and was open to his brother bishops whom he indeed saw as brothers, to the People of God, and to all people of goodwill. John XXIII gave his successors and all other Catholics a stunning and successful model to follow.

Bibliography

This book is intended for the general reader, and the bibliography reflects that. Twenty-one councils over eighteen centuries have generated an enormous literature; Vatican II alone has spawned more than one thousand books of varying value. This bibliography recommends titles that the general reader can access, although in several cases it also includes great works of scholarship. There are some councils (Lateran I, II, III) for which there are no studies available to the general reader, who should consult the larger works. Since this work is projected for English-speaking readers, the titles are all English-language ones.

English Texts of the Councils' Decrees:

Abbot, Walter, general ed. *The Documents of Vatican II*. New York: Herder & Herder, 1966. (N.B. Many English translations of Vatican II's documents are available.)

Broderick, John F., SJ, ed. *Documents of Vatican Council I*. Collegeville, MN: Liturgical Press, 1971.

Schroeder, Henry J., ed. *Canons and Decrees of the Council of Trent*. Latin text and English translation. St. Louis: B. Herder Book Company, 1941.

Tanner, Norman P., SJ, ed. *Decrees of the Ecumenical Councils*. London: Sheed & Ward, 1990; Washington: Georgetown University Press, 1990. Includes all the texts from all of the councils in both the original languages (Greek and Latin) and in English translation. An immensely valuable work.

General Works on Councils:

Bellitto, Christopher. *The General Councils: A History of the Twenty-One Church Councils from Nicea to Vatican II*. Mahwah, NJ: Paulist Press, 2002.

Hughes, Philip. *The Church in Crisis: A History of the Twenty Great Councils*. London: Burns & Oates, 1961. An older work that does not include Vatican II but is still of value.

Huizing, Peter, and Knut Walf, eds. *The Ecumenical Council: Its Significance in the Constitution of the Church*. Edinburgh: T&T Clark, 1983.

Jedin, Hubert. *Ecumenical Councils in the Catholic Church.* English translation by Ernest Graf, OSB. New York: Herder & Herder, 1959. Written before Vatican II but by the modern era's foremost authority on councils.

Tanner, Norman, SJ. *The Councils of the Church: A Short History.* New York: Crossroad, 2001.

General Works:

Duffy, Eamon. *Saints and Sinners: A History of the Popes.* New Haven, CT: Yale University Press, 1997. Reliable and readable general account.

Jedin, Hubert, general ed. *History of the Church.* 10 vols. New York: Crossroad, 1971. The councils can be seen against the background of church in these volumes, which can be consulted individually. Individual volumes on particular eras in church history can also be helpful. This is a superb resource. (In the text, individual contributors will be cited this way: Roger Aubert, *Hist Ch* viii, 318, which means that the text cites an article by Roger Aubert in *History of the Church,* volume viii, p. 318.)

Kelly, J. N. D. *Oxford Dictionary of Popes.* New York: Oxford University Press, 2005. Given the close relation of the councils to the popes, this guide to all the popes greatly helps comprehension of the councils.

Levillain, Philippe, general ed. *The Papacy: An Encyclopedia.* 3 vols. London: Routledge, 2002. Entries on all the popes and on most of the ecumenical councils.

Livingstone, Elizabeth, ed. *The Oxford Dictionary of the Christian Church.* 3rd ed. rev. New York: Oxford University Press, 2005. A quick and easy-to-use reference work compiled by scholars. Helpful in checking up on the endless number of people and things related to the councils.

Nevins, Albert, ed. *The Maryknoll Catholic Dictionary.* Wilkes-Barre, PA: Dimension Books, 1965.

The Earliest Councils (Nicea I to Constantinople IV):

Allen, Pauline. *Sophronius of Jerusalem and Seventh-Century Heresy.* New York: Oxford University Press, 2009.

Chadwick, Henry. *East and West: The Making of a Rift in the Church from Apostolic Times to the Council of Florence.* New York: Oxford University Press, 2003.

Davis, Leo Donald, SJ. *The First Seven Ecumenical Councils.* Wilmington, DE: Michael Glazier, 1987.

Eno, Robert. *The Rise of the Papacy.* Wilmington, DE: Michael Glazier, 1990.

Ferguson, Everett, general ed. *Encyclopedia of Early Christianity.* 2 vols. London: Garland Press, 1997. Contains articles on the early councils but also on the many personalities and issues involved.

Frend, W. H. C. *The Rise of the Monophysite Movement.* 2nd ed. Cambridge: Cambridge University Press, 1979.

———. *Saints and Sinners in the Early Church.* Wilmington, DE: Michael Glazier, 1985.

Gero, Stephen. *Byzantine Iconoclasm during the Reign of Constantine V.* Louvain: Corpus SCO, 1977.

Hanson, R. P. C. *The Search for the Christian Doctrine of God.* Edinburgh: T&T Clark, 1988.

Harvey, Susan Ashbrook, and David Hunter, eds. *The Oxford Handbook of Early Christian Studies.* New York: Oxford University Press, 2008. A superb introduction to ancient Christianity; see particularly "Arius and Arians" by J. Rebecca Lyman (236–57), "Creeds, Councils, and Canons" by Everett Ferguson (427–45), "Doctrine of God" by Lewis Ayres (864–85), and "Christ and Christologies" by Brian E. Daley, SJ (886–905).

Hussey, J. M. *The Orthodox Church during the Byzantine Period.* Oxford: Clarendon Press, 1986.

Kelly, J. N. D. *Early Christian Creeds.* 3rd ed. London: Continuum, 2006.

L'Huillier, Peter. *The Church of the Ancient Councils.* Crestwood, NY: St. Vladimir's Seminary Press, 1996.

Noble, Thomas F. X. *Image, Iconoclasm, and the Carolingians.* Philadelphia: University of Pennsylvania Press, 2009.

Price, Richard, and Mary Whitby, eds. *Chalcedon in Context: Church Councils 400–700.* Liverpool: Liverpool University Press, 2009.

Richards, Jeffrey. *The Popes and the Papacy in the Early Middle Ages.* London: Routledge & Kegan Paul, 1986.

Young, Frances. *From Nicea to Chalcedon.* London: SCM Press, 1983.

Medieval Papal Councils (Lateran I to Lyons II):

Lynch, Joseph. *The Medieval Church.* London: Longman, 1992.

Moore, J. C., ed. *Innocent III and His World.* London: Aldershot, 1999.

Morris, Colin. *The Papal Monarchy: The Western Church from 1050 to 1250.* Oxford: Clarendon Press, 1989.

Sayers, Jane. *Innocent III: Leader of Europe 1198–1216.* London: Longman, 1994.

Avignon and the Conciliar Period:

Alberigo, Giuseppe, ed. *Christian Unity: The Council of Ferrara-Florence 1438/39–1989.* Leuven: Leuven University Press, 1991.

Black, Antony. *Monarchy and Community: Political Ideas in the Later Conciliar Period, 1430–1450.* Cambridge: Cambridge University Press, 1970.

Christianson, Gerald, Thomas Izbicki, and Christopher Bellitto, eds. *The Church, the Councils, and Reform: The Legacy of the Fifteenth Century.* Washington: Catholic University of America Press, 2008.

Gill, Joseph, SJ. *The Council of Florence.* Cambridge: Cambridge University Press, 1959.

Minnich, Nelson. *The Fifth Lateran Council (1512–1517)*. Brookfield, VT: Ashgate Publishing Company, 1993.

Oakley, Francis. *The Conciliarist Tradition*. New York: Oxford University Press, 2003.

———. *The Western Church in the Later Middle Ages*. Ithaca, NY: Cornell University Press, 1979.

Stieber, Joachim. *Pope Eugenius IV, the Council of Basel, and the Secular and Ecclesiastical Authorities in the Empire*. Leiden: E. J. Brill, 1978.

Stump, Philip. *The Reforms of the Council of Constance*. Leiden: E. J. Brill, 1994.

Tierney, Brian. *Foundations of the Conciliar Theory*. Cambridge: Cambridge University Press, 1955.

Trent:

Birely, Robert. *The Refashioning of Catholicism, 1450–1700*. Washington: Catholic University of America Press, 1999.

Bossy, John. *Christianity in the West 1400–1700*. Oxford: Oxford University Press, 1985.

Bulman, Raymond, and Frederick Perrella, eds. *From Trent to Vatican II*. New York: Oxford University Press, 2006.

Jedin, Hubert. *Crisis and the Closure of the Council of Trent*. London: Sheed & Ward, 1967.

———. *A History of the Council of Trent*. 2 vols. Translated by Ernest Graf, OSB. London: Nelson, 1957–61. The basic work; only the first two volumes are available in English.

Lindberg, Carter. *The European Reformations*. Oxford: Blackwell Publishers, 1996.

McGrath, Alistair. *Reformation Thought*. Oxford: Blackwell Publishers, 1988.

McNally, Robert E., SJ. "The Council of Trent and Vernacular Bibles." *Theological Studies* 276 (1966): 204–27.

Murphy, Paul. *Ruling Peacefully: Cardinal Ercole Gonzaga and Patrician Reform in Sixteenth-Century Italy*. Washington: Catholic University of America Press, 2007.

O'Malley, John, SJ. *Trent and All That*. Cambridge: Harvard University Press, 2000.

Vatican I:

Butler, Cuthbert. *The Vatican Council 1869–1870*. 2 vols. London: Longmans, Green and Company, 1932.

Chadwick, Owen. *A History of the Popes, 1830–1914*. Oxford: Clarendon Press, 1998.

Coppa, Frank J. *Politics and the Papacy in the Modern World*. Westport, CT: Praeger Publishers, 2008. Covers 1789–1978; very good for the period before and just after Vatican I.

Hasler, August. *How the Pope Became Infallible*. Garden City, NY: Doubleday & Company, 1981.

Hennesey, James, SJ. *The First Council of the Vatican: The American Experience*. New York: Herder & Herder, 1983. Still the best book-length study of the U.S. bishops at the council.

Mioni, Anthony, ed. *The Popes Against Modern Errors: 16 Papal Documents*. Rockford, IL: Tan Books and Publishers, 1999. A handy collection of papal documents from the nineteenth and early twentieth centuries; several relate to Vatican I.

Vatican II:

Alberigo, Giuseppe. *A Brief History of Vatican II*. Maryknoll, NY: Orbis Books, 2006. The best text for the general reader.

Alberigo, Giuseppe, and Joseph Komonchak, eds. *History of Vatican II*. 5 vols. Maryknoll, NY: Orbis Books, 1995–2003. The standard multivolume history in English.

O'Malley, John, SJ. *Tradition and Transition: Historical Perspectives on Vatican II*. Wilmington, DE: Michael Glazier, 1989.

———. *What Happened at Vatican II*. Cambridge, MA: Harvard University Press, 2008. Now the basic and best one-volume history of the council.

Pennington, M. Basil, OCSO. *Vatican II: We've Only Just Begun*. New York: Crossroad, 1994.

Ratzinger, Joseph. *Theological Highlights of Vatican II*. Mahwah, NJ: Paulist Press, 1966.

Rush, Ormond. *Still Interpreting Vatican II: Some Hermeneutical Principles*. Mahwah, NJ: Paulist Press, 2004.

Schultenover, David, ed. *Vatican II: Did Anything Happen?* New York: Continuum, 2007.

Sullivan, Maureen. *101 Questions and Answers on Vatican II*. Mahwah, NJ: Paulist Press, 2002. Although not a history, this a very handy introductory volume.

Wicks, Jared, SJ. "Further Light on Vatican Council II." *Catholic Historical Review* 95 (2009): 546–59.

———. "More Light on Vatican II." *Catholic Historical Review* 94 (2008): 75–101.

———. "New Light on Vatican II." *Catholic Historical Review* 92 (2006): 609–28.

———. *Professor Ratzinger at Vatican II: A Chapter in the Life of Pope Benedict XI*. New Orleans: Loyola University of New Orleans, 2007.

Index

There have been twenty-one universal gatherings—ecumenical councils—of the Catholic Church. The first opened in 325, the last closed in 1965, and the names of many ring out in the history of the church: Nicea, Chalcedon, Trent, Vatican II. Though centuries separate the councils, each occurred when the church faced serious crises, sometimes with doctrinal matters, sometimes with moral or even political matters, and sometimes with discerning the church's relation to the world. The councils determined much of what the Catholic Church is and believes. Additionally, many councils impacted believers in other Christian traditions and even in other faiths.

In this accessible, readable, and yet substantial account of the councils Joseph Kelly provides both the historical context for each council as well as an account of its proceedings. Readers will discover how the councils shaped the debate for the following decades and even centuries, and will appreciate the occasional portraits of important conciliar figures from Emperor Constantine to Pope John XXIII.

Joseph F. Kelly, PhD, is professor of religious studies at John Carroll University in Cleveland, Ohio. He is author of *The Origins of Christmas, An Introduction to the New Testament for Catholics, The Collegeville Church History Timeline,* and *The Birth of Jesus According to the Gospels,* all published by Liturgical Press.

"In clear and concise language, Kelly describes the political and theological context of the councils that made Catholicism what it is today."

Thomas J. Reese, SJ
Senior Fellow, Woodstock Theological Center
Georgetown University, Washington, DC

ISBN 978-0-8146-5376-0

U.S. $24.95